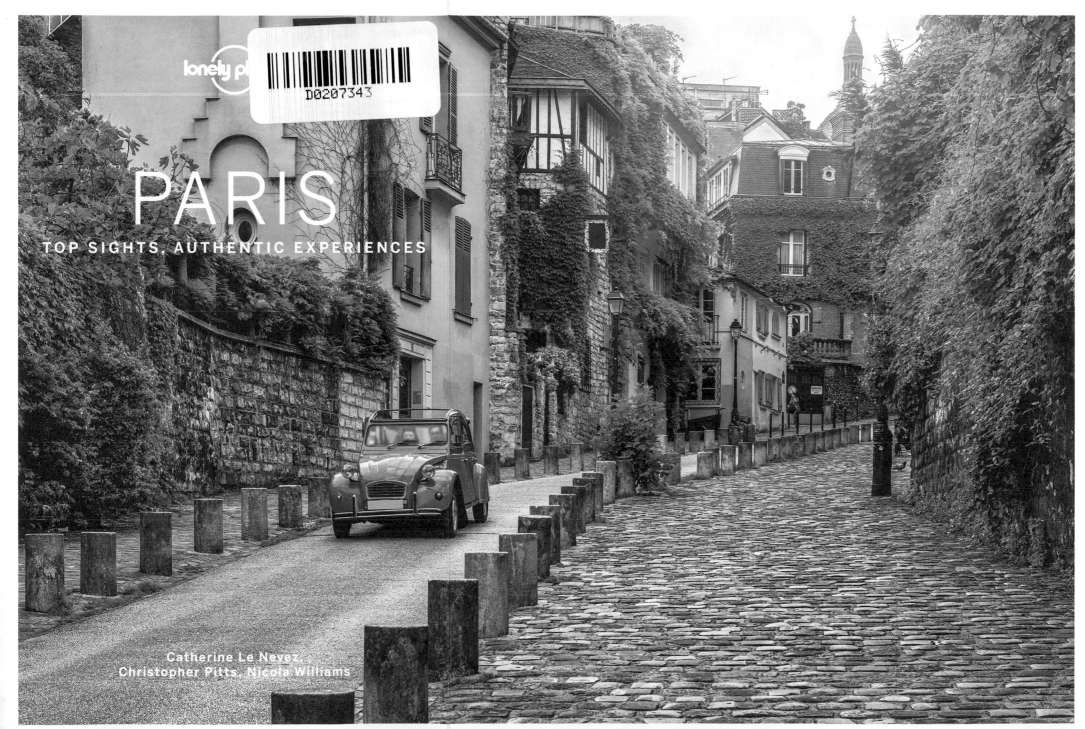

PARIS

TOP SIGHTS, AUTHENTIC EXPERIENCES

Catherine Le Nevez,
Christopher Pitts, Nicola Williams

Welcome to Paris

Paris' monument-lined boulevards, museums, classical bistros and boutiques are enhanced by a new wave of multimedia galleries, creative wine bars, design shops and tech start-ups.

The French capital is awash with landmarks – the Eiffel Tower, and Arc de Triomphe among them – along with a trove of specialist museums and galleries. Creamy-stone, grey-metal-roofed apartment buildings, lamp-lit bridges and geometrically laid-out formal parks are equally integral to the city's fabric.

Contrary to its magnificently preserved cityscapes, however, *la Ville Lumière* (the City of Light; a moniker Paris acquired due to its leading role in the Age of Enlightenment) has never stood still, but has constantly evolved, spearheading industrial, artistic, scientific and architectural endeavours. This innovative spirit continues today, with pioneering green transport initiatives and dazzling new architectural projects that include skyscraping towers along the periphery and re-energised urban spaces, many as part of the city's ambitious Grand Paris (Greater Paris) expansion. Creativity is evident everywhere, from neobistro kitchens and cutting-edge bars to fashion ateliers and vibrant street art, plus a digital art museum in a former foundry and the 1920s former railway depot housing Station F, the world's largest start-up hub.

Creativity is evident everywhere, from neobistro kitchens and cutting-edge bars to fashion ateliers and vibrant street art...

Montmartre (p60)
CATARINA BELOVA/SHUTTERSTOCK ©

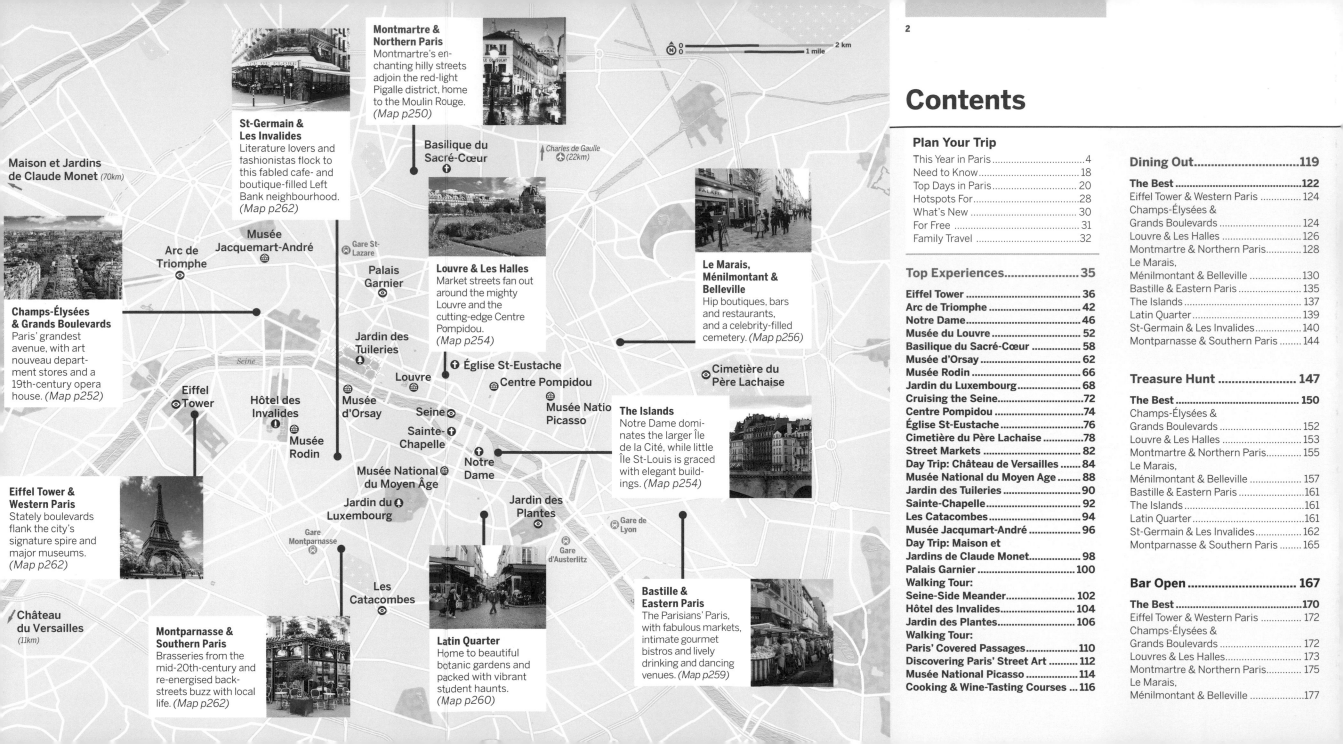

Maison et Jardins de Claude Monet (70km)

Montmartre & Northern Paris
Montmartre's enchanting hilly streets adjoin the red-light Pigalle district, home to the Moulin Rouge. (Map p250)

St-Germain & Les Invalides
Literature lovers and fashionistas flock to this fabled cafe- and boutique-filled Left Bank neighbourhood. (Map p262)

Basilique du Sacré-Cœur

Charles de Gaulle (22km)

Arc de Triomphe

Musée Jacquemart-André

Gare St-Lazare

Palais Garnier

Louvre & Les Halles
Market streets fan out around the mighty Louvre and the cutting-edge Centre Pompidou. (Map p254)

Le Marais, Ménilmontant & Belleville
Hip boutiques, bars and restaurants, and a celebrity-filled cemetery. (Map p256)

Champs-Élysées & Grands Boulevards
Paris' grandest avenue, with art nouveau department stores and a 19th-century opera house. (Map p252)

Jardin des Tuileries

Louvre

Église St-Eustache

Centre Pompidou

Cimetière du Père Lachaise

Eiffel Tower

Hôtel des Invalides

Musée d'Orsay

Seine

Musée Natio Picasso

Seine

Sainte-Chapelle

Musée Rodin

The Islands
Notre Dame dominates the larger Île de la Cité, while little Île St-Louis is graced with elegant buildings. (Map p254)

Eiffel Tower & Western Paris
Stately boulevards flank the city's signature spire and major museums. (Map p262)

Musée National du Moyen Âge

Notre Dame

Jardin des Plantes

Jardin du Luxembourg

Gare Montparnasse

Gare de Lyon

Gare d'Austerlitz

Château du Versailles (11km)

Les Catacombes

Montparnasse & Southern Paris
Brasseries from the mid-20th-century and re-energised backstreets buzz with local life. (Map p262)

Latin Quarter
Home to beautiful botanic gardens and packed with vibrant student haunts. (Map p260)

Bastille & Eastern Paris
The Parisians' Paris, with fabulous markets, intimate gourmet bistros and lively drinking and dancing venues. (Map p259)

2 km
1 mile

Contents

In Focus

Survival Guide

Plan Your Trip
This Year in Paris

2020

YOANN MORIN/SHUTTERSTOCK ©

Paris

*Art fairs, music festivals, open-air cinemas and epicurean events are just some
of the highlights of Paris' calendar in 2020, with many more in the works: check
www.parisinfo.com for updates.*

Clockwise from left: Nuit Blanche (p15); Paris Plages (p12); Iced-tea cocktail; Rafael Nadal at the French Open (p10)

2020

TOMMY LAREY/SHUTTERSTOCK ©

★ Top Festivals & Events

Paris Plages, July (p12)
Bastille Day, July (p12)
Paris Cocktail Week, January (p6)
French Open, May (p10)
Nuit Blanche, October (p15)

LEONARD ZHUKOVSKY/SHUTTERSTOCK ©. MADAMOUR CHRISTOPHE/GETTY IMAGES ©

Plan Your Trip
This Year in Paris

January

The frosty first month of the year isn't the most festive in Paris, but cocktails – as well as the winter soldes *(sales) – brighten the mood.*

✥ Epiphany
6 Jan

On this Christian feast day (aka Three Kings' Day), patisseries bake frangipane-filled puff-pastry *galettes des rois* (kings' cakes), which conceal a *fève* (small trinket). Whoever finds the *fève* is crowned 'king' for the day and wears the cardboard crown that comes with the cake.

✥ Louis XVI
Commemorative Mass
19 Jan

On the Sunday closest to 21 January, royalists attend a mass at the Chapelle Expiatoire (www.monuments-nationaux.fr) marking the execution by guillotine of King Louis XVI in 1793.

♟ Paris Cocktail Week
late Jan

Participating cocktail bars all over the city create signature cocktails for Paris Cocktail Week (www.pariscocktailweek.fr). There are also workshops, guest bartenders, masterclasses and food pairings.

✥ Chinese New Year
25 Jan

Paris' largest lantern-lit festivities and dragon parades take place in the city's main Chinatown in the 13e. Parades are also held in Belleville and Le Marais.

BATAREYKIN/ALAMY STOCK PHOTO ©; BELOW: CORIN/SHUTTERSTOCK ©

02

February

Festivities still aren't in full swing in February, but couples descend on France's romantic capital for Valentine's Day, when virtually all restaurants offer special menus.

👁 **Rétromobile** 5–9 Feb
Some 600 vintage cars are displayed over five days at the Parc des Expositions at Porte de Versailles, 15e, during this motor enthusiasts' showcase (pictured above; www.retromobile.com).

Le Rêveur de la Forêt to 23 Feb
The Dreamer in the Forest exhibition at the Musée Zadkine (from 27 September) explores the metaphoric and literal 'border' with the wilderness, the 'genesis' of the forest ecosystem, and 'holy woods', encompassing the forest's ancient and contemporary myths and beliefs (www.zadkine.paris.fr).

🍴 **Salon International de l'Agriculture** 22 Feb–1 Mar
At this appetising nine-day international agricultural fair (www.salon-agriculture.com), produce and animals from all over

⛸ **Outdoor Ice Skating**
All winter, ice-skating rinks pop up around the city, including in some truly picturesque spots, such as the Grande Arche de la Défense rooftop. Skating is usually free, but you'll need to pay for skate hire if you don't have your own. Check www.parisinfo.com, as specific venues change from year to year.

France are turned into delectable fare at the Parc des Expositions at Porte de Versailles, 15e.

Plan Your Trip
This Year in Paris

March

03

Blooms appear in Paris' parks and gardens, leaves start greening the city's avenues and festivities begin to flourish. And days get longer – the last Sunday morning of the month ushers in daylight-saving time.

🌺 Livre Paris   20–23 Mar
France's largest international book fair (pictured above; www.livreparis.com) takes place over four days at the Parc des Expositions at Porte de Versailles, 15e.

🏃 La Verticale de la Tour Eiffel   mid-Mar
Elite athletes and amateur runners drawn from a lottery scale the stairs of the Eiffel Tower during this vertical race (www.verticaletoureiffel.fr).

🔒 Foire de Chatou   mid-Mar
Some 500 antique and secondhand dealers, jewellers and art galleries set up at this 10-day fair (www.foiredechatou.com) held on the Île des Impressionnistes,

a 10-minute journey by RER to Rueil-Malmaison with a free shuttle from the station.

☆ Banlieues Bleues   mid-Mar–mid-Apr
Big-name acts perform during the Suburban Blues (www.banlieuesbleues.org) jazz, blues and R&B festival at venues in Paris' northern suburbs.

☆ Cinéma du Réel   late Mar
Dozens of French and international documentary films screen both in and out of competition at this prestigious 10-day festival (www.cinemadureel.org), which takes place at venues including the Centre Pompidou.

GUIMEAO/SHUTTERSTOCK ©

April

Sinatra sang about April in Paris, and the month sees the city's 'charm of spring' in full swing, with chestnuts blossoming and cafe terraces coming into their own.

🏃 Salon du Running early Apr

In the run-up to the Marathon International de Paris, the three-day Salon du Running (www.salondurunning.fr) draws over 80,000 visitors (including competitors picking up their bibs) and 200-plus professional exhibitors at the Parc des Expositions, Porte de Versailles, 15e.

🏃 Marathon International de Paris early Apr

On your marks...the Paris International Marathon (pictured above; www.schneiderelectricparis marathon.com), usually held on the second Sunday of April, starts on av des Champs-Élysées, 8e, and finishes on av Foch, 16e, attracting some 55,000 runners from around 145 countries.

🎡 Foire du Trône mid-Apr–late May/early Jun

Dating back over a millennium, from 957 AD, this huge funfair (www.foire dutrone.com) is held on the Pelouse de Reuilly of the Bois de Vincennes from around Easter to late May/early June.

🎡 Foire de Paris late Apr–early May

Gadgets, widgets, food and wine feature at this huge 12-day contemporary-living fair (www.foiredeparis.fr), held at the Parc des Expositions at Porte de Versailles, 15e.

Plan Your Trip
This Year in Paris

VIEW.CANTE/ALAMY STOCK PHOTO ©

May

05

The temperate month of May has more public holidays than any other in France. Watch out for widespread closures, particularly on May Day (1 May).

👁 La Nuit Européenne des Musées
mid-May

Key museums across Paris stay open late for the European Museums Night (www.nuitdesmusees.culturecommunication.gouv.fr), on one Saturday in May, with free entry.

✖ Taste Paris
mid-May

A highlight on foodies' calendars, the four-day gourmet festival Taste Paris (pictured above; www.paris.tastefestivals.com) incorporates tastings, cooking classes and demonstrations by some of Paris' most acclaimed chefs.

👁 Portes Ouvertes des Ateliers d'Artistes de Belleville
late May

More than 200 painters, sculptors and other artists at over 100 Belleville studios open their doors to visitors over four days

🏃 French Open
late May–early Jun

The glitzy Internationaux de France de Tennis Grand Slam (www.rolandgarros.com) hits up from late May to early June at Stade Roland Garros at the Bois de Boulogne.

(Friday to Monday) in late May (www.ateliers-artistes-belleville.fr).

June

Paris is positively jumping in June, thanks to warm temperatures, a host of outdoor events and long daylight hours, with twilight lingering until late.

🍷 Paris Beer Week   early Jun
Craft beer's popularity in Paris peaks during Paris Beer Week (www.laparisbeerweek.com), held, despite the name, over 10 days, when events take place across the city's bars, pubs, breweries, specialist beer shops and other venues.

☆ Fête de la Musique   21 Jun
This national music festival (www.fetedela musique.culturecommunication.gouv.fr) welcomes in summer on the solstice with fabulous staged and impromptu live performances of jazz, reggae, classical and more all over the city.

☆ Paris Jazz Festival   late Jun–mid-Jul
Jazz concerts swing every Saturday and Sunday afternoon from late June to mid-July in the Bois de Vincennes' Parc Floral de Paris during the Paris Jazz Festival (www.parisjazzfestival.fr).

🎊 Marche des Fiertés (Pride)   late Jun
The colourful Saturday-afternoon Marche des Fiertés (pictured above; www.inter-lgbt.org) celebrates LGBT+ pride with a march that incorporates over-the-top floats and outrageous costumes, and crosses Paris via Le Marais.

☆ La Goutte d'Or en Fête   late Jun–early Jul
Raï, reggae and rap feature at this three-day world-music festival (www.gouttedorenfete.wordpress.com) on square Léon in the 18e's Goutte d'Or neighbourhood.

Plan Your Trip
This Year in Paris

July

During the Parisian summer, 'beaches' line the banks of the Seine, while shoppers hit the summer soldes (sales).

☆ La Fête du Cinéma
early Jul

Selected cinemas across Paris offer filmgoers a unique entry fee of €4 per session over three days sometime around early July (www.feteducinema.com).

✻ Bals des Pompiers
13 & 14 Jul

Bookending the city's Bastille Day celebrations, traditional Bals des Pompiers (Firemen's Balls) see dancing at many Parisian fire stations from 9pm to 4am on 13 and 14 July.

✻ Bastille Day
14 Jul

The capital celebrates France's national day on 14 July with a morning military parade along av des Champs-Élysées (pictured above) and fly-past of fighter aircraft and helicopters. *Feux d'artifice* (fireworks) light up the sky above the Champ de Mars by night.

⚐ Paris Plages
mid-Jul–early Sep

'Paris Beaches' – complete with sunbeds, umbrellas, atomisers, lounge chairs and palm trees – set up along Paris' riverbanks in two main zones, the Parc Rives de Seine, and the Bassin de la Villette (with swimming pools in the canal).

⚐ Tour de France
late Jul

The last of the 21 stages of this legendary, 3500km-long cycling event (www.letour.com) finishes with a dash up av des Champs-Élysées on the third or fourth Sunday of July.

August

Parisians desert the city in droves during the summer swelter when, despite an influx of tourists, many restaurants and shops shut. It's a prime time to cycle, with far less traffic on the roads.

☆ **Cinéma En Plein Air de la Villette** mid-Jul–mid-Aug
Free film screenings take place under the stars in Parc de la Villlette (pictured above; www.lavillette.com).

☆ **Classique au Vert** mid-Aug–early Sep
In the Bois de Vincennes, the Parc Floral de Paris hosts classical-music concerts (www.classiqueauvert.paris.fr) amid the greenery on August and September weekends.

☆ **Rock en Seine** late Aug
Headlining acts rock the Domaine National de St-Cloud, on the city's southwestern edge, at this popular three-day music festival (www.rockenseine.com).

☆ **Silhouette** late Aug–early Sep
Out-of-the-box short films by independent film-makers screen in competition alongside open-air concerts and workshops during this nine-day film festival (www.association-silhouette.com).

Plan Your Trip
This Year in Paris

September

Tourists leave and Parisians come home: la rentrée *marks residents' return to work and study after the summer break. Cultural life shifts into top gear and the weather is often at its blue-skied best.*

☆ Jazz à La Villette   early Sep
This 10-day jazz festival (https://jazzala villette.com) in the first half of September has sessions in Parc de la Villette, at the Cité de la Musique and at surrounding venues.

☆ Festival d'Automne   mid-Sep–Dec
The long-running Autumn Festival of arts (www.festival-automne.com) incorporates painting, music, dance and theatre at venues throughout the city.

☆ Techno Parade   mid-Sep
On one Saturday in mid-September, floats carrying musicians and DJs pump up the volume as they travel through the city's streets during the Techno Parade (www.technoparade.fr).

☉ Journées Européennes du Patrimoine   19–20 Sep
The third weekend in September sees Paris open the doors of otherwise off-limits buildings – embassies, government ministries and so forth – during European Heritage Days (www.journeesdupatrimoine. culturecommunication.gouv.fr).

🎟 Journée Sans Voiture   mid-Sep
Pedestrians and cyclists reclaim Paris' streets from mid-morning to early evening on one Sunday in mid-September on this annual car-free day (pictured above).

October

October heralds an autumnal kaleidoscope in the city's parks and gardens, along with bright, crisp days, cool, clear nights and excellent cultural offerings. Daylight saving ends on the last Sunday morning of the month.

✿ Fête des Vendanges de Montmartre   mid-Oct

This five-day festival (www.fetedesvend angesdemontmartre.com), held on the second weekend in October celebrates Montmartre's grape harvest with costumes, concerts, food events and a parade.

⊙ Foire Internationale d'Art Contemporain   mid-Oct

Scores of galleries are represented at this contemporary-art fair (www.fiac.com), held over four days.

☆ Pitchfork Music Festival Paris   late Oct/early Nov

The Grande Halle de la Villette at the Parc de la Villette is the venue for this three-day fest (www.pitchforkmusicfestival.fr; MIA performance pictured above) of pop, rock, indie and electro music.

✿ Nuit Blanche   5–6 Oct

From sundown until sunrise on the first Saturday and Sunday of October, museums stay open, along with bars and clubs, for one 'White Night' (ie 'All-Nighter').

✕ Salon du Chocolat   late Oct–early Nov

Chocaholics won't want to miss this five-day chocolate festival's tastings, workshops, demonstrations and more at Paris Expo Porte de Versailles, 15e (www.salonduchocolat.fr) There are special activities for kids.

Plan Your Trip
This Year in Paris

November

Dark, chilly days and long, cold nights see Parisians take refuge indoors: the opera and ballet seasons are going strong and there are plenty of cosy bistros and bars.

☆ Africolor   mid-Nov–late Dec
From mid-November to late December, this five-week-long African-music festival (www.africolor.com) is primarily held in outer suburbs, such as St-Denis, St-Ouen and Montreuil.

❄ Illuminations
de Noël   mid-Nov–early Jan
For the holiday season, festive lights sparkle along the av des Champs-Élysées (pictured above), rue du Faubourg Saint-Honoré and av Montaigne, all in the 8e, and others, while window displays enchant kids and adults alike at department stores including Galeries Lafayette and Le Printemps.

🍷 Beaujolais Nouveau   21 Nov
At midnight on the third Thursday (ie Wednesday night) in November – as soon as French law permits – the opening of the first bottles of cherry-bright, six-week-old Beaujolais Nouveau is celebrated in Paris wine bars, with more celebrations on the Thursday itself.

2020

NOVIKOV ALEKSEY/SHUTTERSTOCK ©

12

December

Twinkling fairy lights, brightly decorated Christmas trees and shop windows, and outdoor ice-skating rinks make December a magical month to be in the City of Light.

🏇 Salon du
Cheval de Paris   late Nov–early Dec

Sporting events and competitions including show jumping and dressage, plus a horseback parade through Paris, are part of the nine-day Paris Horse Fair (www.salon-cheval.com).

🎄 Christmas Eve Mass   24 Dec

Mass is celebrated at midnight on Christmas Eve at many Paris churches – arrive early to find a place.

👁 Le Festival
du Merveilleux   late Dec–early Jan

The magical private museum Musée des Arts Forains (www.arts-forains.com), filled with fairground attractions of yesteryear, opens from late December, with enchanting rides, attractions and festive shows.

🎄 New Year's Eve   31 Dec

Bd St-Michel, 5e, place de la Bastille, 11e, the Eiffel Tower, 7e, and especially av des Champs-Élysées (pictured above), are the Parisian hotspots for welcoming in the New Year.

Plan Your Trip
Need to Know

Daily Costs

Budget:
Less than €100

- Dorm bed: €25–50

- Espresso/glass of wine/*demi* (half-pint of beer)/cocktail: from €2/3.50/3.50/9

- Metro ticket: €1.90

- Baguette sandwich: €4.50–6.50

- Frequent free concerts and events

Midrange:
€100–250

- Double room: €130–250

- Two-course meal: €20–40

- Admission to museums: free to around €15

- Admission to clubs: free to around €20

Top end:
More than €250

- Double room at historic luxury hotel: from €250

- Gastronomic-restaurant *menu*: from €40

- Private two-hour city tour: from €150

- Premium ticket to opera/ballet performance: from €160

Advance Planning

Two months before Book accommodation, organise opera, ballet or cabaret tickets, check events calendars to find out what festivals will be on, and make reservations for high-end/popular restaurants.

Two weeks before Sign up for a local-led tour and start narrowing down your choice of museums, prepurchasing tickets online where possible to minimise ticket queues.

Two days before Pack your comfiest shoes to walk Paris' streets.

Useful Websites

Lonely Planet (www.lonely planet.com/paris) Destination information, hotel bookings, traveller forum and more.

Paris Info (www.parisinfo. com) Comprehensive tourist-authority website.

Sortiraparis (www.sortira paris.com) Up-to-date calendar listing what's on around town.

Bonjour Paris (www.bonjour paris.com) New openings, old favourites and upcoming events.

HiP Paris (www.hipparis.com) Not only vacation rentals ('Haven in Paris') but articles and reviews by expat locals, too.

Currency
Euro (€)

Language
French

Visas
Generally no restrictions for EU citizens. Usually not required for most other nationalities for stays of up to 90 days.

Money
ATMs widely available. Visa and MasterCard accepted in most hotels, shops and restaurants; fewer accept American Express.

Mobile Phones
Check with your provider about roaming costs before you leave home, or ensure your phone's unlocked to use a French SIM card (available cheaply in Paris).

Time
Central European Time (GMT/UTC plus one hour)

Tourist Information
Paris Convention & Visitors Bureau (p232), Paris' main tourist office, is at the Hôtel de Ville. It sells tickets for tours and several attractions, plus museum and transport passes.

For more, see the **Survival Guide** (p231)

When to Go

Spring and autumn are ideal. Summer is the main tourist season, but many establishments close during August. Sights are quieter during winter.

Paris

Arriving in Paris

Charles de Gaulle Airport Trains (RER), buses and night buses to the city centre €6 to €18; taxi €50 to €55, 15% higher evenings and Sundays.

Orly Airport Trains (Orlyval then RER), buses and night buses to the city centre €8.70 to €13.25; T7 tram to Villejuif–Louis Aragon then metro to centre (€3.80); taxi €30 to €35, 15% higher evenings and Sundays.

Beauvais Airport Buses (€17) to Porte Maillot then metro (€1.90); taxi during the day/night around €170/210 (probably more than the cost of your flight!).

Gare du Nord train station Within central Paris; served by metro (€1.90).

Getting Around

Walking is a pleasure in Paris, and the city also has one of the most efficient and inexpensive public-transport systems in the world, making getting around a breeze.

Metro & RER The fastest way to get around. Metros run from about 5.30am and finish around 1.15am (around 2.15am on Friday and Saturday nights), depending on the line. RER commuter trains operate from around 5.30am to 1.20am daily.

Bicycle Virtually free pick-up, drop-off Vélib' bikes have docking stations across the city; electric bikes are also available.

Bus Good for parents with prams/strollers and people with limited mobility.

Boat The Batobus is a handy hop-on, hop-off service stopping at nine key destinations along the Seine.

Arrondissements

Within the *périphérique* (ring road), Paris is divided into 20 *arrondissements* (city districts), which spiral clockwise like a snail shell from the centre (see map p238). *Arrondissement* numbers (1er, 2e etc) form an integral part of all Parisian addresses. Each *arrondissement* has its own personality, but it's the *quartiers* (quarters, ie neighbourhoods), which often overlap *arrondissement* boundaries, that give Paris its village atmosphere.

Sleeping

Paris' wealth of accommodation spans all budgets, but it's often *complet* (full) well in advance. Reservations are recommended year-round and essential during the warmer months (April to October) and all public and school holidays. See p205 for info on where to stay.

Plan Your Trip
Top Days in Paris

KAVALENKAU/SHUTTERSTOCK ©

Central Right Bank

The central Right Bank is the ideal place to kick off your Parisian trip. As well as the ancient art and artefacts in Paris' mightiest museum, the Louvre, you'll also see groundbreaking modern and contemporary art inside the striking Centre Pompidou.

❶ Jardin des Tuileries (p90)

Start your day with a stroll through the elegant Jardin des Tuileries, stopping to view Monet's enormous *Water Lilies* at the Musée de l'Orangerie and/or photography exhibits at the Jeu de Paume.

➲ Jardin des Tuileries to Musée du Louvre

🏃 Stroll through the gardens to the Louvre.

❷ Musée du Louvre (p52)

Visiting the world's largest museum could easily consume a full day, but tickets are valid all day, so you can come and go as you please. Various tours (guided and self-guided) help you maximise your time.

➲ Musée du Louvre to Chez La Vieille

🏃 From the Louvre's Cour Carée, walk east via rue de Rivoli.

Day
01

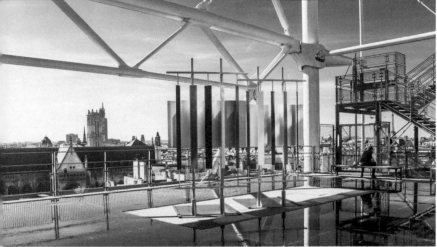

NIKOLPETR/SHUTTERSTOCK © CENTRE GEORGES POMPIDOU, PARIS, FRANCE. STUDIO PIANO & ROGERS, ARCHITECTS (1971-1977)

❸ Lunch at Chez La Vieille (p127)

Dine on updated versions of timeless bistro dishes at Chez La Vieille.

➲ Chez La Vieille to Jardin du Palais Royal

🚶 Walk northwest via rue St-Honoré to place du Palais Royal.

❹ Jardin du Palais Royal (p101)

Browse the colonnaded arcades of the exquisite Jardin du Palais Royal.

➲ Jardin du Palais Royal to Église St-Eustache

🚶 Head back down rue St-Honoré, turn north onto rue du Louvre and east on rue Coquillière.

❺ Église St-Eustache (p76)

One of Paris' most beautiful churches, Église St-Eustache has a magnificent organ – catch a classical concert here if you can.

➲ Église St-Eustache to Centre Pompidou

🚶 Continue east on rue Rambuteau to place Georges-Pompidou.

❻ Centre Pompidou (p74)

Head to the late-opening Centre Pompidou for amazing modern and contemporary art.

➲ Centre Pompidou to Breizh Café

🚶 Keep heading east on rue Rambuteau, then turn northeast on rue Vieille du Temple

❼ Dinner at Breizh Café (p130)

Dine on savoury *galettes* and sweet crêpes at this authentic Breton crêperie.

➲ Breizh Café to Le Mary Céleste

🚶 Take rue Vieille du Temple northeast and turn east on rue Froissart

❽ Drinks at Le Mary Céleste (p179)

Le Marais really comes into its own at night, with a cornucopia of hip clubs and top-notch cocktail bars such as Le Mary Céleste.

From left: Jardin des Tuileries (p90); Centre Pompidou (p74)

Plan Your Trip
Top Days in Paris

Western & Southern Paris

It's a day of Parisian icons today – from the triumphal span of the Arc de Triomphe to the world-famous avenue, the Champs-Élysées, and, of course, the city's stunning art nouveau Eiffel Tower, plus some surprises, such as floating nightclubs.

❶ Arc de Triomphe (p42)

Climb the mighty Arc de Triomphe for a pinch-yourself Parisian panorama. Back down on ground level, take the time to check out the intricate sculptures and historic bronze plaques, and pay your respects at the Tomb of the Unknown Soldier.

◗ Arc de Triomphe to Champs-Élysées

🚶 Walk downhill along the Champs-Élysées.

❷ Champs-Élysées (p152)

Promenade along Paris' most glamorous avenue, the Champs-Élysées, and perhaps give your credit card a workout in the adjacent Triangle d'Or (Golden Triangle), home to flagship *haute couture* (high fashion) houses.

◗ Champs-Élysées to Musée du Quai Branly

Ⓜ Line 9 from Franklin D Roosevelt to Alma Marceau

❸ Musée du Quai Branly – Jacques Chirac (p40)

Cross the Pont d'Alma and turn right along quai Branly to check out indigenous art as

Day

02

KIEV.VICTOR/SHUTTERSTOCK ©

well as the awesome architecture of the Musée du Quai Branly – Jacques Chirac. Dine at the museum's Café Branly or head to its elegant restaurant, Les Ombres (named 'the Shadows' for the webbed patterns cast by the adjacent Eiffel Tower).

○ Musée du Quai Branly to Palais de Tokyo

⚘ Cross the Passerelle Debilly. Walk uphill along rue de la Manutention, turning east on av du Président Wilson.

❹ Palais de Tokyo (p41)

This stunning building takes on major temporary cutting-edge exhibits – the rooftop, for example, has been the setting for attention-getting projects such as the transient Hotel Everland and the see-through restaurant Nomiya.

○ Palais de Tokyo to Eiffel Tower

Ⓜ Line 9 from Iéna to Trocadéro

❺ Eiffel Tower (p36)

Exiting the Trocadéro metro station, walk east through the Jardins du Trocadéro for

the ultimate Eiffel Tower snapshot, and cross Pont d'Iéna to the tower itself. Sunset is the best time to ascend the Eiffel Tower, to experience both the dazzling views during daylight and then the twinkling Ville Lumière (City of Light) by night. (Pre-purchase your tickets to minimise queuing.)

○ Eiffel Tower to Le Cassenoix

⚘ Walk southeast through Parc du Champ de Mars, turn southwest on av Joseph Bouvard then rue Desaix to Le Cassenoix.

❻ Dinner & Drinks

Dining inside the Eiffel Tower itself is unforgettable. Alternatively, book ahead for cracking modern French cuisine at Le Cassenoix (p144). Take metro line 6 to party aboard floating nightclubs such as Bateau El Alamein (p185).

From left: Arc de Triomphe (p42); Musée du Quai Branly – Jacques Chirac (p40)

Plan Your Trip
Top Days in Paris

BENEDEK/GETTY IMAGES ©

The Islands & Left Bank

Begin the day in the exquisite gothic masterpiece of Sainte-Chapelle, then venture across to Paris' elegant Left Bank to see impressionist masterpieces in the Musée d'Orsay, and to visit the city's oldest church and loveliest gardens.

❶ Sainte-Chapelle (p92)

Start your day at the exquisite Sainte-Chapelle. Consecrated in 1248, the chapel's stained glass forms a curtain of glazing on the 1st floor. From here you can walk five minutes across the Île de la Cité to see Notre Dame cathedral, still standing, and still impressive after being ravaged by fire in April 2019.

➲ Sainte-Chapelle to Musée d'Orsay

Ⓜ RER from St-Michel–Notre Dame to Gare Musée d'Orsay.

❷ Musée d'Orsay (p62)

Set inside a magnificent art nouveau former railway station, the Musée d'Orsay is filled with impressionist tours de force by masters including Renoir, Monet, Van Gogh,

Day
03

Degas and dozens more. It's also an ideal place to dine at casual Café Campana or the ornate Restaurant Musée d'Orsay.

○ Musée d'Orsay to Église St-Germain des Prés

Ⓜ Solférino to Sèvres-Babylone (line 12), then change for Mabillon (line 10).

❸ Église St-Germain des Prés

Paris' oldest church (www.eglise-saintgermain despres.fr; 3 place St-Germain des Prés, 6e; ⏰9am-8pm; Ⓜ St-Germain des Prés) sits in the heart of the buzzing St-Germain des Prés district, with chic boutiques and historic literary cafes, including Les Deux Magots (p183), just opposite.

○ Église St-Germain des Prés to Jardin du Luxembourg

🚶 Head south on rue Bonaparte to place St-Sulpice and continue on to rue Vaugirard.

❹ Jardin du Luxembourg (p68)

Enter this lovely garden from rue Vaugirard and stroll among its chestnut groves, paths and statues.

○ Jardin du Luxembourg to Bouillon Racine

🚶 From rue Vaugirard, take rue Monsieur-le-Prince northwest to rue Racine.

❺ Dinner at Bouillon Racine (p140)

Feast on French classics in this art nouveau jewel. Afterwards, head to Shakespeare & Company for late-night book shopping.

From left: Église St-Germain des Prés; Fontaine des Médicis (p71), Jardin du Luxembourg

Plan Your Trip
Top Days in Paris

ANTOINE2K/SHUTTERSTOCK ©

Northern & Eastern Paris

Montmartre's slinking streets and steep staircases lined with crooked ivy-clad buildings are especially enchanting to meander in the early morning when there are fewer tourists. Afterwards, explore charming Canal St-Martin and futuristic Parc de la Villette before drinking, dining and dancing in lively Bastille.

❶ Musée de Montmartre (p61)

Brush up on the area's fascinating history at the local museum, the Musée de Montmartre. Not only was Montmartre home to seminal artists, but Renoir and Utrillo are among those who lived in this very building.

➲ Musée de Montmartre to Sacré-Cœur

🏃 Walk east to Sacré-Cœur along rue Cortot, rue du Mont Cenis then rue Azais.

❷ Sacré-Cœur (p58)

Head to the hilltop Sacré-Cœur basilica and, for an even more extraordinary panorama over Paris, climb up into the basilica's main dome. Regular metro tickets are valid on the funicular that shuttles up and down the steep Butte de Montmartre.

➲ Sacré-Cœur to Le Bistrot de la Galette

🏃 Head west, past place du Tertre, along rue Norvins and turn left onto rue Lepic.

Day

04

SAMANTHAINALAODHLSEN/SHUTTERSTOCK ©

❸ Lunch at Le Bistrot de la Galette (p130)

Below historic Montmartre windmill Moulin de la Galette, Le Bistrot de la Galette serves house-speciality *feuilletés* (pastry puffs) made from locally hand-milled flour.

➲ Le Bistrot de la Galette to Canal St-Martin

Ⓜ Line 2 Blanche to Jaurès.

❹ Canal St-Martin (p153)

A postcard-perfect vision of iron foot-bridges, swing bridges and shaded tow paths, Canal St-Martin's banks (and the surrounding streets) are lined with a steadily growing number of hip cafes and boutiques. Also here is cultural centre Point Éphemère; its restaurant, Animal Kitchen, combines gourmet cuisine with music from Animal Records.

➲ Canal St-Martin to Parc de la Villette

Ⓜ Line 5 Jacques Bonsergent to Porte de Pantin.

❺ Parc de la Villette (p200)

In addition to its striking geometric gardens, innovative Parc de la Villette has a slew of attractions, including the kid-friendly Cité des Sciences et de l'Industrie museum and the Cité de la Musique – Philharmonie de Paris complex.

➲ Parc de la Villette to Le Bistrot Paul Bert

Ⓜ Porte de Pantin to République (line 5), changing for Faidherbe-Chaligny (line 8).

❻ Dinner at Le Bistrot Paul Bert (p136)

After a pre-dinner *apéro* (aperitif) at back-street favourite cherry-red Le Pure Café, head around the corner to enjoy exceptional bistro classics at Le Bistrot Paul Bert. After dinner head west to the Bastille neighbourhood's buzzing bars; there's a great concentration on rue de Lappe.

From left: Canal St-Martin (p153); Cité des Sciences et de l'Industrie, Parc de la Vilette (p32)

Plan Your Trip
Hotspots For...

ART LOVERS

◉ **Maison et Jardins de Claude Monet** Take a day trip to Monet's former house and beautiful gardens. (p98; pictured above)

◉ **Musée National Picasso** View this exceptional collection inside a 17th-century mansion. (p114)

🍷 **La Belle Hortense** Art and literary events take place at this wine bar. (p178)

🍷 **La Palette** Braque was among the artists who frequented this cafe; today it's popular with art dealers. (p185)

🛍 **Magasin Sennelier** Former clients of this 1887-founded art-supply shop include Cézanne and Picasso. (p163)

EPICUREANS

◉ **Musée du Louvre** Follow the Louvre's 'Art of Eating' thematic trail. (p52)

🍴 **Le Cordon Bleu** Cooking classes by the Seine at one of the world's most prestigious culinary campuses. (p116)

🛍 **La Grande Épicerie de Paris** Stock up on luxury food items at Le Bon Marché's spectacular food hall. (p163)

✗ **Bustronome** Dine on gourmet cuisine aboard a glass-roofed bus cruising Paris' boulevards. (p125)

✗ **Marché d'Aligre** Shop for fresh produce and delectable specialities at this outstanding Parisian market. (p83; pictured below)

ACTIVE OUTDOORS

⊙ **Jardin du Luxembourg** Paris' most popular park is perfect for a stroll, run, sports or kids' activities. (p68)

⊙ **Eiffel Tower** Get up-close tower views while scaling 720 steps to the 2nd floor. (p36)

⚡ **Paris à Vélo, C'est Sympa!** Explore Paris on a bike tour. (p203)

⚡ **Piscine Joséphine Baker** Swim in this striking pool floating on the Seine. (p200)

⚡ **Bois de Boulogne** Explore Paris' western woods by rowing boat or bicycle. (p202)

ART NOUVEAU BUFFS

⊙ **Eiffel Tower** The graceful latticed metalwork of Paris' 'iron lady' is art nouveau architecture at its best. (p36)

⊙ **Musée d'Orsay** The former railway station housing this monumental museum justifies a visit alone. (p62)

✖ **Bouillon Racine** Classical cooking in an art nouveau showpiece. (p141)

🛍 **Galeries Lafayette** Glorious department store topped by a stunning stained-glass dome. (p152; pictured above)

☆ **Le Carreau du Temple** This old covered market in Le Marais is now a cutting-edge cultural and community centre. (p193)

FASHION FANS

⊙ **Musée Yves Saint Laurent Paris** See sketches and couture creations by avant-garde designer YSL. (p105; pictured above)

⚡ **Galeries Lafayette** Attend free fashion shows at this resplendent department store. (p152)

🛍 **Triangle d'Or** Flit between flagships such as Chanel in Paris' Golden Triangle. (p155)

🛍 **Chercheminippes** Search for vintage treasures at this string of boutiques. (p163)

✖ **Lasserre** Style icon Audrey Hepburn was a former patron of this Michelin-starred restaurant. (p125)

Plan Your Trip
What's New

Contemporary Art Landmark

Topped by a soaring frescoed cupola, Paris' former grain market and stock exchange, the circular Bourse de Commerce, has been dramatically reinvented to showcase contemporary art over three floors of galleries at Collection Pinault – Paris (p77).

Eat Streets

A gourmand's fantasy land, Beaupassage (p128) brings together some of the country's most feted chefs, artisans and purveyors, who collectively hold 17 Michelin stars, in one Left Bank 'mini district'.

Parisian History Redux

Paris' history museum, the pair of 16th- and 17th-century *hôtels particuliers* (private mansions) in Le Marais housing the Musée

Carnavalet (p115) reopen in early 2020 following four years of renovations.

Palatial Splendour

On place de la Concorde, monumental palace Hôtel de la Marine (p91), built by Louis XV to house the royal furnishings and later used as the French navy's headquarters until 2015, will open to the public for guided tours in 2020.

Economics & Banking Museum

Footsteps from leafy Parc Monceau, a turreted, neo-renaissance 19th-century townhouse built for banker Emile Gaillard forms the backdrop for Citéco (p97), Paris' new economics and banking museum, where highlights include historical currency displays.

Above: Collection Pinault – Paris (p77), Bourse de Commerce

Plan Your Trip
For Free

PAUL GUEU/SHUTTERSTOCK ©

Free Museums

If you can, time your trip to be here on the first Sunday of the month, when you can visit many national museums and a handful of monuments for free (some during certain months only).

European citizens under 26 get free entry to national museums and monuments.

At any time you can visit the permanent collections of Paris' *musées municipaux* (www.paris.fr/musees) for free (some only when temporary exhibitions aren't taking place).

Free Churches & Cemeteries

Some of the city's most magnificent buildings are its churches and other places of worship. Not only exceptional architecturally and historically, they contain exquisite art, artefacts and other priceless treasures. Best of all, entry to general areas within them is, in most cases, free.

Do respect the fact that, although many of Paris' places of worship are also major tourist attractions, Parisians come here to pray and celebrate significant events on religious calendars as part of their daily lives. Keep noise to a minimum, obey photography rules (check signs), dress appropriately and try to avoid key times (eg Mass) if you're sightseeing only.

Free Music

Concerts, DJ sets and recitals regularly take place for free (or for the cost of a drink) at venues throughout the city.

Busking musicians and performers entertain crowds on Paris' streets and squares and even aboard the metro.

Free Literary Events

This literary-minded city is an inspired place to catch a reading, author signing or writing workshop. English-language bookshops such as Shakespeare & Company and Abbey Bookshop host literary events throughout the year and can point you towards others.

Free Festivals & Events

Loads of Paris' festivals and events are free, such as the summertime Paris Plages riverside beaches.

Above: Fête des Vendanges de Montmartre parade (p15)

Plan Your Trip
Family Travel

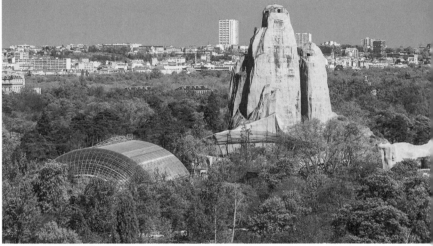

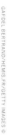

Sights & Activities

In addition to classic playgrounds, Paris' parks also have a host of children's activities.

° The toy boats, marionettes (puppets), pony rides and carousel of the Jardin du Luxembourg (p68).

° The new millennium playgrounds of Parc de la Villette (p200).

° The fabulous interactive museum **Cité des Sciences et de l'Industrie** (☑01 40 05 80 00; www.cite-sciences.fr; 30 av Corentin Cariou, Parc de la Villette, 19e; per attraction adult/child €12/9; ☺10am-6pm Tue-Sat, to 7pm Sun; MPorte de la Villette).

° Bois de Boulogne's Jardin d'Acclimatation (p202) amusement park.

° Animal-mad kids will love the lions, cougars, white rhinos and other creatures at the Bois de Vincennes' state-of-the-art Parc Zoologique de Paris (p202); the kid-friendly natural-history–focused Muséum National d'Histoire Naturelle (p107); and the shark tank inside the **Cinéaqua aquarium** (☑01 40 69 23 23; www.cineaqua.com; av des Nations Unies, 16e; adult/child €20.50/13; ☺10am-7pm; MTrocadéro).

° The Louvre (p52) can be a treat, particularly following thematic trails such as hunting for lions or galloping horses.

° Every kid, big and small, loves a voyage down the Seine with Bateaux-Mouches (p73) or Bateaux Parisiens (p232). But the one-hour 'Paris Mystery' tours designed especially for children by Vedettes de Paris (p72) are extra special.

° Further afield, theme parks within day-trip distance include Disneyland Paris (www.disneylandparis.com) and Parc Astérix (www.parcasterix.fr).

Eating Out with Kids

Many restaurants accept little diners (confirm ahead), but they're expected to behave. Children's menus are common, although most restaurants don't have high chairs. A wave of gourmet pizza, pasta,

NIKONAFT/SHUTTERSTOCK ©

bagel and burger restaurants throughout the city offer kid-friendly fare. In fine
weather, good options include picking
up sandwiches and crêpes from a street
stall or packing a market-fresh picnic and
heading to parks and gardens where kids
can play to their hearts' content.

Getting Around with Kids

Paris' narrow streets and metro stairways
are a trial if you have a stroller (pram or
pushchair) in tow; buses offer an easier,
scenic alternative. Children under four
years of age travel free on public transport
and generally receive free admission to
sights. For older kids, discounts vary
from place to place – anything from a euro
off for over-fours to free entry up to the
age of 18.

Need to Know

Babysitting *L'Officiel des Spectacles* (www.offi.
fr) lists *gardes d'enfants* (babysitters); some
hotels organise sitters for guests.

★ Best Parks & Playgrounds

Jardin du Luxembourg (p68)

Parc de la Villette (p200)

Parc Montsouris (p201)

Bois de Boulogne (p202)

Bois de Vincennes (p201)

Equipment Rent strollers, scooters, car seats,
travel beds and more while in Paris from companies such as Kidelio (www.kidelio.com).

Paris Mômes (www.parismomes.fr) Outstanding
bimonthly magazine on Parisian kid culture (up
to 12 years); print off playful kids' guides for
major art exhibitions before leaving home.

From left: Parc Zoologique de Paris (p202); Grand
Bassin (p70), Jardin du Luxembourg

TOP EXPERIENCES

The very best to see & do

Eiffel Tower

Paris today is unimaginable without its signature spire. Originally only constructed as a temporary 1889 Exposition Universelle exhibit, it went on to become the defining fixture of the city's skyline.

Great For...

ⓘ Need to Know

Map p262; ☎08 92 70 12 39; www.toureiffel. paris; Champ de Mars, 5 av Anatole France, 7e; adult/child lift to top €25/12.50, lift to 2nd fl €16/8, stairs to 2nd fl €10/5; ⊘lifts & stairs 9am-12.45am mid-Jun–Aug, lifts 9.30am-11.45pm, stairs 9.30am-6.30pm Sep–mid-Jun; Ⓜ Bir Hakeim or RER Champ de Mars–Tour Eiffel

★ **Top Tip**

Head here at dusk for the best daytime vistas and glittering night-time city views.

Named after its designer, Gustave Eiffel, the Tour Eiffel was built for the 1889 Exposition Universelle (World's Fair). It took 300 workers, 2.5 million rivets and two years of nonstop labour to assemble. Upon completion the tower became the tallest human-made structure in the world (324m or 1063ft) – a record held until the completion of the Chrysler Building in New York (1930). A symbol of the modern age, it faced massive opposition from Paris' artistic and literary elite, and the 'metal asparagus', as some Parisians snidely called it, was originally slated to be torn down in 1909. It was spared only because it proved an ideal platform for the transmitting antennas needed for the newfangled science of radiotelegraphy.

Tickets & Queues

Visitors must pass through security at the bullet-proof glass barriers surrounding the tower's base.

Ascend as far as the 2nd floor, either on foot or by lift (elevator), from where it is lift-only to the top floor. Pushchairs must be folded in lifts and you are not allowed to take bags or backpacks larger than aeroplane-cabin size.

Buying tickets in advance online usually means you avoid the monumental queues at the ticket offices. Print your ticket or show it on a smartphone screen. If you can't reserve your tickets ahead of time, expect waits of well over an hour in high season.

Stair tickets can't be reserved online. They are sold at the south pillar, where the staircase can also be accessed: the climb

Top floor observation deck

consists of 360 steps to the 1st floor and another 360 steps to the 2nd floor.

If you have reservations for either restaurant, you are granted direct access to the lifts.

1st Floor

Of the tower's three floors, the 1st (57m) has the most space but the least impressive views. The glass-enclosed **Pavillon Ferrié** houses an immersion film along with a small cafe and souvenir shop, while the outer walkway features a discovery circuit to help visitors learn more about the tower's ingenious design. Check out the sections of glass flooring that proffer a

dizzying view of the ant-like people walking on the ground far below.

This level also hosts the **58 Tour Eiffel** (Map p262; ☎08 25 56 66 62; www.restaurants-toureiffel.com; 1st fl, Eiffel Tower, Champ de Mars, 7e; menus lunch €39, dinner €86-125; ⊙11.30am-3.30pm & 6.30-11pm; ⚹🚼; ⓂBir Hakeim or RER Champ de Mars–Tour Eiffel) restaurant.

Not all lifts stop at the 1st floor; (check before ascending), but it's an easy walk down from the 2nd floor.

The 1st floor's commercial areas are powered by two sleek wind turbines within the tower.

2nd Floor

Views from the 2nd floor (115m) are the best – impressively high but still close enough to see the details of the city below. Telescopes and panoramic maps placed around the tower pinpoint locations in Paris and beyond. Story windows give an overview of the lifts' mechanics, and the vision well allows you to gaze through glass panels to the ground. Also up here are toilets, a souvenir shop and gastronomic restaurant **Le Jules Verne** (Map p262; www.toureiffel.paris; 2nd fl, Eiffel Tower, Champ de Mars, 7e; ⓂBir Hakeim or RER Champ de Mars–Tour Eiffel).

Top Floor

Views from the wind-buffeted top floor (276m) stretch up to 60km on a clear day, though at this height the panoramas are more sweeping than detailed. Celebrate your ascent with a glass of bubbly (€13 to €22) from the Champagne bar (open 11am to 10.30pm, to midnight in July and August). Afterwards peep into Gustave Eiffel's restored top-level office where lifelike wax models of Eiffel and his daughter Claire greet Thomas Edison.

> ### ☑ Don't Miss
>
> Views of the tower from the Jardins du Trocadéro outside Palais de Chaillot.

GIL.MANSHIN/SHUTTERSTOCK ©

> ### ✗ Take a Break
>
> At the tower's two restaurants, snack bars, macaron bar or top-floor Champagne bar.

To access the top floor, take a separate lift on the 2nd floor (closed during heavy winds).

Nightly Sparkles

Every hour on the hour, the entire tower sparkles for five minutes with 20,000 6-watt lights. They were first installed for Paris' millennium celebration in 2000 – it took 25 mountain climbers five months to install the current bulbs and 40km of electrical cords. For the best view of the light show, head across the Seine to the Jardins du Trocadéro.

What's Nearby?

Parc du Champ de Mars   Park

(Map p262; Champ de Mars, 7e; ☉24hr; MÉcole Militaire or RER Champ de Mars–Tour Eiffel) Running southeast from the Eiffel Tower, the grassy Champ de Mars – an ideal summer picnic spot – was originally used as a parade ground for the cadets of the 18th-century **École Militaire**, the vast French-classical building at the southeastern end of the park, which counts Napoléon Bonaparte among its graduates. The steel-and-etched-glass **Wall for Peace Memorial** (http://wallforpeace.org), erected in 2000, is by Clara Halter.

Musée du Quai Branly – Jacques Chirac   Museum

(Map p262; ☎01 56 61 70 00; www.quaibranly.fr; 37 quai Branly, 7e; adult/child €10/free; ☉11am-7pm Tue, Wed & Sun, 11am-9pm Thu-Sat, plus 11am-9pm Mon during school holidays; MAlma Marceau or RER Pont de l'Alma) A tribute to the diversity of human culture, Musée du Quai Branly's highly inspiring overview of indigenous and folk art spans four main sections – Oceania, Asia, Africa and the Americas. An impressive array of masks, carvings, weapons, jewellery and more make up the body of the rich collection, displayed in a refreshingly unorthodox interior without rooms or high walls. Look out for excellent temporary exhibitions and performances.

Palais de Chaillot   Historic Building

(Map p262; place du Trocadéro et du 11 Novembre, 16e; MTrocadéro) The two curved, colonnaded wings of this building (built for the 1937 International Expo) and central terrace afford an exceptional panorama of the **Jardins du Trocadéro**, Seine and Eiffel Tower.

The eastern wing houses the standout **Cité de l'Architecture et du Patrimoine** (☎01 58 51 52 00; www.citedelarchitecture.fr; adult/child €8/free; ☉11am-7pm Wed & Fri-Mon, to 9pm Thu), devoted to French architecture and heritage, as well as the **Théâtre National de Chaillot** (☎01 53 65 30 00; www.theatre-chaillot.fr), staging dance and theatre.

Eiffel Tower from Jardins du Trocadéro

The **Musée de la Marine** (Maritime Museum; ☎01 53 65 69 69; www.musee-marine. fr), closed for renovations until 2021, and the **Musée de l'Homme** (Museum of Humankind; ☎01 44 05 72 72; www.museedelhomme.fr; adult/child €10/free; ⊙10am-6pm Wed-Mon) are housed in the western wing.

Palais de Tokyo Gallery

(Map p252; ☎01 81 97 35 88; www.palaisde tokyo.com; 13 av du Président Wilson, 16e; adult/child €12/free; ⊙noon-midnight Wed-Mon; Ⓜléna) The Tokyo Palace, created for the 1937 Exposition Internationale des Arts et Techniques dans la Vie Moderne (International Exposition of Art and Technology in Modern Life), has no permanent collection. Instead, its shell-like interior of concrete and steel is a stark backdrop to interactive contemporary-art exhibitions and installations. Its bookshop is fabulous for art and design magazines, and its eating and drinking options are magic.

★ **Did You Know?**

Slapping a fresh coat of paint on the tower is no easy feat. It takes a 25-person team 18 months to complete the 60-tonnes-of-paint task, redone every seven years.

★ **Man on a Wire**

In 1989 tightrope artist Philippe Petit walked up an inclined 700m cable across the Seine, from Palais Chaillot to the Eiffel Tower's 2nd floor. The act, performed before an audience of 250,000 people, was held to commemorate the French Republic's bicentennial.

Arc de Triomphe

If anything rivals the Eiffel Tower as the symbol of Paris, it's this magnificent 1836-built triumphal arch commemorating Napoléon's 1805 victory at Austerlitz, which he commissioned the following year.

Great For...

ⓘ Need to Know

Map p252; www.paris-arc-de-triomphe. fr; place Charles de Gaulle, 8e; viewing platform adult/child €12/free; ⊕10am-11pm Apr-Sep, to 10.30pm Oct-Mar; Ⓜ Charles de Gaulle–Étoile)

★ **Top Tip**

Don't risk getting skittled by traffic by taking photos while crossing the Champs-Élysées.

History

Napoléon's armies never did march through the Arc de Triomphe showered in honour. At the time it was commissioned, his victory at Austerlitz seemed like a watershed moment that confirmed the tactical supremacy of the French army, but a mere decade later Napoléon had already fallen from power and his empire had crumbled.

The Arc de Triomphe was never fully abandoned – simply laying the foundations had taken an entire two years – and in 1836, after a series of starts and stops under the restored monarchy, the project was finally completed. In 1840 Napoléon's remains were returned to France and passed under the arch before being interred at Invalides.

Accessing the Arch

Don't try to cross the traffic-choked roundabout above ground! Stairs on the Champs-Élysées' northeastern side lead beneath the Place de l'Étoile (Place Charles de Gaulle) to pedestrian tunnels that bring you out safely beneath the arch.

There are lifts at the arch to access the terrace, but only for visitors with limited mobility or those travelling with young children.

Underside of the Arc de Triomphe

Beneath the Arch

Beneath the arch at ground level lies the **Tomb of the Unknown Soldier**. Honouring the 1.3 million French soldiers who lost their lives in WWI, the Unknown Soldier was laid to rest in 1921, beneath an eternal flame that is rekindled daily at 6.30pm.

Also here are a number of bronze plaques laid into the ground. Take the time to try and decipher some: these mark significant moments in modern French history, such as the proclamation of the Third French Republic (4 September 1870) and the return of Alsace and Lorraine to French rule (11 November 1918). The most notable plaque is the text from Charles de Gaulle's famous London broadcast on 18 June 1940, which sparked the French Resistance to life.

Sculptures

The arch is adorned with four main sculptures, six panels in relief, and a frieze running beneath the top. The higher panels depict a series of important victories for the Revolutionary and imperial French armies, from Egypt to Austerlitz, while the detailed frieze is divided into two sections: the *Departure of the Armies* and the *Return of the Armies*. Don't miss the **multimedia section** beneath the viewing platform, which provides more detail and historical background for each of the sculptures.

Viewing Platform

Climb the 284 steps to the viewing platform at the top of the 50m-high arch and you'll be suitably rewarded with magnificent panoramas over western Paris. From here, a dozen broad avenues – many of them named after Napoléonic victories and illustrious generals – radiate towards every compass point. The Arc de Triomphe is the highest point in the line of monuments known as the *axe historique* (historic axis, also called the grand axis); it offers views that swoop east down the Champs-Élysées to the gold-tipped obelisk at place de la Concorde (and beyond to the Louvre's glass pyramid), and west to the skyscraper district of La Défense, where the colossal Grande Arche marks the axis' western terminus.

☑ **Don't Miss**

Some of the best vistas in Paris from the top of the arch.

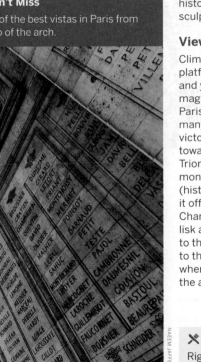

NAEEM JAFFER/GETTY IMAGES ©

✕ **Take a Break**

Right near the arch, **Publicis Drugstore** (Map p252; ☎01 44 43 75 07; www.publicis drugstore.com; 133 av des Champs-Élysées, 8e; ⊗8am-2am Mon-Fri, 10am-2pm Sat & Sun; MCharles de Gaulle-Étoile) is handy for a meal, drink or snack.

Rose window

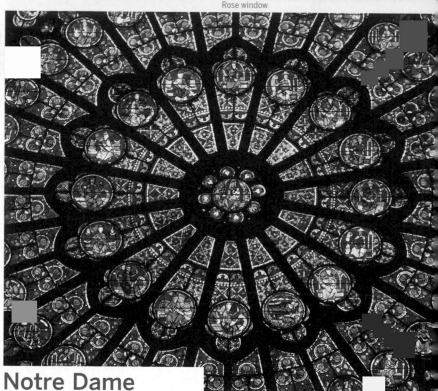

ARTEM NEDOLUZHKO/SHUTTERSTOCK ©

Notre Dame

A vision of stained-glass rose windows, flying buttresses and frightening gargoyles, Paris' glorious cathedral is the city's geographic and spiritual heart – so much so that distances from Paris to every part of metropolitan France are measured from its location.

Great For...

❶ Notre Dame Closed

The cathedral suffered a devastating fire in 2019. Visitors will most likely not be able to enter Notre Dame for many years.

Fire of April 2019

A blaze broke out under the cathedral's roof on the evening of 15 April 2019. Though firefighters were able to control the fire and ultimately save the church, it suffered devastating damage.

The fire destroyed most of the roof and toppled its spire, a 19th-century addition. However, the oldest parts of the cathedral – notably the two bell towers, the rose windows and the west facade – were all saved.

At the time of the fire, Notre Dame was undergoing a planned restoration, and this spared several statues and other artifacts, which had been taken off site to be restored.

Despite the damage, the awesome exterior of the cathedral, and its surrounding squares, are well worth a visit – for the sublime gothic architecture and the church's historical and cultural significance.

Towers and rose window facade

Cité
St-Michel–
Notre Dame
St-Michel
Seine
R du Cloître Notre Dame
Pont au Double
Notre Dame

ⓘ Need to Know

Map p254; ☎01 42 34 56 10, towers 01 53 10 07 00; www.notredamedeparis.fr; 6 Parvis Notre Dame – place Jean-Paul-II, 4e; ⓂCité

★ Top Tip

One of the best views of the cathedral's forest of flying buttresses is from square Jean XXIII, the little park behind the cathedral.

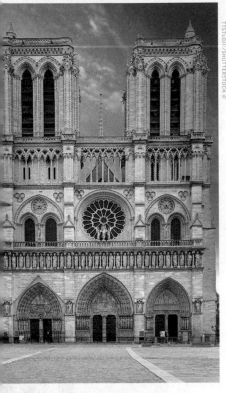

Rebuilding Notre Dame

After the fire, French President Emmanuel Macron said he'd like the cathedral to be rebuilt by 2024, in time for the Olympic Games, but others estimate that a full restoration could take decades.

There is debate over the form that the restoration should take: should it be restored to its original era, to the 19th-century update or something more modern still?

Though it will be a long while before visits to the interior can resume, the cathedral's significance has not dimmed. The gothic structure stands strong and continues to inspire awe and devotion more than 800 years after it was first built.

Architecture

Built on a site occupied by earlier churches and, a millennium prior, a Gallo-Roman temple, the construction of Notre Dame was begun in 1163 and largely completed by the early 14th century. The cathedral was badly damaged during the Revolution, prompting architect Eugène Emmanuel Viollet-le-Duc to oversee extensive renovations between 1845 and 1864.

Notre Dame is known for its sublime balance, though if you look closely you'll see all sorts of minor asymmetrical elements introduced to avoid monotony, in accordance with standard Gothic practice. These include the slightly different shapes of each of the three main portals, whose statues were once brightly coloured to make them more effective as a *Biblia pauperum* – a 'Bible of the poor' to help the illiterate faithful understand Old Testament stories, the Passion of the Christ and the lives of the saints.

The grand dimensions of the cathedral are immediately evident: the interior alone is 127m long, 48m wide and 35m high, and can accommodate some 6000 worshippers.

Rose Windows

A cathedral highlight, the three rose windows are Notre Dame's most spectacular feature. All three windows appear to have survived the 2019 fires, with no catastrophic damage.

Towers

Gargoyles grimace and grin on the rooftop Galerie des Chimères (Gargoyles Gallery), around the cathedral's bell towers. These grotesque statues divert rainwater from the roof to prevent masonry damage, with the water exiting through their elongated open mouths. They also, purportedly, ward off evil spirits. Although they appear medieval, they were installed by Eugène Viollet-le-Duc in the 19th century.

In the South Tower hangs Emmanuel, the cathedral's original 13-tonne bourdon bell (all of the cathedral's bells are named). During the night of 24 August 1944, when the Île de la Cité was retaken by French, Allied and Resistance troops, the tolling of the Emmanuel announced Paris' approaching liberation. Emmanuel's peal purity comes from the precious gems and jewels Parisian women threw into the pot when it was recast from copper and bronze in 1631.

As part of 2013's celebrations for Notre Dame's 850th anniversary since construction began, nine new bells were installed, replicating the original medieval chimes.

Point Zéro

Distances from Paris to every part of metropolitan France are measured from this bronze star, embedded in the paving stones of Place Jean-Paul II, the vast square in front of Notre Dame. When the sun floods onto the cathedral's exquisitely sculptured front facade, the square is packed, making it a challenge to locate the **Point Zéro des Routes de France** (Map p254; Parvis Notre Dame – place Jean-Paul II, 4e; MCité). The square is also graced by a statue of Charlemagne (AD 742–814), emperor of the Franks, on horseback.

Coloured archival photo of Notre Dame circa 1910

Notre Dame

TIMELINE

1160 Maurice de Sully becomes bishop of Paris. Mission: to grace growing Paris with a lofty new cathedral.

1182–90 The choir with double ambulatory is finished and work starts on the nave and side chapels.

1200–50 The ❶ **west facade**, with rose window, three portals and two soaring towers, goes up. Everyone is stunned.

1345 Some 180 years after the foundation stone was laid, the Cathédrale de Notre Dame is complete. It is dedicated to *notre dame* (our lady), the Virgin Mary.

1789 Revolutionaries smash the original Gallery of Kings, pillage the cathedral and melt all its bells except the great bell ❷ **Emmanuel**. The cathedral becomes a Temple of Reason then a warehouse.

1831 Victor Hugo's novel *The Hunchback of Notre Dame* inspires new interest in the half-ruined Gothic cathedral.

1845–64 Architect Viollet-le-Duc undertakes its restoration. Twenty-eight new kings are sculpted for the west facade. The heavily decorated ❸ **portals** and spire are reconstructed. The neo-Gothic treasury is built.

1860 The area in front of Notre Dame is cleared to create the ❹ **parvis**, an al fresco classroom where Parisians can learn a catechism illustrated on sculpted portals.

1935 A rooster bearing part of the relics of the Crown of Thorns, St Denis and Ste Geneviève is put on top of the cathedral spire to protect those who pray inside.

1991 The architectural masterpiece of Notre Dame and its Seine-side riverbanks become a Unesco World Heritage Site.

2013 Notre Dame celebrates 850 years since construction began with a bevy of new bells and restoration works.

2019 A fire causes devastating damage to the cathedral interior, destroys most of the roof and topples the spire.

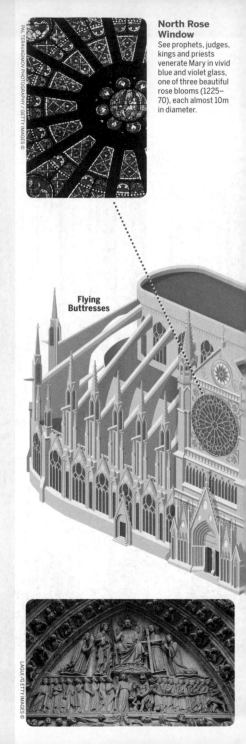

North Rose Window
See prophets, judges, kings and priests venerate Mary in vivid blue and violet glass, one of three beautiful rose blooms (1225–70), each almost 10m in diameter.

PAL TERAVAGIMOV PHOTOGRAPHY / GETTY IMAGES ©

Flying Buttresses

LAGUI /GETTY IMAGES ©

Treasury

The cash reserve of French kings – who ordered chalices, crucifixes, baptism fonts and other sacred gems to be melted down in the Mint during times of financial strife (war, famine and so on) – was stored in the Notre Dame treasury.

In the April 2019 fire, priceless relics, such as the prized Ste-Couronne (Holy Crown), purportedly the wreath of thorns placed on Jesus' head before he was crucified, were saved by a human chain of rescue workers.

Spire & Roof

Two-thirds of the roof, and the 19th-century spire, were destroyed in the April 2019 fire.

BRIAN A JACKSON / SHUTTERSTOCK ©

SYADCHKA / SHUTTERSTOCK ©

Great Bell
The peal of Emmanuel, the cathedral's great bell, is so pure thanks to precious gems and jewels Parisian women threw into the pot when it was recast from copper and bronze in 1631. Admire its original siblings in Square Jean XXII.

Chimera Gallery
The north tower is graced with grimacing gargoyles and grotesque chimera, including celebrity chimera Stryga, who has wings, horns, a human body and sticking-out tongue. This bestial lot wards off demons.

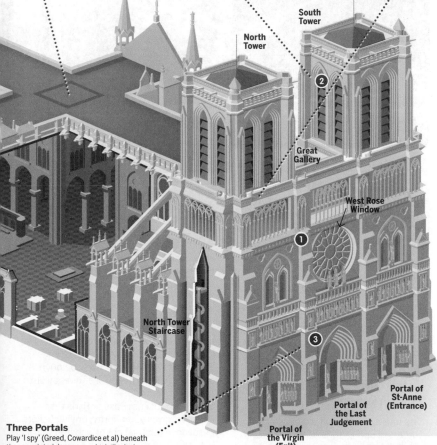

South Tower

North Tower

Great Gallery

West Rose Window

①

②

North Tower Staircase

③

Portal of St-Anne (Entrance)

Portal of the Last Judgement

Portal of the Virgin (Exit)

④ Parvis Notre Dame

Three Portals
Play 'I spy' (Greed, Cowardice et al) beneath these sculpted doorways, which illustrate the seasons, life and the 12 vices and virtues alongside the Bible.

Musée du Louvre

The Mona Lisa and the Venus de Milo are just two of the priceless treasures resplendently housed inside the fortress turned royal palace turned France's first national museum.

Few art galleries are as prized or as daunting as the Louvre, Paris' pièce de résistance that no first-time visitor to the city can resist. This is, after all, one of the world's largest and most diverse museums, showcasing 35,000 works of art. It would take nine months to glance at every piece, rendering advance planning essential.

Visiting

You need to queue twice to get in: once for security and then again to buy tickets. The longest queues are outside the Grande Pyramide; use the Carrousel du Louvre entrance (99 rue de Rivoli or direct from the metro).

A Paris Museum Pass or Paris City Passport gives you priority; buying tickets in advance (on the Louvre website) will also help expedite the process.

Great For...

☑ Don't Miss

The museum's thematic trails – from the 'Art of Eating' to 'Love in the Louvre'.

ℹ️ Need to Know

Map p254; 📞01 40 20 53 17; www.louvre.
fr; rue de Rivoli & quai des Tuileries, 1er;
adult/child €15/free, free 1st Sat of month
6-9.45pm; ⊙9am-6pm Mon, Thu, Sat &
Sun, to 9.45pm Wed, Fri & 1st Sat of month;
Ⓜ Palais Royal–Musée du Louvre

✕ Take a Break

The Hall Napoléon sells sandwiches;
ideal for a Jardin des Tuileries (p85)
picnic.

★ Top Tip

Search the Louvre's website for its
schedule of room closures.

Self-guided thematic trails range from
Louvre masterpieces and the art of eating
to family-friendly topics. Download trail
brochures from the website.

Other good options are the free Louvre:
My Visit app, or renting a Nintendo 3DS
multimedia guide (€5; ID required). More
formal, English-language **guided tours**
(Map p254; 📞01 40 20 52 63; adult/child €12/7;
⊙11am & 2pm daily except 1st Tue & Sun of
month, plus 7pm Wed; Ⓜ Palais Royal–Musée
du Louvre) depart from the Hall Napoléon.
Reserve a spot up to 14 days in advance or
sign up on arrival at the museum.

In late 2014, the Louvre embarked on a
30-year renovation plan, with the aim of
modernising the museum to make it more
accessible. Phase 1 increased the number
of main entrances in order to reduce security wait times. It also revamped the central
Hall Napoléon to vastly improve what was
previously bewildering chaos. Important
changes to come include increasing the
number of English-language signs and
artwork texts.

Palais du Louvre

The Louvre today rambles over four floors
and through three wings: the **Sully Wing**
creates the four sides of the Cour Carrée
(literally 'Square Courtyard') at the eastern
end of the complex; the **Denon Wing**
stretches 800m along the Seine to the
south; and the northern **Richelieu Wing**
skirts rue de Rivoli. The building started life
as a fortress built by Philippe-Auguste in
the 12th century – medieval remnants are
still visible on the lower ground floor (Sully
Wing). In the 16th century it became a royal
residence and, after the Revolution, in 1793
it was turned it into a national museum.

Over the centuries French governments
amassed the paintings, sculptures and

artefacts displayed today. The 'Grand Louvre' project inaugurated by the late President Mitterrand in 1989 doubled the museum's exhibition space, and both new and renovated galleries have since opened, including the state-of-the-art **Islamic art galleries** (lower ground floor, Denon) in the stunningly restored Cour Visconti.

Priceless Antiquities

Whatever your plans are, don't rush by the Louvre's astonishing cache of treasures from antiquity: both **Mesopotamia** (ground floor, Richelieu) and **Egypt** (ground and 1st floors, Sully) are well represented, as seen in the *Code of Hammurabi* (Room 227, ground floor, Richelieu) and *The Seated Scribe* (Room 635, 1st floor, Sully). Room 307 (ground floor, Sully Wing)

holds impressive friezes and an enormous **two-headed-bull column** from the Darius Palace in ancient Iran, while an enormous seated **statue of Pharaoh Ramesses II** highlights the temple room (Room 324, Sully).

Also worth a look are the mosaics and figurines from the Byzantine empire (lower ground floor, Denon), and the Greek statuary collection, culminating with the world's most famous armless duo, the **Venus de Milo** (Room 346, ground floor, Sully) and the **Winged Victory of Samothrace** (Room 703, 1st floor, Denon).

French & Italian Masterpieces

The **1st floor of the Denon Wing**, where the *Mona Lisa* is found, is easily the most popular part of the Louvre – and with good

Sphinx sculpture, Egypt Collection

reason. Rooms 700 to 702 are hung with monumental French paintings, many iconic: look for the *Consecration of the Emperor Napoléon I* (David), *The Raft of the Medusa* (Géricault) and *Grande Odalisque* (Ingres).

Rooms 710, 711, 712 and 716 are also must-visits. Filled with classic works by **Renaissance** masters (Raphael, Titian, Uccello, Botticini), this area culminates in the crowds around the *Mona Lisa*. But you'll find plenty else to contemplate, such as the superbly detailed *Wedding Feast at Cana* (Room 711). Boticelli's frescoes grace Room 706. On the ground floor of the Denon Wing, take time for the Italian sculptures, including Michelangelo's *The Dying Slave* and Canova's *Psyche and Cupid* (Room 403).

Mona Lisa

Easily the Louvre's most admired work (and world's most famous painting) is Leonardo da Vinci's *La Joconde* (in French; *La Gioconda* in Italian), the lady with that enigmatic smile known as *Mona Lisa* (Room 711, 1st floor, Denon). *Mona* (*monna* in Italian) is a contraction of *madonna,* and Gioconda is the feminine form of the surname Giocondo. Canadian scientists used infrared technology to peer through paint layers and confirm the identity of the painting's subject as Lisa Gherardini (1479–1542?), wife of Florentine merchant Francesco de Giocondo. Scientists also discovered that her dress was covered in a transparent gauze veil typically worn in early-16th-century Italy by pregnant women or new mothers; it's surmised that the work was painted to commemorate the birth of her second son around 1503, when she was aged about 24.

The Pyramid Inside & Out

Almost as stunning as the masterpieces inside is the 21m-high glass pyramid designed by Chinese-born American architect IM Pei that bedecks the main entrance to the Louvre in a dazzling crown. Beneath Pei's Grande Pyramide is the **Hall Napoléon**, the main entrance area, comprising an information booth, temporary exhibition hall, bookshop, souvenir store, cafe and auditoriums.

☑ **Don't Miss**

The Mesopotamian and Egyptian collections; the Denon Wing's 1st floor, including, of course, *Mona Lisa*.

INJONG SEO/SHUTTERSTOCK ©

★ **Louis XV's Crown**

French kings wore their crowns only once – at their coronation. Lined with embroidered satin and topped with openwork arches and a fleur-de-lis, Louis XV's 1722-crafted crown (Room 705, 1st floor, Denon) was originally adorned with pearls, sapphires, rubies, topazes, emeralds and diamonds.

The Louvre

A HALF-DAY TOUR

Successfully visiting the Louvre is a fine art. Its complex labyrinth of galleries and staircases spiralling across three wings and four floors renders discovery a snakes-and-ladders experience. Initiate yourself with this three-hour itinerary – a playful mix of *Mona Lisa*–obvious and up-to-the-minute unexpected.

Arriving in the newly renovated **❶ Cour Napoléon** beneath IM Pei's glass pyramid, pick up colour-coded floor plans at an information stand, then ride the escalator up to the Sully Wing and swap passport or credit card for a multimedia guide (there are limited descriptions in the galleries) at the wing entrance.

The Louvre is as much about spectacular architecture as masterful art. To appreciate this, zip up and down Sully's Escalier Henri II to admire **❷ Venus de Milo**, then up parallel Escalier Henri IV to the palatial displays in **❸ Cour Khorsabad**. Cross Room 236 to find the escalator up to the 1st floor and the opulent **❹ Napoléon III apartments**. Next traverse 25 consecutive galleries (thank you, floor plan!) to flip conventional contemplation on its head with Cy Twombly's **❺ The Ceiling**, and the hypnotic **❻ Winged Victory of Samothrace**, which brazenly insists on being admired from all angles. End with the impossibly famous **❼ Raft of the Medusa**, **❽ Mona Lisa** and **❾ Virgin & Child**.

TOP TIPS

➡ Don't even consider entering the Louvre's maze of galleries without a floor plan, free from the information desk in the Hall Napoléon.

➡ The Denon Wing is always packed; visit on late nights (Wednesday or Friday) or trade Denon in for the notably quieter Richelieu Wing.

➡ Tickets to the Louvre are valid for the whole day, meaning that you can nip out for lunch.

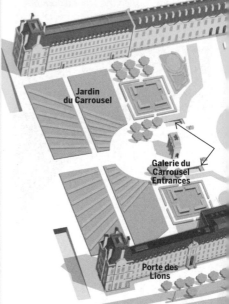

BRIAN KINNEY/SHUTTERSTOCK ©

Napoléon III Apartments
1st Floor, Richelieu
Napoléon III's gorgeous gilt apartments were built from 1854 to 1861, featuring an over-the-top decor of gold leaf, stucco and crystal chandeliers that reaches a dizzying climax in the Grand Salon and State Dining Room.

Jardin
du Carrousel

Galerie du
Carrousel
Entrances

Porte des
Lions

LOUVRE AUDITORIUM

Classical-music concerts are staged several times a week at the Louvre Auditorium (off the main entrance hall). Don't miss the Thursday lunchtime concerts featuring emerging composers and musicians. The season runs from September to April or May, depending on the concert series.

Mona Lisa
Room 711, 1st Floor, Denon
No smile is as enigmatic or bewitching as hers. Da Vinci's diminutive *La Joconde* hangs opposite the largest painting in the Louvre – sumptuous, fellow Italian Renaissance artwork *The Wedding at Cana*.

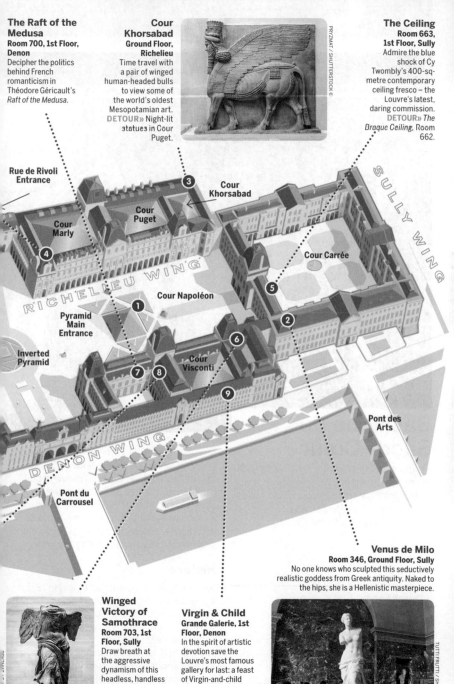

The Raft of the Medusa
Room 700, 1st Floor, Denon
Decipher the politics behind French romanticism in Théodore Géricault's *Raft of the Medusa*.

Cour Khorsabad
Ground Floor, Richelieu
Time travel with a pair of winged human-headed bulls to view some of the world's oldest Mesopotamian art.
DETOUR» Night-lit statues in Cour Puget.

The Ceiling
Room 663, 1st Floor, Sully
Admire the blue shock of Cy Twombly's 400-sq-metre contemporary ceiling fresco – the Louvre's latest, daring commission.
DETOUR» *The Braque Ceiling,* Room 662.

Rue de Rivoli Entrance

Cour Marly

Cour Puget

Cour Khorsabad

RICHELIEU WING

SULLY WING

Cour Carrée

Cour Napoléon

Pyramid Main Entrance

Inverted Pyramid

Cour Visconti

DENON WING

Pont des Arts

Pont du Carrousel

Winged Victory of Samothrace
Room 703, 1st Floor, Sully
Draw breath at the aggressive dynamism of this headless, handless Hellenistic goddess.
DETOUR» The razzle-dazzle of the Apollo Gallery's crown jewels.

Virgin & Child
Grande Galerie, 1st Floor, Denon
In the spirit of artistic devotion save the Louvre's most famous gallery for last: a feast of Virgin-and-child paintings by Da Vinci, Raphael, Domenico Ghirlandaio, Giovanni Bellini and Francesco Botticini.

Venus de Milo
Room 346, Ground Floor, Sully
No one knows who sculpted this seductively realistic goddess from Greek antiquity. Naked to the hips, she is a Hellenistic masterpiece.

GIUSEPPE TORRE/GETTY IMAGES ©

Basilique du Sacré-Cœur

Staircased, ivy-clad streets slink up the hill of the fabled artists' neighbourhood of Montmartre to a funicular that glides up to the dove-white domes of Paris' landmark basilica, Sacré-Cœur.

Great For...

☑ Don't Miss

Dizzying vistas across Paris, especially from up inside the basilica's main dome.

More than just a place of worship, the distinctive dove-white domed Basilique du Sacré-Cœur (Sacred Heart Basilica) is a veritable experience. Reached by 270 steps, the parvis (forecourt) in front of the basilica provides a postcard-perfect city panorama. Buskers and street artists perform on the steps, while picnickers spread out on the hillside park.

History

Sacré-Cœur's construction began in 1875, in the wake of France's humiliating defeat by Prussia and the subsequent chaos of the Paris Commune. Following Napoléon III's surrender to Otto von Bismarck in September 1870, angry Parisians, with the help of the National Guard, continued to hold out against Prussian forces – a harrowing siege that lasted four long winter months. By the time a ceasefire was negotiated in

ℹ️ Need to Know

Map p250; 📞01 53 41 89 00; www.sacre-
coeur-montmartre.com; Parvis du Sacré-
Cœur, 18e; basilica free, dome adult/child
€6/4, cash only; ⊘basilica 6am-10.30pm,
dome 8.30am-8pm May-Sep, 9am-5pm Oct-
Apr; MAnvers, Abbesses

✕ Take a Break

Head to **L'Été en Pente Douce** (Map
p250; 📞01 42 64 02 67; http://lete-en-pente-
douce.business.site; 8 rue Paul Albert, 18e;
mains €10.50-17; ⊘noon-midnight;
MChâteau Rouge) for French classics.

★ Top Tip

To skip walking up the hill, use a regular
metro ticket aboard the funicular.

early 1871, the split between the radical
working-class Parisians (supported by
the National Guard) and the conservative
national government (supported by the
French army) had become insurmountable.

Over the next several months, the
rebels, known as Communards, managed
to overthrow the reactionary government
and take over the city. It was a particularly
chaotic and bloody moment in Parisian
history, with mass executions on both
sides and a wave of rampant destruction
that spread throughout Paris. Montmartre
was a key Communard stronghold. It was
on the future site of Sacré-Cœur that the
rebels won their first victory and it was
consequently the first neighbourhood to be
targeted when the French army returned
in full force in May 1871. Ultimately, many
Communards were buried alive in the
gypsum mines beneath the Butte.

The Basilica

Within the historical context, the construction of an enormous basilica to expiate the
city's sins seemed like a gesture of peace
and forgiveness – indeed, the seven million
French francs needed to construct the
church's foundations came solely from the
contributions of local Catholics. However,
the Montmartre location was certainly no
coincidence: the conservative old guard
desperately wanted to assert its power in
what was then a hotbed of revolution. The
battle between the two camps – Catholic
versus secular, royalist versus republican –
raged on and in 1882 the construction of
the basilica was even voted down by the
city council on the grounds that it would
continue to fan the flames of civil war. It
was overturned in the end by a technicality.

The Romano-Byzantine–style basilica's
travertine stone exudes calcite, ensuring

it remains white despite weathering and pollution. Six successive architects oversaw construction of the basilica, and it wasn't until 1919 that Sacré-Cœur was finally consecrated, contrasting with the surrounding area's bohemian lifestyle.

Sacré-Cœur's interior is enlivened by the glittering apse mosaic *Christ in Majesty*, designed by Luc-Olivier Merson in 1922 and one of the largest in the world.

On Sundays, you can hear the organ being played during Mass and Vespers.

The Dome

Outside, to the west of the main entrance, 300 spiralling steps lead you to the basilica's dome, which affords one of Paris' most spectacular panoramas; it's said you can see for 30km on a clear day. Weighing in at 19 tonnes, the bell in the tower above, called La Savoyarde, is the largest in France.

What's Nearby?

Place du Tertre   Square
(Map p250; 18e; Ⓜ Abbesses) Today filled with visitors, buskers and portrait artists, place du Tertre was originally the main square of the village of Montmartre before it was incorporated into the city proper.

Dalí Paris   Gallery
(Map p250; ☑ 01 42 64 40 10; www.daliparis.com; 11 rue Poulbot, 18e; adult/child €12/9; ⊙ 10am-8.30pm Jul & Aug, to 6.30pm Sep-Jun; Ⓜ Abbesses) More than 300 works by Salvador Dalí (1904–89), the flamboyant Catalan surrealist printmaker, painter, sculptor and

self-promoter, are on display at this basement museum located just west of place du Tertre. The collection includes Dalí's strange sculptures, lithographs, and many of his illustrations and furniture, including the famous *Mae West Lips Sofa*.

Clos Montmartre   Vineyard

(Map p250; 18 rue des Saules, 18e; MLamarck–Caulaincourt) Epitomising Montmartre's enchanting village-like atmosphere, the *quartier* (neighbourhood) has its own small vineyard. Planted in 1933, its 2000

vines produce an average of 800 bottles of wine a year. Each October the grapes are pressed, fermented and bottled in Montmartre's town hall, then sold by auction to raise funds for local community projects. It's closed to the public except for a handful of special events.

Musée de Montmartre   Museum

(Map p250; ☎01 49 25 89 39; www.museede montmartre.fr; 12 rue Cortot, 18e; adult/child €9.50/5.50, garden only €4; ⊙10am-10pm Jul & Aug, to 7pm Apr-Jun & Sep, to 6pm Oct-Mar; MLamarck–Caulaincourt) This delightful 'village' museum showcases paintings, lithographs and documents illustrating Montmartre's bohemian, artistic and hedonistic past – one room is dedicated entirely to the French cancan. It's housed in a 17th-century manor where several artists, including Renoir and Raoul Dufy, had their studios in the 19th century. You can also visit the studio of painter Suzanne Valadon, who lived and worked here with her son Maurice Utrillo and partner André Utter between 1912 and 1926.

Moulin Blute Fin   Windmill

(Moulin de la Galette; Map p250; 75–77 rue Lepic, 18e; MAbbesses) Sister windmill to surviving **Moulin Radet** (83 rue Lepic) on the same street, this abandoned 18th-century windmill ground flour on its hillock perch above rue Lepic. It later became known as Moulin de la Galette after the *guinguette* (dance hall) – immortalised in Renoir's painting, *Bal du Moulin de la Galette* (1876), now in the Musée d'Orsay – that sprang up around its base in the 1830s.

JOPSTOCK/GETTY IMAGES ©

★ Top Tip

Allow time to stroll the Musée de Montmartre gardens, named after Renoir, who painted his masterpieces *Bal du Moulin de la Galette* and *Jardin de la rue Cortot* while working in his studio here from 1875 to 1877.

Sculpture hall in the central nave

Musée d'Orsay

After the Louvre, this eye-catching art gallery, at home in a former railway station overlooking the River Seine, is a one-stop shop for some of the world's most celebrated paintings by impressionist, postimpressionist and art nouveau artists. The museum's cavernous interiors, vintage monumental clocks and contemporary-styled galleries are as dazzling as the art itself.

Great For...

❶ Need to Know

Map p262; ☎ 01 40 49 48 14; www.musee-orsay.fr; 1 rue de la Légion d'Honneur, 7e; adult/child €14/free; ⊗ 9.30am-6pm Tue, Wed & Fri-Sun, to 9.45pm Thu; Ⓜ Assemblée Nationale, RER Musée d'Orsay)

★ **Top Tip**

Musée d'Orsay admission drops to €11 after 4.30pm (after 6pm on Thursday).

History

The Gare d'Orsay railway station was designed by competition-winning architect Victor Laloux. Even on its completion, just in time for the 1900 Exposition Universelle, painter Edouard Detaille declared that the new station looked like a *palais des beaux arts* (palace of fine arts). But although it had its own hotel and all the mod cons of the day – including separate lifts for luggage and passengers – by 1939 the increasing electrification of the rail network meant the platforms were too short for mainline trains, and within a few years all rail services ceased.

The station was used as a mailing centre during WWII, and in 1962 Orson Welles filmed Franz Kafka's *The Trial* in the then-abandoned building. It was saved from being demolished and replaced with a hotel complex by a Historical Monument listing in 1973, before the government set about establishing the palatial museum.

Transforming the languishing building into the country's premier showcase for art from 1848 to 1914 was the grand project of President Valéry Giscard d'Estaing, who signed off on it in 1977. The museum opened its doors in 1986. Major renovations between 2008 and 2011 incorporated a re-energised layout and increased exhibition space.

Paintings

Most visitors make a beeline for the world's largest collection of impressionist and post-impressionist art, the highlights of which include Manet's *On the Beach* and *Woman*

Musée d'Orsay from the Seine

with Fans; Monet's gardens at Giverny and *The Rue Montorgueil, Paris. Celebration of June 30, 1878*; Cézanne's card players, *Apples and Oranges* and *Blue Vase*; Renoir's *Ball at the Moulin de la Galette* and *Young Girls at the Piano*; Degas' ballerinas; Toulouse-Lautrec's cabaret dancers; Pissarro's *The Seine and the Louvre*; Sisley's *View of the Canal St-Martin*, and Van Gogh's self-portraits, *Bedroom in Arles* and *Starry Night over the Rhône*. Less high-profile but classified as a National Treasure is James

Tissot's 1868 painting *The Circle of the Rue Royale*.

Decorative & Graphic Arts

Household items such as hat and coat stands, candlesticks, desks, chairs, book cases, vases, pot-plant holders, free-standing screens, wall mirrors, water pitchers, plates, goblets and bowls become works of art in the hands of their creators, who incorporated exquisite design elements from the era.

Drawings, pastels and sketches from major artists are another of the d'Orsay's lesser-known highlights. Look for Georges Seurat's *The Black Bow* (c 1882), which uses crayon on paper to define forms by contrasting between black and white, and Paul Gaugin's poignant self-portrait (c 1902–03), drawn near the end of his life.

Visiting

Combined tickets with the Musée de l'Orangerie (p90; €18) and the Musée Rodin (p66; €21) are valid for a single visit to the museums within three months.

The museum is busiest Tuesday and Sunday, followed by Thursday and Saturday. Save time by buying tickets online and head directly to entrance C.

For a thorough introduction to the museum, 90-minute 'Masterpieces of the Musée d'Orsay' guided tours (€6; in English) run at 11am and 2pm on Tuesday to Saturday. Kids under 13 aren't permitted on adult tours (family tours are available). An audioguide costs €5.

Non-professional photography is permitted but flash photography, selfie sticks and tripods are not. There's an excellent gift and bookshop.

✕ Take a Break

On the 5th floor, one of the museum's two monumental clocks keeps watch in the shimmering, orange-and-turquoise **Café Campana** (mains €14-18; ⊙10.30am-5pm Tue, Wed & Fri-Sun, to 9pm Thu).

DMITRY ZINOVYEV/SHUTTERSTOCK ©

☑ Don't Miss

The magnificent sculptures, including works by Degas, Gauguin, Camille Claudel, Renoir and Rodin.

Musée Rodin from the garden

Musée Rodin

Paris' most romantic museum displays Auguste Rodin's sculptural masterpieces in his former workshop and showroom, the 1730-built, beautifully restored Hôtel Biron, as well as in its rambling rose gardens.

Sculptor, painter, sketcher, engraver and collector Auguste Rodin donated his entire collection to the French state in 1908 on the proviso they dedicate his former workshop and showroom to displaying his works. They're now installed not only in the mansion itself, but also in its rose-filled garden – one of the most peaceful places in central Paris.

Great For...

☑ Don't Miss

Rodin's collection of works by artists including Van Gogh, Renoir and Camille Claudel.

Sculptures

The first large-scale cast of Rodin's famous sculpture **The Thinker** (*Le Penseur*), made in 1902, resides in the garden. It was conceived by Rodin to represent intellect and poetry (it was originally titled *The Poet*).

The Gates of Hell (*La Porte de l'Enfer*) was commissioned in 1880 as the entrance for a never-built museum, and Rodin worked on his sculptural masterpiece up

The Cathedral, Auguste Rodin

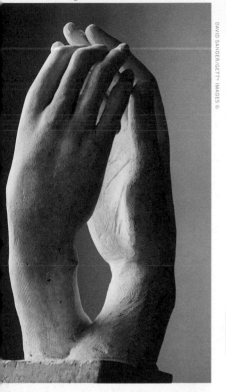

ⓘ Need to Know

Map p262; ☎01 44 18 61 10; www.musee-rodin.fr; 79 rue de Varenne, 7e; adult/child €10/free, garden only €4/free; ⊗10am-5.45pm Tue-Sun; Ⓜ Varenne or Invalides

✕ Take a Break

Paris' oldest restaurant, **À la Petite Chaise** (Map p262; ☎01 42 22 13 35; www.alapetitechaise.fr; 36 rue de Grenelle, 7e; 2-/3-course lunch menu €25/33, 3-course dinner menu €36.50, mains €21; ⊗noon-2pm & 7-11pm; Ⓜ Sèvres-Babylone), still serves excellent traditional fare.

★ Top Tip

Cheaper garden-only entry is available.

until his death in 1917. Standing 6m high and 4m wide, its 180 figures comprise an intricate scene from Dante's *Inferno*.

Marble monument to love **The Kiss** *(Le Baiser)* was originally part of *The Gates of Hell*. The sculpture's entwined lovers caused controversy on completion due to Rodin's then-radical depiction of women as equal partners in ardour.

The museum also features many sculptures by Camille Claudel, Rodin's protégé and muse.

Rodin at the Hôtel Biron

Extensive renovations to the museum between 2012 and 2015 – the first since Rodin worked here until his death in 1917 – included the creation of Biron Grey, a new colour of paint by British company Farrow & Ball.

The 'Rodin at the Hôtel Biron' room incorporates original furniture to recreate the space as it was when he lived and worked here.

Visiting

Prepurchase tickets online to avoid queuing. Audioguides cost €6. A combined ticket with the Musée d'Orsay costs €21; combination tickets are valid for a single visit to each of the museums within three months.

What's Nearby?

Hôtel Matignon   Landmark

(Map p262; 57 rue de Varenne, 7e; Ⓜ Solférino) Hôtel Matignon has been the official residence of the French prime minister since the start of the Fifth Republic (1958). It's closed to the public.

Palais du Luxembourg

Jardin du Luxembourg

The city's most beautiful park, the Jardin du Luxembourg, is an inner-city oasis encompassing 23 gracefully laid-out hectares of formal terraces, chestnut groves and lush lawns.

Great For...

ℹ Need to Know

Map p260; www.senat.fr/visite/jardin; 6e; ⊙hours vary; Ⓜ Mabillon, St-Sulpice, Rennes, Notre Dame des Champs, RER Luxembourg

★ Top Tip

For a quick snack or drink, kiosks and cafes are dotted throughout the park.

The Jardin du Luxembourg has a special place in Parisians' hearts. Napoléon dedicated the gardens to the children of Paris, and many residents spent their childhood prodding little wooden sailboats with long sticks on the octagonal pond, watching puppet shows, and riding the carousel or ponies. All those activities are still here today, as are modern playgrounds and sporting and games venues.

History

The Jardin du Luxembourg's history stretches further back than Napoléon's dedication. The gardens are a backdrop to the Palais du Luxembourg, built in the 1620s for Marie de Médici, Henri IV's consort, to assuage her longing for the Pitti Palace in Florence. The Palais is now home to the French Senate, which, in addition to parliamentary-assembly activities like voting on legislation, is charged with promoting the palace and its gardens.

Numerous overhauls over the centuries have given the Jardin du Luxembourg a blend of traditional French- and English-style gardens that is unique in Paris.

Grand Bassin

All ages love the octagonal **Grand Bassin** (MMabillon or RER Luxembourg), a serene ornamental pond where adults can lounge and kids can play with 1920s **toy sailboats** (sailboat rental per 30min €4; ☺11am-6pm Apr-Oct; MNotre Dame des Champs, RER Luxembourg). Nearby, littlies can take **pony rides** (☑06 07 32 53 95; www.animaponey.com; 600m/900m pony ride €6/8.50; ☺3-6pm Wed,

Sculptures in the Jardin du Luxembourg

Sat, Sun & school holidays; Ⓜ Notre Dames des Champs, RER Luxembourg) or romp around the **playgrounds** (adult/child €1.20/2.50; ⊘hours vary; Ⓜ Notre Dame des Champs, RER Luxembourg) – the green half is for kids aged seven to 12 years, the blue half for under-sevens.

Puppet Shows

Puppetry is an ancient tradition in France and alfresco puppet shows at the Jardin du Luxembourg's bijou **Théâtre**

✕ Take a Break

Park picnics aside, nearby options include family-style French cuisine at historic **Polidor** (Map p260; www.polidor. com; 41 rue Monsieur le Prince, 6e; menus €22 & €35, mains €13-20; ⊘noon-2.30pm & 7pm-12.30am Mon-Sat, to 11pm Sun; Ⓜ Odéon).

BRIAN KINNEY/SHUTTERSTOCK ©

du Luxembourg (☏01 43 29 50 97; www. marionnettesduluxembourg.fr; tickets €6.40; ⊘Wed, Sat & Sun, daily during school holidays; Ⓜ Notre Dame des Champs) are as entertaining as marionette shows come – regardless of whether you speak French or are a child. Show times vary; check the program online and arrive 30 minutes before.

Palais du Luxembourg

The **Palais du Luxembourg** (www.senat.fr; rue de Vaugirard, 6e; Ⓜ Mabillon, RER Luxembourg) was built in the 1620s and has been home to the Sénat (French Senate) since 1958. It's occasionally visitable by guided tour.

East of the palace is the ornate, Italianate **Fontaine des Médici** (Ⓜ Mabillon, RER Luxembourg), built in 1630. During Baron Haussmann's 19th-century reshaping of the roads, the fountain was moved 30m and the pond and dramatic statues of the giant bronze Polyphemus discovering the white-marble lovers Acis and Galatea were added.

Musée du Luxembourg

Prestigious temporary art exhibitions take place in the beautiful **Musée du Luxembourg** (☏01 40 13 62 00; www.museedu luxembourg.fr; 19 rue de Vaugirard, 6e; most exhibitions €13; ⊘10.30am-7pm Sat-Thu, to 10pm Fri; Ⓜ St-Sulpice, RER Luxembourg).

Around the back of the museum, lemon and orange trees, palms, grenadiers and oleanders shelter from the cold in the palace's orangery.

☑ Don't Miss

Discovering the park's many sculptures, which include statues of Stendhal, Chopin, Baudelaire and Delacroix.

Tour boat passing under the Pont des Arts

ADRIENNE PITTS/LONELY PLANET ©

Cruising the Seine

The lifeline of Paris, the Seine sluices through the city, spanned by 37 bridges. Cruises along the river are an idyllic way to observe its Unesco World Heritage–listed riverbanks.

Great For...

☑ Don't Miss

Floating past Parisian landmarks such as the Louvre and Notre Dame.

Boat Trips & Cruise Companies

Batobus (www.batobus.com; adult/child 1-day pass €17/8, 2-day pass €19/10; ☺10am-9.30pm late Apr-Aug, shorter hours Sep-late Apr) An alternative to traditional boat tours, this handy hop-on, hop-off service stops at the Eiffel Tower, Champs-Élysées, Musée d'Orsay, Musée du Louvre, St-Germain des Prés, Hôtel de Ville, Notre Dame and Jardin des Plantes. Single- and multiday tickets allow you to spend as long as you like sightseeing between stops.

Vedettes de Paris (Map p262; ☎01 44 18 19 50; www.vedettesdeparis.fr; Port de Suffren, 7e; adult/child €15/7; ☺10.30am-8.30pm May-Nov, hours vary Dec-Apr; MBir Hakeim or RER Pont de l'Alma) These one-hour sightseeing cruises on smaller boats are a more intimate experience than with the major companies. Themed cruises

❶ Need to Know

There are no barriers at the water's edge; keep a close eye on young children.

✕ Take a Break

Many cruise companies offer brunch, lunch and dinner cruises with high-quality food.

★ Top Tip

Floodlights illuminate the iconic riverside buildings at night.

languages (every 30 minutes 10am to 11pm April to September, hourly 10.30am to 10.30pm October to March), and a host of themed lunch and dinner cruises. It has two locations: one by the Eiffel Tower, the other south of Notre Dame.

include imaginative 'Mysteries of Paris' tours for kids (adult/child €15/9).

Vedettes du Pont Neuf (Map p254; ☎01 46 33 98 38; www.vedettesdupontneuf.com; square du Vert Galant, 1er; adult/child €14/7; ⊙10.30am-10.30pm; MPont Neuf) One-hour cruises depart year-round from Vedettes' centrally located dock at the western tip of Île de la Cité; commentary is in French and English. Tickets are cheaper if you buy in advance online (adult/child €12/5). Check the website for details of its one-hour lunch cruises (adult/child €37/29) and two-hour dinner cruises (€71/35).

Bateaux Parisiens (Map p262; ☎08 25 01 01 01; www.bateauxparisiens.com; Port de la Bourdonnais, 7e; adult/child €15/7; 🛜; MBir Hakeim or RER Pont de l'Alma) This vast operation runs hour-long river circuits with audioguides in 14

Bateaux-Mouches (Map p252; ☎01 42 25 96 10; www.bateaux-mouches.fr; Port de la Conférence, 8e; adult/child €14/6; ⊙10am-10.30pm Mon-Fri, 10.15am-9.20pm Sat & Sun Apr-Sep, every 40min 11am-9.20pm Oct-Mar; MAlma Marceau) The largest river cruise company in Paris, Bateaux-Mouches is a favourite with tour groups. Departing just east of the Pont de l'Alma on the Right Bank, its 70-minute cruises have commentary in French and English.

Paris Canal Croisières (Map p262; ☎01 42 40 96 97; www.pariscanal.com; quai Anatole France, 7e; adult/child €22/14; ⊙Mar–mid-Dec; MSolférino, RER Musée d'Orsay) Seasonal 2½-hour Seine-and-canal cruises depart from quai Anatole France near the Musée d'Orsay (morning cruises) and from Parc de la Villette (afternoon cruises).

Centre Pompidou exterior

SAILORR/SHUTTERSTOCK. © CENTRE GEORGES POMPIDOU, PARIS, FRANCE. STUDIO PIANO & ROGERS, ARCHITECTS (1971-1977)

Centre Pompidou

The primary-coloured, inside-out Centre Pompidou building houses France's national modern and contemporary art museum, the Musée National d'Art Moderne (MNAM), showcasing creations from 1905 to the present day.

Galleries and exhibitions, hands-on workshops, dance performances, a bookshop, a design boutique, cinemas and other entertainment venues here are an irresistible cocktail.

Architecture & Views

Former French President Georges Pompidou wanted an ultracontemporary artistic hub and he got it: competition-winning architects Renzo Piano and Richard Rogers designed the building inside out, with utilitarian features like plumbing, pipes, air vents and electrical cables forming part of the external facade.

Although it's just six storeys high, the city's low-rise cityscape means stupendous views extend from its roof (reached by external escalators enclosed in tubes). Rooftop admission is included in museum

Great For...

☑ Don't Miss

The sweeping panorama of Paris from the rooftop.

Châtelet–Les Halles

Ⓜ Les Halles Ⓜ
Ⓜ Rambuteau
**Centre 🏛
Pompidou**
R du Renard
R de Rivoli
Châtelet Ⓜ
Ⓜ Hôtel de Ville

❶ Need to Know

Map p254; ☑️01 44 78 12 33; www.centre
pompidou.fr; place Georges Pompidou, 4e;
museum, exhibitions & panorama adult/
child €14/free, panorama only ticket €5/free;
⊙11am-9pm Wed-Mon, temporary exhibits to
11pm Thu; 🕾; ⓂRambuteau

✕ Take a Break

For a meal or a casual drink, head to
nearby **Café La Fusée** (Map p254; ☑️01 42
76 93 99; 168 rue St-Martin, 3e; ⊙9am-2am
Mon-Sat, 10am-2am Sun; ⓂRambuteau,
Étienne Marcel).

★ Top Tip

The Centre Pompidou opens late; head
here around 5pm to avoid daytime
crowds.

and exhibition admission – or buy a panorama ticket (€5) just for the roof.

Musée National d'Art Moderne

Europe's largest collection of modern art
fills the bright and airy, well-lit galleries of the National Museum of Modern
Art, covering two complete floors of the
Pompidou. On a par with the permanent
collection are the two temporary exhibition halls (on the ground floor/basement
and the top floor), which showcase some
memorable blockbuster exhibits. Also of
note is the fabulous children's gallery on
the 1st floor.

The permanent collection changes
every two years, but the basic layout
generally stays the same. The 5th floor
showcases artists active between 1905
and 1970 (give or take a decade), mixing

up works by Picasso, Matisse, Chagall and
Kandinsky with lesser-known contem-
poraries; the 4th floor focuses on more
contemporary creations, roughly from the
1990s onward, with monumental paintings, installation pieces, sculpture and
video taking centre stage.

Atelier Brancusi

West of the Centre Pompidou main
building, this reconstruction of the **studio**
(Map p254; www.centrepompidou.fr; 55 rue
de Rambuteau, 4e; incl in admission to Centre
Pompidou adult/child €14/free; ⊙2-6pm
Wed-Mon; ⓂRambuteau) of Romanian-born
sculptor Constantin Brancusi (1876–1957)
contains over 100 sculptures in stone and
wood. You'll also find drawings, pedestals
and photographic plates from his original
Paris studio.

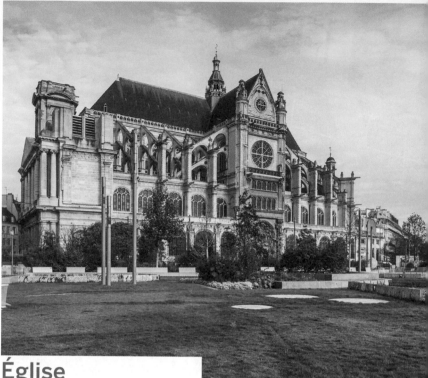

MICHAEL LEE/GETTY IMAGES ©

Église St-Eustache

One of the most beautiful churches in Paris, St-Eustache is majestic, architecturally magnificent and musically outstanding.

Great For...

☑ **Don't Miss**

Free Sunday-afternoon organ recitals, which are a real treat.

St-Eustache was constructed between 1532 and 1632 and is primarily Gothic. Artistic highlights include a work by Rubens, Raymond Mason's colourful bas-relief of market vendors (1969) and Keith Haring's bronze triptych (1990) in the side chapels.

Outside the church is a gigantic sculpture of a head and hand entitled *L'Écoute* (Listen; 1986) by Henri de Miller.

One of France's largest organs, above the church's western entrance, has 101 stops and 8000 pipes dating from 1854. Free organ recitals at 5.30pm on Sunday are a must for music lovers; there are also various concerts during the week.

What's Nearby?
Jardin Nelson Mandela   Park

(Map p254; 1er; ⏰24hr; Ⓜ Les Halles or RER Châtelet–Les Halles) A refreshing counterpoint to the built-up surrounds, this

MAZIARZ/SHUTTERSTOCK ©

ℹ️ Need to Know

Map p254; www.st-eustache.org; 2 impasse St-Eustache, 1er; ⏱9.30am-7pm Mon-Fri, 10am-7.15pm Sat, 9am-7.15pm Sun; Ⓜ️Les Halles or RER Châtelet–Les Halles

✖️ Take a Break

Alain Ducasse's **Champeaux** (Map p254; 📞01 53 45 84 50; www.restaurant-champeaux.com; La Canopée, Forum des Halles, Porte Rambuteau, 1er; mains €18-34; ⏱noon-midnight Sun-Wed, to 1am Thu-Sat; Ⓜ️Les Halles or RER Châtelet–Les Halles) is in the renovated Les Halles.

★ Top Tip

Choral concerts are also occasionally held here.

2018-inaugurated park spans 4 hectares of meadow-like gardens, fountains and kids' playgrounds. Its 500-plus trees include elms, birches, magnolias and Japanese cherry blossoms.

Collection Pinault – Paris   Museum

(Map p254; www.collectionpinaultparis.com; 2 rue de Viarmes, 1er; Ⓜ️Les Halles or RER Châtelet–Les Halles) Paris' newest art museum occupies the Bourse de Commerce, an 18th-century rotunda that once held the city's grain market and stock exchange. Japaneses architect Tadao Ando designed the ambitious interior, where three floors of galleries will display contemporary works collected by François Pinault, who previously teamed up with Ando to open Venice's Palazzo Grassi and Punta della Dogana. Exhibitions will span varying scales and media, from painting, sculpture, photography and video to installations. At the time of research it was slated to open in autumn 2019.

Forum des Halles   Notable Building

(Map p254; www.forumdeshalles.com; 1 rue Pierre Lescot, 1er; ⏱shops 10am-8pm Mon-Sat, 11am-7pm Sun; Ⓜ️Les Halles or RER Châtelet–Les Halles) Paris' main wholesale food market stood here for nearly 800 years before being replaced by this underground shopping mall in 1971. Long considered an eyesore by many Parisians, the mall's exterior was finally demolished in 2011 to make way for its golden-hued translucent canopy, unveiled in 2016. Below, four floors of stores (131 in total), 23 restaurants, cafes and fast food outlets, and entertainment venues including cinemas and a swimming pool, extend down to the city's busiest metro hub.

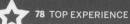

DANIEL CANDAL/GETTY IMAGES ©

Cimetière du Père Lachaise

Paris is a collection of villages and this sprawling cemetery of cobbled lanes and elaborate tombs, with a 'population' of over one million, qualifies as one in its own right.

Great For...

☑ Don't Miss

Oscar Wilde, Jim Morrison, Édith Piaf and countless other famous names.

The world's most visited cemetery was founded in 1804, and initially attracted few funerals because of its distance from the city centre. The authorities responded by exhuming famous remains and resettling them here. Their marketing ploy worked and Cimetière du Père Lachaise has been Paris' most fashionable final address ever since.

Famous Occupants

Paris residency was the only criterion for being buried in Père Lachaise, hence the cemetery's cosmopolitan population, which includes Irish playright Oscar Wilde and 1960s rock god Jim Morrison. Other famous occupants buried here are the composer Chopin; the playwright Molière; the poet Apollinaire; writers Balzac, Proust, Gertrude Stein and Colette; the actors

Tomb of Oscar Wilde

MACH PHOTOS/SHUTTERSTOCK ©

❶ Need to Know

Map p256; ☎01 55 25 82 10; www.pere-lachaise.com; 16 rue du Repos & 8 bd de Ménilmontant, 20e; ☺8am-6pm Mon-Fri, from 8.30am Sat, from 9am Sun mid-Mar–Oct, shorter hours Nov–mid-Mar; Ⓜ Père Lachaise, Gambetta

✖ Take a Break

Book ahead for neobistro fare at nearby Le Servan (p133).

★ Top Tip

Arriving at Gambetta metro station allows you to walk downhill through the cemetery.

entertaining cemetery historian Thierry Le Roi (www.necro-romantiques.com).

What's Nearby?

L'Atelier des Lumières   Museum

(Map p256; ☎01 80 98 46 00; www.atelier-lumieres.com; 38-40 rue St-Maur, 11e; adult/child €14.50/9.50; ☺10am-6pm Mon-Thu, to 10pm Fri & Sat, to 7pm Sun; Ⓜ Voltaire) A former foundry dating from 1835 that supplied iron for the French navy and railroads now houses Paris' first digital art museum, opened in 2018. The 1500-sq-metre La Halle mounts dazzling light projections that take over the bare walls. Long programs lasting around 30 minutes are based on historic artists' works; there's also a shorter contemporary program. Screenings are continuous. In the separate Le Studio space, you can discover emerging and established digital artists.

Simone Signoret, Sarah Bernhardt and Yves Montand; the painters Pissarro, Seurat, Modigliani and Delacroix; the *chanteuse* Édith Piaf alongside her two-year-old daughter; and the dancer Isadora Duncan.

Visiting

The cemetery has five entrances, two of which are on bd de Ménilmontant.

To save time searching for famous graves, pick up cemetery maps at the **conservation office** (Bureaux de la Conservation; ☎01 55 25 82 10; 16 rue du Repos, 20e; ☺8.30am-12.30pm & 2-5pm Mon-Fri; Ⓜ Philippe Auguste, Père Lachaise) near the main bd de Ménilmontant entrance.

Alternatively, pre-book a themed guided tour (in French and English) led by

Cimetière du Père Lachaise

A HALF-DAY TOUR

There is a certain romance to getting lost in Cimetière du Père Lachaise, a jungle of graves spun from centuries of tales. But to search for one grave among one million in this 44-hectare land of the dead is no joke – narrow the search with this itinerary.

From the main bd de Ménilmontant entrance (metro Père Lachaise or Philippe Auguste), head up av Principale, turn right onto av du Puits and collect a map from ❶ **the Bureaux de la Conservation**.

Backtrack along av du Puits, turn right onto av Latérale du Sud, scale the stairs and bear right along chemin Denon to New Realist artist ❷ **Arman**, film director ❸ **Claude Chabrol** and ❹ **Chopin**.

Follow chemin Méhul downhill, cross av Casimir Périer and bear right onto chemin Serré. Take the second left (chemin Lebrun – unsigned), head uphill and near the top leave the footpath to weave through graves on your right to rock star ❺ **Jim Morrison**. Back on chemin Lauriston, continue uphill to roundabout ❻ **Rond-Point Casimir Périer**.

Admire the funerary art of contemporary photographer ❼ **André Chabot**, av de la Chapelle. Continue uphill for energising city views from the ❽ **chapel** steps, then zig-zag to ❾ **Molière & La Fontaine**, on chemin Molière.

Cut between graves onto av Tranversale No 1 – spot potatoes atop ❿ **Parmentier's** headstone. Continue straight onto av Greffülhe and left onto av Tranversale No 2 to rub ⓫ **Monsieur Noir's** shiny crotch.

Navigation to ⓬ **Édith Piaf** and the ⓭ **Mur des Fédérés** is straightforward. End with angel-topped ⓮ **Oscar Wilde** near the Porte Gambetta entrance.

TOP TIPS

➡ Père Lachaise is a photographer's paradise any time of the day or year, but best are sunny autumn mornings after the rain.

➡ Cemetery-lovers will appreciate themed guided tours (two hours) led by entertaining cemetery historian Thierry Le Roi (www.necro-romantiques.com).

BRUNO DE HOGUES / GETTY IMAGES ©

Chopin, Division 11
Add a devotional note to the handwritten letters and flowers brightening the marble tomb of Polish composer/pianist Frédéric Chopin (1810–49), who spent his short adult life in Paris. His heart is buried in Warsaw.

Jim Morrison, Division 6
The original bust adorning the disgracefully dishevelled grave of Jim Morrison (1943–71), lead singer of The Doors, was stolen. Pay your respects to rock's greatest legend – no chewing gum or padlocks please.

HUANG ZHENG / SHUTTERSTOCK ©

André Chabot, Division 20

Contemporary photographer André Chabot (b 1941) shoots funerary art, hence the bijou 19th-century chapel he's equipped with monumental granite camera – and a QR code – in preparation for the day he departs.

Molière & La Fontaine, Division 25

Parisians refused to leave their local *quartier* for Père Lachaise so in 1817 the authorities moved in popular playwright Molière (1622–73) and poet Jean de la Fontaine (1621–95). The marketing strategy worked.

Oscar Wilde, Division 89

Irish writer Oscar Wilde (1854–1900) was forever scandalous: check the enormous packet of the sphinx on his tomb, sculpted by British-American sculptor Jacob Epstein 11 years after Wilde died.

André Chabot, Division 20

84

Porte Gambetta Entrance

av des Combattants Étrangers morts pour la France

88

av Circulaire

Crematorium

av Tranversale No 3

89

14

Chapel

51 50

av Tranversale No 1

av Tranversale No 2

93

8

chemin Bertholle

av de Saint Morys

92

Monsieur Noir, Division 92

Cemetery sex stud Mr Black, alias 21-year-old journalist Victor Noir (1848–70), was shot by Napoléon III's nephew in a botched duel. Urban myth means women rub his crotch to boost fertility.

21

24

chemin Molière 25

11

av Greffülhe

94

7

20

9

42

av de la Chapelle

26

10

41

95

6

Rond-Point Casimir Périer

39

av Pacthod

Commemorative war memorials

14

chemin Lauriston

12 97 **13**

5

6

76

Édith Piaf, Division 97

The archbishop of Paris might have refused Parisian diva Édith Piaf (1915–63) the Catholic rite of burial, but that didn't stop more than 100,000 mourners attending her internment at Père Lachaise.

5

chemin Lebrun

96

av Circulaire

Mur des Fédérés, Division 76

This plain brick wall was where 147 Communard insurgents were lined up and shot in 1871. Equally emotive is the sculpted walkway of commemorative war memorials surrounding the mass grave.

Porte de la Réunion

Cheese for sale in the Marché d'Aligre

PREMIER PHOTO/SHUTTERSTOCK ©

Street Markets

Not simply places to shop, the city's street markets are social gatherings for the entire neighbourhood, and visiting one will give you a true appreciation of Parisian life.

Stall after stall of cheeses, stacked baguettes, sun-ripened tomatoes, freshly lopped pigs' trotters, horsemeat sausages, spit-roasted chickens, glass bottles of olives and olive oils, quail eggs, duck eggs boxes of chanterelle mushrooms and knobbly truffles, long-clawed langoustines and prickly sea urchins on beds of crushed ice – along with belts, boots, wallets, cheap socks, chic hats, colourful scarves, striped t-shirts, wicker baskets, wind-up toys, buckets of flowers… Paris' street markets are a feast for the senses.

Great For...

☑ **Don't Miss**

The city's wonderful covered food markets.

Top Choices

Marché Bastille (Map p259; bd Richard Lenoir, 11e; ⊘7am-2.30pm Thu, to 3pm Sun; ⓂBastille, Bréguet–Sabin) **If you only get to one open-air street market in Paris, this one – stretching**

Marché Bastille

MUSEMAGE/GETTY IMAGES ©

between the Bastille and Richard Lenoir metro stations – is among the very best. Its 150-plus stalls are piled high with fruit and vegetables, meats, fish, shellfish, cheeses and seasonal specialities such as truffles. You'll also find clothing, leather handbags and wallets, and a smattering of antiques.

Marché d'Aligre (Map p259; rue d'Aligre, 12e; ⊙8am-1pm Tue-Sun; Ⓜ Ledru-Rollin) A favourite with chefs and locals, this chaotic street market's stalls are piled with fruit, vegetables and seasonal delicacies such as truffles. Behind them, specialist shops stock cheeses, coffee, chocolates, meat, seafood and wine. More are located in the adjoining covered market hall,

Marché Beauvau (Map p259; place d'Aligre, 12e; ⊙9am-2pm & 4-7.30pm Tue-Sat, 9am-2pm Sun; Ⓜ Ledru-Rollin). The small but bargain-filled flea market **Marché aux Puces d'Aligre** (Map p259; place d'Aligre, 12e; ⊙8am-1pm Tue-Sun; Ⓜ Ledru-Rollin) takes place on the square.

Marché Raspail (Map p262; bd Raspail, 6e, btwn rue de Rennes & rue du Cherche Midi, 6e; ⊙7am-2.30pm Tue & Fri, organic market 9am-1.30pm Sun; Ⓜ Rennes) ✿ A traditional open-air market on Tuesday and Friday, Marché Raspail is especially popular on Sunday, when it's filled with *biologique* (organic) produce.

Marché Biologique des Batignolles (Map p252; 34 bd des Batignolles, 17e; ⊙9am-3pm Sat; Ⓜ Place de Clichy, Rome) ✿ Abuzz with market stalls, this busy boulevard in northern Paris is renowned for its organic produce. Many of the stalls offer tastings and everything is super fresh.

Marché de Belleville (Map p256; bd de Belleville, 11e & 20e; ⊙7am-2.30pm Tue & Fri; Ⓜ Belleville) Belleville Market has filled busy thoroughfare bd de Belleville with open-air fruit, veg and other fresh-produce stalls since 1860. Food shopping aside, it provides a fascinating insight into the large, vibrant multiethnic community of this eastern neighbourhood.

Château de Versailles from the Orangerie

DIMA MOROZ/SHUTTERSTOCK ©

Day Trip: Château de Versailles

This monumental, 700-room palace and sprawling estate – with its gardens, fountains, ponds and canals – is a Unesco World Heritage–listed wonder situated an easy 40-minute train ride from central Paris.

Great For...

☑ Don't Miss

Summertime 'dancing water' displays set to baroque- and classical-era music.

Amid magnificently landscaped formal gardens, this splendid and enormous palace was built in the mid-17th century during the reign of Louis XIV – the Roi Soleil (Sun King) – to project the absolute power of the French monarchy, which was then at the height of its glory. The château has undergone relatively few alterations since its construction, though almost all the interior furnishings disappeared during the Revolution and many of the rooms were rebuilt by Louis-Philippe (r 1830–48).

Some 30,000 workers and soldiers toiled on the structure, the bills for which all but emptied the kingdom's coffers.

Work began in 1661 under the guidance of architect Louis Le Vau (Jules Hardouin-Mansart took over from Le Vau in the mid-1670s); painter and interior designer Charles Le Brun; and landscape

Galerie des Glaces (Hall of Mirrors)

❶ Need to Know

📞01 30 83 78 00; www.chateauversailles.fr; place d'Armes; adult/child passport ticket incl estate-wide access €20/free, with musical events €27/free, palace €18/free except during musical events; ⏰9am-6.30pm Tue-Sun Apr-Oct, to 5.30pm Tue-Sun Nov-Mar; Ⓜ RER Versailles-Château–Rive Gauche

✕ Take a Break

Rue de Satory and rue de la Paroisse are lined with restaurants.

★ Top Tip

Arrive early morning and avoid Tuesday, Saturday and Sunday, Versailles' busiest days.

artist André Le Nôtre, whose workers flattened hills, drained marshes and relocated forests as they laid out the seemingly endless **gardens** (www.chateauversailles.fr; place d'Armes; free except during musical events; ⏰gardens 8am-8.30pm Apr-Oct, to 6pm Nov-Mar, park 7am-8.30pm Apr-Oct, 8am-6pm Nov-Mar), ponds and fountains.

Le Brun and his hundreds of artisans decorated every moulding, cornice, ceiling and door of the interior with the most luxurious and ostentatious of appointments: frescoes, marble, gilt and woodcarvings, many with themes and symbols drawn from Greek and Roman mythology. The King's Suite of the Grands Appartements du Roi et de la Reine (King's and Queen's State Apartments), for example, includes rooms dedicated to Hercules, Venus, Diana, Mars and Mercury. The opulence reaches

its peak in the Galerie des Glaces (Hall of Mirrors), a 75m-long ballroom with 17 huge mirrors on one side and, on the other, an equal number of windows looking out over the gardens and the setting sun.

To access areas that are otherwise off limits and to learn more about Versailles' history, prebook a 90-minute **guided tour** (📞01 30 83 77 88; www.chateauversailles.fr; Château de Versailles; tours €10, plus palace entry; ⏰English-language tours 11am, 1.30pm & 3pm Tue-Sun) of the Private Apartments of Louis XV and Louis XVI and the Royal Opera House or Royal Chapel. Tours also cover the most famous parts of the palace.

The château is situated in the leafy, bourgeois suburb of Versailles, 22km southwest of central Paris. Take the frequent RER C5 (return €7.10) from Paris' Left Bank RER stations to Versailles-Château–Rive Gauche station.

Versailles

A DAY IN COURT

Visiting Versailles – even just the State Apartments – may seem overwhelming at first, but think of it as a house where people ate, drank, worked, slept and conspired and you'll be on the right path.

Some two decades into his long reign, Louis XIV began turning his father's hunting lodge into a palace large enough to house his entire court (to keep closer tabs on the 6000-strong army of courtiers). Sparing no expense, the Sun King employed the greatest artists and craftspeople of the day and by 1682 he'd created the most extravagant dormitory in history.

The royal schedule was as accurate and predictable as a Swiss watch. By following this itinerary of rooms you can recreate the king's day, starting with the **❶ King's Bedchamber** and the **❷ Queen's Bedchamber**, where the royal couple was roused at about the same time. The royal procession then leads through the **❸ Hall of Mirrors** to the **❹ Royal Chapel** for morning Mass and returns to the **❺ Council Chamber** for late-morning meetings with ministers. After lunch the king might ride or hunt or visit the **❻ King's Library**. Later he could join courtesans for an 'apartment evening' starting from the **❼ Hercules Drawing Room** or play billiards in the **❽ Diana Drawing Room** before supping at 10pm.

VERSAILLES BY NUMBERS

Rooms 700 (11 hectares of roof)

Windows 2153

Staircases 67

Gardens and parks 800 hectares

Trees 200,000

Fountains 50 (with 620 nozzles)

Paintings 6300 (measuring 11km laid end to end)

Statues and sculptures 2100

Objets d'art and furnishings 5000

Visitors 5.3 million per year

Queen's Bedchamber
Chambre de la Reine
The queen's life was on constant public display and even the births of her children were watched by crowds of spectators in her own bedchamber. DETOUR » The Guardroom, with a dozen armed men at the ready.

Guardroom

South Wing

LUNCH BREAK

Contemporary French cuisine at Alain Ducasse's restaurant Ore, or a picnic in the park.

Hercules Drawing Room
Salon d'Hercule
This salon, with its stunning ceiling fresco of the strong man, gave way to the State Apartments, which were open to courtiers three nights a week. DETOUR» Apollo Drawing Room, used for formal audiences and as a throne room.

Hall of Mirrors
Galerie des Glaces

The solid-silver candelabra and furnishings in this extravagant hall, devoted to Louis XIV's successes in war, were melted down in 1689 to pay for yet another conflict. DETOUR» The antithetical Peace Drawing Room, adjacent.

WALTER G / SHUTTERSTOCK ©

King's Bedchamber
Chambre du Roi

The king's daily life was anything but private and even his *lever* (rising) at 8am and *coucher* (retiring) at 11.30pm would be witnessed by up to 150 sycophantic courtiers.

Council Chamber
Cabinet du Conseil

This chamber, with carved medallions evoking the king's work, is where the monarch met his various ministers (state, finance, religion etc) depending on the days of the week.

King's Library
Bibliothèque du Roi

The last resident, bibliophile Louis XVI, loved geography and his copy of *The Travels of James Cook* (in English, which he read fluently) is still on the shelf here.

Diana Drawing Room
Salon de Diane

With walls and ceiling covered in frescoes devoted to the mythical huntress, this room contained a large billiard table reserved for Louis XIV, a keen player.

Peace Drawing Room

② **③**

Hall of Mirrors

① **⑤**

Marble Courtyard

Apollo Drawing Room

Entrance

⑥ **⑧**

Entrance

North Wing

⑦

To Royal Opera

④

Royal Chapel
Chapelle Royale

This two-storey chapel (with gallery for the royals and important courtiers, and the ground floor for the B-list) was dedicated to St Louis, patron of French monarchs. DETOUR» The sumptuous Royal Opera.

COJATO / BUDGET TRAVEL ©

SAVVY SIGHTSEEING

Avoid Versailles on Monday (closed), Tuesday (Paris' museums close, so visitors flock here) and Sunday, the busiest day. Also, book tickets online so you don't have to queue.

Gallery of the Kings of Judah, Musée National du Moyen Age

Musée National du Moyen Age

Accessed by a state-of-the-art entrance opened in 2018, the National Museum of the Middle Ages brims with medieval statuary, stained glass and The Lady and the Unicorn *series of tapestries.*

Great For...

☑ Don't Miss

The tapestries and the Gallo-Roman bathhouse.

Gallo-Roman Bathhouse

The Gallo-Roman bathhouse was built around AD 200. Look for the fragment of mosaic *Love Riding a Dolphin*, as well as a gorgeous marble bathtub from Rome. Outside the museum, remnants of the other rooms – a *palestra* (exercise room), *tepidarium* (warm bath) and *calidarium* (hot bath) – are visible.

Tapestries

It is believed that the unicorn tapestries – representing the five senses and an enigmatic sixth, perhaps the heart – were originally commissioned by the Le Viste family in Paris in the late 15th century. Discovered in 1814 in Château de Boussac, they were acquired by the museum in 1882.

MAZIARZ/SHUTTERSTOCK ©

Medieval gate adjacent to the museum entrance

NIKOLPETR/SHUTTERSTOCK ©

ⓘ Need to Know

Map p260; ☏01 53 73 78 00; www.musee-moyenage.fr; 28 rue du Sommerard, 5e; adult/child €5/free, 1st Sun of month free; ⓧ9.15am-5.45pm Wed-Mon; Ⓜ Cluny–La Sorbonne

✖ Take a Break

Bouillon Racine (p141) serves outstanding French fare in art nouveau surrounds.

★ Top Tip

The museum will remain partly open throughout renovations due for completion in late 2020.

A copy of Foucault's pendulum, first hung from the dome in 1851 to demonstrate the rotation of the earth, takes pride of place.

Hôtel de Cluny

The 15th-century Hôtel de Cluny, reopening in late 2020, was initially the residential quarters of the Cluny Abbots.

What's Nearby?

Panthéon   Mausoleum

(Map p260; ☏01 44 32 18 00; www.paris-pantheon.fr; place du Panthéon, 5e; adult/child €9/free; ⓧ10am-6.30pm Apr-Sep, to 6pm Oct-Mar; Ⓜ Maubert-Mutualité or RER Luxembourg) The Panthéon's stately neoclassical dome is an icon of the Parisian skyline. Its vast interior is an architectural masterpiece: originally an abbey church dedicated to Ste Geneviève and now a mausoleum, it has served since 1791 as the resting place of some of France's greatest thinkers, including Voltaire, Rousseau, Braille and Hugo.

Musée National Eugène Delacroix   Museum

(Map p254; ☏01 44 41 86 50; www.musee-delacroix.fr; 6 rue de Furstenberg, 6e; adult/child €7/free; ⓧ9.30am-5pm Wed-Mon, to 9pm 1st Thu of month; Ⓜ Mabillon) In a courtyard off a pretty tree-shaded square, this museum is housed in the romantic artist's home and studio at the time of his death in 1863. It contains a collection of his oil paintings, watercolours, pastels and drawings, including many of his more intimate works, such as *An Unmade Bed* (1828) and his paintings of Morocco. A ticket from the Musée du Louvre (p51) allows same-day entry here (you can also buy tickets here and skip the Louvre's ticket queues).

View of the Louvre from the Jardin des Tuileries

ANMBPH/SHUTTERSTOCK ©

Jardin des Tuileries

Filled with fountains, classical sculptures and magnificent panoramas at every turn, this quintessentially Parisian 28-hectare formal park constitutes part of the Banks of the Seine Unesco World Heritage Site.

Great For...

☑ **Don't Miss**

Monet's enormous mural-like *Water Lilies* in the Musée de l'Orangerie.

The park was laid out in its present form in 1664 by André Le Nôtre, who also created the gardens at Versailles.

Musée de l'Orangerie   Museum

(☎01 44 77 80 07; www.musee-orangerie.fr; place de la Concorde, 1er; adult/child €9/free; ☺9am-6pm Wed-Mon; MConcorde) Monet's extraordinary cycle of eight enormous *Decorations des Nymphéas* (Water Lilies) occupies two huge oval rooms purpose-built in 1927 on the artist's instructions. The lower level houses more of Monet's impressionist works and many by Sisley, Renoir, Cézanne, Gauguin, Picasso, Matisse and Modigliani, as well as Derain's *Arlequin et Pierrot*. The orangery and photography gallery Jeu de Paume are all that remains of the former Palais des Tuileries, which was razed during the Paris Commune in 1871. Audioguides cost €5.

WYSIATI/GETTY IMAGES ©

❶ Need to Know

Map p252; rue de Rivoli, 1er; ⏰7am-9pm Apr-late Sep, 7.30am-7.30pm late Sep-Mar; Ⓜ Tuileries, Concorde

✕ Take a Break

Enjoy famed hot chocolate at Angelina (p174).

★ Top Tip

Place de la Concorde (Map p252; 8e; Ⓜ Concorde) offers a 360-degree Parisian panorama at the park's northwestern end.

Jeu de Paume — Gallery

(📞01 47 03 12 50; www.jeudepaume.org; 1 place de la Concorde, 1er; adult/child €10/free; ⏰11am-9pm Tue, to 7pm Wed-Sun; Ⓜ Concorde) The Galerie du Jeu de Paume, which stages innovative photography exhibitions, is housed in an erstwhile *jeu de paume* (royal tennis court) of the former Palais des Tuileries in the northwestern corner of the Jardin des Tuileries (p85). Cinema screenings and concert performances also take place – check the agenda online.

What's Nearby?

Arc de Triomphe du Carrousel — Monument

(place du Carrousel, 1er; Ⓜ Palais Royal–Musée du Louvre) This triumphal arch, erected by Napoléon to celebrate his battlefield successes of 1805, rises from the **Jardin du Carrousel**, the gardens immediately next to the Louvre. The eastern counterpoint to the more famous Arc de Triomphe, it is one of several monuments that comprise the *axe historique* (historical axis), which terminates with the statue of Louis XIV next to the Pyramide du Louvre.

Hôtel de la Marine — Palace

(www.hotel-de-la-marine.paris; 2 place de la Concorde, 8e; Ⓜ Concorde) Built to house the Garde-Meuble de la Couronne (royal furnishings), the Hôtel de la Marine is one of two grand-scale palaces (along with the Hôtel de Crillon, now a luxury hotel) commissioned by Louis XV in the late 18th century to grace place de la Concorde. After the building was looted during the French Revolution, the French navy was headquartered here until 2015. From spring 2020, it will open to the public, with guided tours providing an insight into its history.

Sainte-Chapelle stained-glass windows

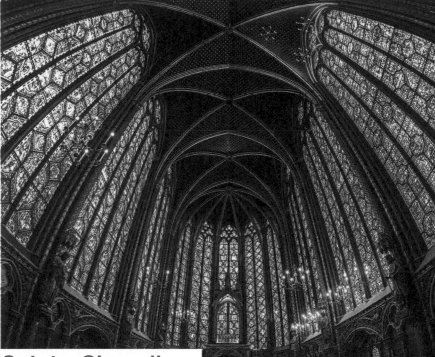

VICHIE81/GETTY IMAGES ©

Sainte-Chapelle

This gemlike Holy Chapel is Paris'
most exquisite Gothic monument.
Try to save it for a sunny day, when
Paris' oldest, finest stained glass is
at its dazzling best.

Sainte-Chapelle was built in just six years
(compared with nearly 200 years for
Notre Dame) and consecrated in 1248.
The chapel was conceived by Louis IX to
house his personal collection of holy relics,
including the famous Ste-Couronne (Holy
Crown), acquired by the French king in
1239 from the emperors of Constantinople.

The chapel's 15 floor-to-ceiling stained-
glass windows – 15.5m high in the nave,
13.5m in the apse – depict 1113 scenes.
From the bookshop, spiral up the staircase
to the king's private upper chapel.

Before arriving, download the 'Sainte
Chapelle Windows' app to 'read' the window
biblical story – from Genesis through to the
resurrection of Christ. Once here, rent an
audioguide (€3) or join a free 45-minute
guided tour in English (daily between 11am
and 3pm).

Great For...

☑ Don't Miss

The ethereal experience of classical-
and sacred-music concerts amid the
stained glass.

Spire of Sainte-Chapelle

❶ Need to Know

Map p254; ☎01 53 40 60 80, concerts 01 42 77 65 65; www.sainte-chapelle.fr; 8 bd du Palais, 1er; adult/child €10/free, joint ticket with Conciergerie €15/free; ⊗9am-7pm Apr-Sep, to 5pm Oct-Mar; Ⓜ Cité

✕ Take a Break

Enjoy artistically presented dishes at Seine-side Sequana (p139).

★ Top Tip

Combination tickets pre-purchased at the Conciergerie allow you to skip the ticket queues.

Even combination-ticket-holders still need to go through the security queue; be sure to leave pocket knives, scissors and the like at your accommodation.

You can peek at Sainte-Chapelle's exterior from across the street (albeit not a patch on its interior), by the law courts' magnificently gilded 18th-century gate facing rue de Lutèce.

What's Nearby?

Conciergerie   Monument

(Map p254; ☎01 53 40 60 80; www.paris-conciergerie.fr; 2 bd du Palais, 1er; adult/child €9/free, joint ticket with Sainte-Chapelle €15/free; ⊗9.30am-6pm; Ⓜ Cité) A royal palace in the 14th century, the Conciergerie later became a prison. During the Reign of Terror (1793–94) alleged enemies of the Revolution were incarcerated here before being brought before the Revolutionary Tribunal next door in the **Palais de Justice**. Top-billing exhibitions take place in the beautiful, Rayonnant Gothic **Salle des Gens d'Armes**, Europe's largest surviving medieval hall.

Of the almost 2800 prisoners held in the dungeons during the Reign of Terror (in various 'classes' of cells, no less) before being sent in tumbrels to the guillotine, the star prisoner was Queen Marie-Antoinette – see a reproduction of her cell. As the counter revolution began, radicals Danton and Robespierre themselves made an appearance at the Conciergeril.

To get the most out of your visit, rent a HistoPad (a tablet-device guide, €5) to explore the Conciergerie in augmented reality and take part in an interactive 3D treasure hunt.

VIACHESLAV LOPATIN/SHUTTERSTOCK ©

Les Catacombes

Paris' most macabre sight is its series of subterranean passages lined with skulls and bones. It's a 1.5km walk through the creepy ossuary and definitely not for the faint-hearted.

Great For...

☑ Don't Miss

Combining a visit to Les Catacombes with a wander through Cimetière du Montparnasse.

In 1785 it was decided to rectify the hygiene problems of Paris' overflowing cemeteries by exhuming the bones and storing them in disused quarry tunnels; the catacombs were created in 1810.

The route through Les Catacombes begins at the spacious 2018-opened entrance on place Denfert-Rochereau. After descending 20m below street level (via 131 narrow, dizzying spiral steps), you follow the dark subterranean passages to reach the ossuary itself (1.5km in all), with a mind-boggling number of bones and skulls of millions of Parisians neatly packed along the walls.

The exit is up 112 steps via a 'transition space' with a gift shop onto 21bis av René Coty, 14e. Bag searches are carried out to prevent visitors 'souveniring' bones.

ⓘ Need to Know

Map p262; ☎01 43 22 47 63; www.
catacombes.paris.fr; place Denfert-
Rochereau, 14e; adult/child €13/free, online
booking incl audioguide €29/5; ⊙10am-
8.30pm Tue-Sun; Ⓜ Denfert-Rochereau

✕ Take a Break

Pick up picnic fare on foodie street rue
Daguerre and head to a nearby park.

★ Top Tip

Wear sturdy shoes for the uneven, often
muddy surface and loose stones.

Visiting

The route through Les Catacombes begins
at the 2018-opened entrance on place
Denfert-Rochereau. A maximum of 200
people are allowed in the tunnels at a time
and queues can be huge – when the queue
extends beyond a 20-minute wait, you'll
be handed a coupon with a return entry
time later that day. Last entry is at 7.30pm.
Online bookings are pricier but include a
worthwhile audioguide and guarantee a
timeslot, whereas standing in the queue
does not, as online ticket holders have
priority.

Bear in mind that the catacombs are not
suitable for young children. Also be aware
that flash photography isn't permitted
and the temperature is a cool 14°C below
ground.

What's Nearby?

Musée Jean Moulin　　　　Museum

(Map p262; ☎01 40 64 39 44; www.museesle
clercmoulin.paris.fr; place Denfert-Rochereau,
14e; Ⓜ Denfert Rochereau) Opposite Les Catacombes' entrance, this history museum
covers the WWII German occupation of
Paris, with its focus on the Resistance and
its leader, Jean Moulin (1899–1943).

**Cimetière du
Montparnasse**　　　　Cemetery

(Map p262; www.paris.fr; 3 bd Edgar Quinet, 14e;
⊙8am-6pm Mon-Fri, 8.30am-6pm Sat, 9am-6pm
Sun; Ⓜ Edgar Quinet) FREE This 19-hectare
cemetery opened in 1824 and is Paris'
second largest after Père Lachaise (p77).
Famous residents include writer Guy de
Maupassant, playwright Samuel Beckett,
sculptor Constantin Brancusi, photogra-
pher Man Ray, industrialist André Citroën,
Captain Alfred Dreyfus of the infamous
Dreyfus Affair, legendary singer Serge
Gainsbourg and philosopher-writers
Jean-Paul Sartre and Simone de Beauvoir.

KIEV.VICTOR/SHUTTERSTOCK ©

Musée Jacquemart-André

The home of art collectors Nélie Jacquemart and Édouard André, this opulent late-19th-century residence offers an absorbing glimpse of the lifestyle of Parisian high society.

Great For...

☑ Don't Miss

The library, hung with canvases by Rembrandt and Van Dyck.

The mansion was designed in the then-fashionable eclectic style, which combined elements from various eras – seen here in the presence of Greek and Roman antiquities, Egyptian artefacts, period furnishings and portraits by Dutch masters.

A wander through its 16 rambling rooms offers an absorbing glimpse of the lifestyle and tastes of Parisian high society: from the art-filled library to the marvellous Jardin d'Hiver (a glass-paned garden room backed by a magnificent double-helix staircase). Upstairs is an impressive collection of Italian Renaissance works by Botticelli, Donatello and Titian, among others.

The building's architect, Henri Parent, was nearly hired to work on the even more prestigious Paris opera house, the Palais Garnier – he was eclipsed only by the then-unknown Charles Garnier.

JULIAN KUMAR/GODONG/GETTY IMAGES ©

Musée Jacquemart-André
🏛
Bd Haussmann
R de Courcelles
R de la Baume
Av Percier
Ⓜ
Miromesnil

❶ Need to Know

Map p252; 📞01 45 62 11 59; www.musee-jacquemart-andre.com; 158 bd Haussmann, 8e; adult/child incl audioguide €16/9.50; ⏱10am-6pm, to 8.30pm Mon during temporary exhibitions; 📶; ⓂMiromesnil

✕ Take a Break

The museum's beautiful *salon de thé* serves lunch, brunch and pastries.

★ Top Tip

Download the free app from the museum's website.

What's Nearby?

Musée Nissim de Camondo   Gallery

(Map p252; 📞01 44 55 57 50; www.madparis.fr; 63 rue de Monceau, 8e; adult/child incl audioguide €9/free; ⏱10am-5.30pm Wed-Sun; ⓂMonceau, Villiers) Housed in a sumptuous mansion modelled on the Petit Trianon at Versailles, this museum displays 18th-century furniture, wood panelling, tapestries, porcelain and other objets d'art collected by Count Moïse de Camondo, a Sephardic Jewish banker who moved from Constantinople to Paris in the late 19th century.

Musée Cernuschi   Museum

(Map p252; 📞01 53 96 21 50; www.cernuschi.paris.fr; 7 av Vélasquez, 8e; ⏱10am-6pm Tue-Sun; ⓂVilliers) **FREE** The Cernuschi Museum comprises an excellent and rare collection of ancient Chinese art (funerary statues, bronzes, ceramics), much of which predates the Tang dynasty (618–907), in addition to diverse pieces from Japan. Milan banker and philanthropist Henri Cernuschi (1821–96), who settled in Paris before the unification of Italy, assembled the collection during an 1871–73 world tour.

Citéco   Museum

(Cité de l'Économie et de la Monnaie; Map p252; www.citeco.fr; 1 place du Général Catroux, 17e; ⓂMalesherbes) A splendidly renovated turreted neo-renaissance townhouse, built by architect Jules Février for banker Emile Gaillard in the late 19th century, is the setting for Paris' new economics and banking museum, which at the time of research was set to open in 2019. Historic French and foreign banknotes, coins and earlier forms of currency, as well as punch presses and typographic elements, are among its collections.

Kitchen of the Maison de Claude Monet

SHISHKIN DMITRY/SHUTTERSTOCK ©

Day Trip: Maison et Jardins de Claude Monet

Monet lived in Giverny from 1883 until his death in 1926, in a rambling house – surrounded by flower-filled gardens – that's now the immensely popular Maison et Jardins de Claude Monet.

Great For...

☑ Don't Miss

Monet's trademark lily pond, immortalised in his *Nymphéas* (Water Lilies) series.

Monet's home for the last 43 years of his life is now a delightful house-museum. His pastel-pink house and Water Lily studio stand on the periphery of the Clos Normand, with its symmetrically laid-out gardens bursting with flowers. Monet bought the Jardin d'Eau (Water Garden) in 1895 and set about creating his trademark lily pond, as well as the famous Japanese bridge (since rebuilt).

The charmingly preserved house and beautiful bloom-filled gardens (rather than Monet's works) are the draws here.

Draped with purple wisteria, the Japanese bridge blends into the asymmetrical foreground and background, creating the intimate atmosphere for which the 'painter of light' was renowned.

Seasons have an enormous effect on Giverny. From early to late spring, daffodils, tulips, rhododendrons, wisteria and irises

Jardin de Claude Monet

SEAN HEATLEY/SHUTTERSTOCK ©

ℹ Need to Know

📞02 32 51 28 21; www.fondation-monet.com;
84 rue Claude Monet; adult/child €9.50/5.50,
incl Musée des Impressionnismes Giverny
€17/9; ⏱9.30am-6pm Easter-Oct

✕ Take a Break

Michelin-starred dishes are exquisite at
country estate **Le Jardin des Plumes**
(📞02 32 54 26 35; www.jardindesplumes.
fr; 1 rue du Milieu; 3-/5-/7-course menus
€50/85/98, mains €38-46; ⏱12.15-1.30pm
& 7.30-9pm Wed-Sun, hotel closed Mon & Tue
Nov-Mar; 🛜♿).

★ Top Tip

Note the sight closes from November to
Easter, along with most accommodation
and restaurants.

appear, followed by poppies and lilies. By
June, nasturtiums, roses and sweet peas
are in flower. Around September, there are
dahlias, sunflowers and hollyhocks.

Combined tickets with Paris' **Musée
Marmottan Monet** (📞01 44 96 50 33; www.
marmottan.fr; 2 rue Louis Boilly, 16e; adult/child
€12/8.50; ⏱10am-6pm Tue, Wed & Fri-Sun, to 9pm
Thu; Ⓜ La Muette) cost €20.50/12 per adult/
child, and combined adult tickets with Paris'
Musée de l'Orangerie (p90) cost €18.50.

Visiting

The tiny country village of Giverny is
74km northwest of Paris. From Paris' Gare
St-Lazare there are up to 15 daily trains to
Vernon (from €9, 45 minutes to one hour),
7km to the west of Giverny, from where
buses, taxis and cycle/walking tracks run
to Giverny.

Shuttle buses (single/return €5/10,
20 minutes, four daily Monday to Friday
Easter to October, five daily Saturday and
Sunday Easter to October) meet most
trains from Paris at Vernon. There are
limited seats, so arrive early for the return
trip from Giverny. Tickets are sold on board;
check the live shuttle schedule on www.
sngo-giverny.fr.

Rent bikes (cash only) at the **Café
L'Arrivée de Giverny** (📞02 32 21 16 01; 1-3
place de la Gare, Vernon; per day €14; ⏱8am-
11pm), opposite the train station in Vernon,
from where Giverny is a signposted 5km
along a direct (and flat) cycle/walking track.

Taxis (📞02 32 51 10 24) usually wait outside the train station in Vernon and charge
around €15 for the one-way trip to Giverny.
There's no taxi rank in Giverny, however, so
you'll need to phone one for the return trip
to Vernon.

Palais Garnier

GIVAGA/SHUTTERSTOCK ©

Palais Garnier

*The fabled 'phantom of the opera'
lurked in this opulent opera house,
which offers behind-the-scenes tours
and stages opera, ballet and music
performances.*

Great For...

☑ Don't Miss

Chagall's ceiling mural (1964), above
the massive chandelier, which depicts
scenes from 14 operas.

Few other Paris monuments have provided
artistic inspiration in the way that the
Palais Garnier has. From Degas' ballerinas
to Gaston Leroux' Phantom and Chagall's
ceiling, the layers of myth painted on
gradually over the decades have bestowed
a particular air of mystery and drama to
its ornate interior. Designed in 1860 by
Charles Garnier (then an unknown 35-year-
old architect), the opera house was part
of Baron Haussmann's massive urban
renovation project.

The opera house is open to visitors during the day, and the building is a fascinating
place to explore even if you're not taking
in a show. Highlights include the opulent
Grand Staircase, the library-museum (1st
floor) and the horseshoe-shaped auditorium (2nd floor), with its extravagant gilded
interior and red velvet seats. Above the

Interior of the Palais Garnier

GARY YIM/SHUTTERSTOCK ©

❶ Need to Know

Map p252; 📞08 92 89 90 90; www.opera
deparis.fr; cnr rues Scribe & Auber, 9e; self-
guided tours adult/child €12/8, guided tours
adult/child €15.50/8.50; ☺self-guided tours
10am-5pm, English-language guided tours
11am & 2.30pm; ⓂOpéra

✕ Take a Break

Close at hand, place de la Madeleine
(p164) is a gourmet fantasyland.

★ Top Tip

Catching a performance (p190) here is
a treat.

massive chandelier is Chagall's gorgeous
ceiling mural (1964), which depicts scenes
from 14 operas.

Visits are either unguided (audioguides
available; €5), or you can reserve a spot
online for an English-language guided tour.
Check the website for updated schedules.

What's Nearby?
Église de la Madeleine   Church

(Church of St Mary Magdalene; Map p252; www.
eglise-lamadeleine.com; place de la Madeleine,
8e; ☺9.30am-7pm; ⓂMadeleine) Place de la
Madeleine is named after the 19th-century
neoclassical church at its centre, the Église
de la Madeleine. Constructed in the style
of a massive Greek temple, 'La Madeleine'
was consecrated in 1842 after almost a
century of design changes and construction delays.

The church is a popular venue for
classical-music concerts (some free);
check the posters outside or the website
for dates.

Jardin du Palais Royal   Gardens

(Map p254; www.domaine-palais-royal.fr; 2 place
Colette, 1er; ☺8am-10.30pm Apr-Sep, to 8.30pm
Oct-Mar; ⓂPalais Royal–Musée du Louvre) The
Jardin du Palais Royal is a perfect spot to
sit, contemplate and picnic between boxed
hedges, or shop in the trio of beautiful
arcades that frame the garden: the **Galerie
de Valois** (east), **Galerie de Montpensier**
(west) and **Galerie Beaujolais** (north).
However, it's the southern end of the
complex, polka-dotted with sculptor Daniel
Buren's 260 black-and-white-striped
columns, that has become the garden's
signature feature.

Walking Tour: Seine-Side Meander

The Seine and its surrounds are Paris at its most seductive. Descend the steps along the quays wherever possible to stroll along the water's edge.

Start Place de la Concorde
Distance 7km
Duration Three hours

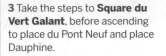

3 Take the steps to **Square du Vert Galant**, before ascending to place du Pont Neuf and place Dauphine.

R Royale
Pl Vendôme
Ⓜ Concorde
Pl de la Concorde Ⓜ
Pyramides Ⓜ
START
Tuileries Ⓜ
Jardin des Tuileries
R de Rivoli
①
Jardin du Carrousel
Q des Tuileries
Seine

Classic Photo

Enjoy fountain views in this elegant 28-hectare garden.

2 Walk through the Jardin de l'Oratoire to the **Cour Carrée** (p53) and exit at the Jardin de l'Infante.

PAVEL L PHOTO AND VIDEO/SHUTTERSTOCK ©

1 After taking in the panorama at place de la Concorde, stroll through the **Jardin des Tuileries** (p90).

MING TANG-EVANS/LONELY PLANET ©

7 End your romantic meander at the tranquil **Jardin des Plantes** (p106). Cruise back along the Seine by Batobus.

RRRAINBOW/GETTY IMAGES ©

4 Curl up with a volume of poetry in the magical **Shakespeare & Company** (p161) bookshop.

ALESSIO CATELLI/SHUTTERSTOCK ©

Take a Break...

Morning or night, try hip **Café Saint Régis** (p137).

5 Cross to Île St-Louis and share an ice cream from *glacier* (ice-cream maker) **Berthillon** (p137).

6 Wander among late-20th-century unfenced sculptures at the **Musée de la Sculpture en Plein Air** (p109).

Aerial view of Les Invalides

Hôtel des Invalides

Flanked by the 500m-long Esplanade des Invalides lawns, this massive military complex built in the 1670s by Louis XIV to house 4000 invalides (disabled war veterans) contains Napoléon's tomb.

Great For...

☑ Don't Miss

France's largest military museum, the Musée de l'Armée.

On 14 July 1789, a mob broke into the building and seized 32,000 rifles before heading on to the prison at Bastille and the start of the French Revolution.

In the **Cour d'Honneur**, the nation's largest collection on the history of the French military is displayed at the **Musée de l'Armée** (Army Museum; www.musee-armee. fr; 129 rue de Grenelle, 7e; included in Hôtel des Invalides entry; ⊘10am-6pm Apr-Oct, to 5pm Nov-Mar; Ⓜ Varenne, La Tour Maubourg). South is **Église St-Louis des Invalides**, once used by soldiers, and **Église du Dôme** (included in Hôtel des Invalides entry; ⊘10am-6pm Wed-Mon, to 9pm Tue Apr-Oct, 10am-5pm Nov-Mar) which, with its sparkling golden dome (1677–1735), is one of the finest religious edifices erected under Louis XIV and was the inspiration for the United States Capitol building. It received the remains

Cannon detail, Hôtel des Invalides

❶ Need to Know

Map p262; www.musee-armee.fr; 129 rue de Grenelle, 7e; adult/child €12/free; ⏲10am-6pm Apr-Oct, to 5pm Nov-Mar; Ⓜ Varenne, La Tour Maubourg

✗ Take a Break

Coutume Café (p183) brews outstanding coffee from its own-roasted beans.

★ Top Tip

Atmospheric classical concerts (ranging from €5 to €30) take place regularly here year-round.

of Napoléon in 1840: the extravagant **Tombeau de Napoléon 1er** comprises six coffins fitting into one another like a Russian doll. Scale models of towns, fortresses and châteaux across France fill the esoteric **Musée des Plans-Reliefs**.

Admission includes entry to all Hôtel des Invalides sights; their individual hours often vary.

What's Nearby?

Musée Yves Saint Laurent Paris   Museum

(Map p252; ☏01 44 31 64 00; www.museeysl paris.com; 5 av Marceau, 16e; adult/child €10/7; ⏲11am-6pm Tue-Thu, Sat & Sun, to 9pm Fri; Ⓜ Alma-Marceau) Housed in the legendary designer's studios (1974–2002), this museum holds retrospectives of YSL's avant-garde designs, from early sketches

to finished pieces. Temporary exhibitions give an insight into the creative process of designing a *haute couture* collection and the history of fashion throughout the 20th century. The building can only accommodate a small number of visitors at a time, so buy tickets online or expect to queue outside.

Petit Palais   Gallery

(Map p252; ☏01 53 43 40 00; www.petitpalais. paris.fr; av Winston Churchill, 8e; ⏲10am-6pm Tue-Sun, to 9pm Fri; Ⓜ Champs-Élysées–Clemenceau) **FREE** This architectural stunner was built for the 1900 Exposition Universelle, and is home to the **Musée des Beaux-Arts de la Ville de Paris** (City of Paris Museum of Fine Arts). It specialises in medieval and Renaissance *objets d'art*, such as porcelain and clocks, tapestries, drawings, and 19th-century French paintings and sculpture; there are also paintings by such artists as Rembrandt, Colbert, Cézanne, Monet, Gauguin and Delacroix. An audioguide costs €5.

Statue of Jean-Baptiste Lamarck, Jardin des Plantes

IMG STOCK STUDIO/SHUTTERSTOCK ©

Jardin des Plantes

Founded in 1626 as a medicinal herb garden for Louis XIII, Paris' 24-hectare botanic gardens are an idyllic spot to stroll or visit the museums or zoo.

Visually defined by the double alley of plane trees that run the length of the park, these sprawling gardens allow you to escape the city concrete for a spell.

Highlights here include peony and rose gardens, an alpine garden, and the gardens of the École de Botanique, used by students of the school and green-fingered Parisians. The gorgeous glass-and-metal **Grandes Serres** (adult/child €7/5; ⊘10am-6pm Apr-Sep, to 5pm Oct-Mar; MJussieu) – a series of four greenhouses – have been in use since 1714, and several of Henri Rousseau's jungle paintings, sometimes on display in the Musée d'Orsay, were inspired by his frequent visits here.

Great For...

☑ Don't Miss

The gardens' beautiful glass-and-metal Grandes Serres (greenhouses).

Tropical plants inside the Grandes Serres

YANN GUICHAOUA-PHOTOS/GETTY IMAGES ©

❶ Need to Know

Map p260; 📞01 40 79 56 01; www.jardin
desplantes.net; place Valhubert & 36 rue
Geoffroy-St-Hilaire, 5e; ⊗8am-6.30pm Apr-
Oct, to 5.30pm Nov-Mar; Ⓜ Gare d'Austerlitz,
Censier Daubenton, Jussieu

✕ Take a Break

Bring a picnic with you (but watch out
for the automatic sprinklers!).

★ Top Tip

A tranquil way to travel to/from here is
by Batobus (p240) along the Seine.

Museums & Zoo

Muséum National
d'Histoire Naturelle   Museum

(Map p260; www.mnhn.fr; place Valhubert & 36
rue Geoffroy-St-Hilaire, 5e; Ⓜ Gare d'Austerlitz,
Censier Daubenton, Jussieu) Despite the name,
the National Museum of Natural History
is not a single building, but a collection
of sites throughout France. Its historic
home is in the Jardin des Plantes, and it's
here that you'll find the greatest number
of branches: taxidermied animals in the
excellent **Grande Galerie de l'Évolution**
(Map p260; 📞01 40 79 54 79; www.grande
galeriedelevolution.fr; 36 rue Geoffroy-St-
Hilaire, 5e; adult/child €10/free, with Galeries
des Enfants €12/9; ⊗10am-6pm Wed-Mon;
Ⓜ Censier Daubenton); fossils and dinosaur
skeletons in the **Galeries d'Anatomie**

Comparée et de Paléontologie (Map p260;
📞01 40 79 56 01; www.mnhn.fr; 2 rue Buffon,
5e; adult/child €9/free; ⊗10am-6pm Wed-Mon;
Ⓜ Gare d'Austerlitz); and meteorites and
crystals in the **Galerie de Minéralogie
et de Géologie** (Map p260; 📞01 40 79 56
01; www.galeriedemineralogieetgeologie.fr; 36
rue Geoffroy-St-Hilaire, 5e; adult/child €7/free;
⊗10am-6pm Wed-Mon Mar-Oct, to 5pm Wed-Mon
Nov-Feb; Ⓜ Censier Daubenton).

Created in 1793, the National Museum
of Natural History became a centre of
significant scientific research in the 19th
century. Of the three museums here, the
four-floor Grande Galerie de l'Évolution is
a particular winner if you're travelling with
kids: life-sized elephants, tigers and rhinos
play safari, and imaginative exhibits on
evolution, extinction and global warming fill
6000 sq metres. The temporary exhibits
are generally excellent. Within this building
is a separate attraction, the **Galerie des
Enfants** (Map p260; www.galeriedesenfants.fr;
36 rue Geoffroy-St-Hilaire, 5e; adult/child €12/9;

⊘10am-6pm Wed-Mon; Ⓜ Censier Daubenton) – a hands-on science museum tailored to children aged from six to 12 years.

La Ménagerie   Zoo

(Le Zoo du Jardin des Plantes; Map p260; www.zoodujardindesplantes.fr; 57 rue Cuvier, 5e; adult/child €13/10; ⊘9am-5.30pm Mar-Oct, to 5pm Nov-Feb; Ⓜ Gare d'Austerlitz) Like the Jardin des Plantes in which it's located, this 170-species zoo is more than a tourist attraction; it also doubles as a research centre for the reproduction of rare and endangered species. During the Prussian siege of 1870, the animals of the day were themselves endangered, when almost all were eaten by starving Parisians.

What's Nearby?

Mosquée de Paris   Mosque

(Map p260; ☑01 45 35 78 17; www.mosquee deparis.net; 2bis place du Puits de l'Ermite, 5e; adult/child €3/2; ⊘9am-noon & 2-7pm Sat-Thu Apr-Sep, 9am-noon & 2-6pm Sat-Thu Oct-Mar; Ⓜ Place Monge, Censier Daubenton) Paris' central mosque, with a striking 26m-high minaret, was completed in 1926 in an ornate art deco Moorish style. You can visit the interior to admire the intricate tile work and calligraphy. A separate entrance leads to the wonderful North African–style **hammam** (Turkish bathhouse; ☑01 43 31 14 32; www.la-mosquee.com; 39 rue Geoffroy-St-Hilaire, 5e), **restaurant** (☑01 45 35 75 17; mains €11-28; ⊘kitchen noon-midnight) and **tearoom** (⊘noon-midnight), and a small souk (actually

Station F

more of a gift shop). Visitors must be modestly dressed.

Musée de la Sculpture en Plein Air   Sculpture

(Map p260; quai St-Bernard, 5e; Ⓜ Gare d'Austerlitz) **FREE** Along quai St-Bernard, this open-air sculpture museum (also known as the Jardin Tino Rossi) has more than 50 late-20th-century unfenced sculptures, and makes a great picnic spot. A salad beneath

ALLOVER IMAGES/ALAMY STOCK PHOTO ©

> ★ **Top Tip**
>
> The natural history museum's Grande Galerie de l'Évolution includes imaginative exhibits on evolution and humankind's effect on the global eco-system – rare specimens dominate the Hall of Threatened and Extinct Species on level 2.

---

a César or a baguette beside a Brancusi is a pretty classy way to see the Seine up close.

Institut du Monde Arabe   Museum

(Arab World Institute; Map p260; ☑01 40 51 38 38; www.imarabe.org; 1 place Mohammed V, 5e; adult/child €8/4; ⊙10am-6pm Tue-Fri, to 7pm Sat & Sun; Ⓜ Jussieu) The Arab World Institute was jointly founded by France and 18 Middle Eastern and North African nations in 1980, with the aim of promoting cross-cultural dialogue. It hosts temporary exhibitions and a fascinating museum of Arabic culture and history (4th to 7th floors). The stunning building, designed by French architect Jean Nouvel, was inspired by latticed-wood windows *(mashrabiya)* traditional to Arabic architecture: thousands of modern-day photoelectrically sensitive apertures cover its sparkling glass facade.

Station F   Research Centre

(https://stationf.co; 55 bd Vincent Auriol, 13e; ⊙English-language tours by reservation 11.30am & 12.30pm Tue & Thu; 🛜; Ⓜ Chevaleret, Bibliothèque) **FREE** The world's largest start-up campus was unveiled by French president Emmanuel Macron in mid-2017. At any one time, some 3000 resident entrepreneurs from all over the world beaver away on ground-breaking new ideas and businesses, supported by 30 high-tech incubators and accelerators in this unique start-up ecosystem. Guided tours take visitors on a 45-minute waltz through the gargantuan steel, glass and concrete hangar – a railway depot constructed in 1927–29 to house new trains servicing nearby Gare d'Austerlitz.

> ☑ **Don't Miss**
>
> The incredible views from the 9th-floor roof terrace of the Institut de Monde Arabe (open 10am to 6pm Tuesday to Sunday).

Walking Tour: Paris' Covered Passages

Stepping into Paris' *passages couverts* (covered shopping arcades) is a superb way to get a feel for what life was like in early-19th-century Paris. This walking tour is tailor-made for a rainy day, but it's best avoided on a Sunday, when some arcades shut.

Start Galerie Véro Dodat
Distance 3km
Duration Two hours

7 There's lots to explore in **Passage Verdeau**: vintage comic books, antiques, old postcards and more.

4 The 1824-built **Passage Choiseul** has discount and vintage clothing, beads and costume jewellery, and cheap eateries.
KIEV.VICTOR/SHUTTERSTOCK ©

Take a Break...
Dine and drink within the arcades.

Classic Photo
Stroll through this elegant passage, designed by Jacques Billaud.

3 The 1826-built **Galerie Colbert** features a huge glass dome and rotunda.
KIEV.VICTOR/SHUTTERSTOCK ©

R St-Augustin

R des Petits Champs
R de Richelieu
R Vivienne

M Pyramides

Av de l'Opéra

Jardin du Palais Royal
R de Valois

1ER

Pl Colette
R du Colonel Driant

R de Rohan

R Croix des Petits Champs

Jardin des Tuileries

Jardin du Carrousel

Palais Royal – Musée du Louvre **M** R de Rivoli

FINISH

R Richer

7

6 Inside **Passage Jouffroy** (1847) there's a wax museum, the Musée Grévin, and wonderful boutiques.

6

Passage des Panoramas

Grands Boulevards Ⓜ

Bd Poissonnière

5

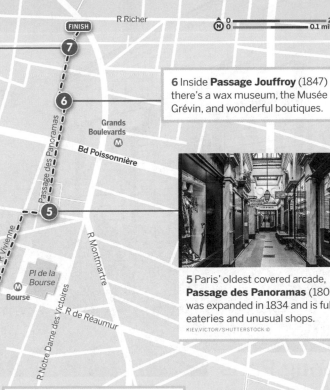

R Vivienne

R Montmartre

Pl de la Bourse Ⓜ

Bourse

R Notre Dame des Victoires

R de Réaumur

5 Paris' oldest covered arcade, **Passage des Panoramas** (1800), was expanded in 1834 and is full of eateries and unusual shops.
KIEV.VICTOR/SHUTTERSTOCK ©

2 Built in 1826, **Galerie Vivienne** is decorated with floor mosaics and bas-reliefs on the walls.

Pl des Victoires

R du Bouloi

R du Louvre

R Coquillière

1 **Galerie Véro Dodat** retains its 19th-century skylights, murals, Corinthian columns, and shopfronts including furniture restorers.
ANDERSPHOTO/SHUTTERSTOCK ©

START

Rue Dénoyez

WARING ABBOTT/CONTRIBUTOR/GETTY IMAGES ©

Discovering Paris' Street Art

The City of Light inspires artists of all genres, including urban art, and vibrant street art continues to splash colour across neighbourhoods city-wide.

Great For...

☑ Don't Miss

Checking out works by French and international artists, including Banksy, at Art 42.

Locations

Rue Dénoyez (Map p256; 20e; M Belleville) One block east of bd de Belleville, narrow rue Dénoyez has some of Paris' most dazzling street art. Everything on the small cobbled street, from litter bins and flower pots to lamp posts and window shutters, is covered in colourful graffiti. Artists' workshops pepper the paved street where local kids kick footballs around and street art 'happenings' break out on summer nights.

Le MUR (Map p256; www.lemur.fr; rue Oberkampf, 11e; M Parmentier) Meaning 'the wall' but also standing for Modulable Urbain Réactif (Modular Urban Reactive), street-art canvas Le MUR is overseen by an arts collective, with hundreds of murals painted on it to date.

Street art in the 13e

ADRIENNE PITTS/LONELY PLANET ©

❶ Need to Know

City funds are set aside to create *murs d'expression* (street-art murals) in all 20 *arrondissements*.

✕ Take a Break

Next to Le MUR, Café Charbon (p178) is great for a drink or bistro fare.

★ Top Tip

See graffiti street artists in action at the workrooms in hip-hop centre La Place (p191).

Compulsory guided tours, generally lasting 1½ to two hours, lead you through 4000 sq metres of subterranean rooms sheltering some 150 works. Entry's free but you need to reserve tours online (ideally several weeks in advance, although last-minute cancellations can arise).

L'Aerosol (www.laerosol.com; 54 rue de l'Évangile, 18e; adult/child €5/3; ⊙11am-9pm Thu-Sat, to 8pm Sun; Ⓜ Marx Dormoy) Street art is showcased at this cavernous museum inside a former SNCF freight railway station. French and international artists here include Mr Chat, Speedy Graphito, Invader and Banksy. You can test out your own tagging skills on the walls outside (BYO aerosols) or ask about taking a street-art course. Festivals, food trucks and a summer roller nightclub also set up here.

Galerie Itinerrance (www.itinerrance.fr; 24 bd du Général d'Armée Jean Simon, 13e; ⊙noon-7pm Tue-Sat; Ⓜ Bibliothèque François Mitterrand) FREE Testament to the 13e's ongoing creative renaissance, this gallery showcases graffiti and street art, and can advise on self-guided and guided street-art tours of the neighbourhood that take in many landmark works by artists represented by the gallery. Exhibitions and events change regularly. Across the train tracks in nearby Chinatown, don't miss the striking twinset of monumental wall murals by Portuguese artist Pantónio showcased on high-rise apartment blocks at 20–22 ave d'Ivry.

Tours

Street Art Paris (☎09 50 75 19 92; www. streetartparis.fr; tours €20; ⊙by reservation) Learn about the history of graffiti on fascinating tours taking in Paris' vibrant street art in Belleville and Montmartre, and on the Left Bank. If you're inspired to try it yourself, book into a 2½-hour mural workshop (€35).

Street Art Museums & Galleries

Art 42 (www.art42.fr; 96 bd Bessières, 17e; ⊙tours in English 7pm every 2nd Tue; Ⓜ Porte de Clichy) FREE Street art and post-graffiti now have their own dedicated space at this 'anti-museum', with works by Banksy, Bom.K, Miss Van, Swoon and Invader (who's behind the Space Invader motifs on buildings all over Paris), among other boundary-pushing urban artists.

TAKASHI IMAGES/SHUTTERSTOCK ©

Musée National Picasso

An exquisite 17th-century mansion in Le Marais is the wonderfully intimate setting for an exceptional collection of works by long-time Paris resident, Pablo Picasso.

Great For...

☑ Don't Miss

The museum's bi-annual temporary exhibitions.

One of Paris' most treasured art collections is showcased inside the mid-17th-century Hôtel Salé, an exquisite private mansion owned by the city since 1964. The Musée National Picasso is a staggering art museum devoted to Spanish artist Pablo Picasso (1881–1973), who spent much of his life living and working in Paris. The collection includes more than 5000 drawings, engravings, paintings, ceramic works and sculptures by the *grand maître* (great master), although they're not all displayed at the same time.

The extraordinary cache of works was donated to the French government by the artist's heirs in lieu of paying inheritance taxes. In addition to the permanent collection, the museum mounts two major temporary exhibitions a year (included in the admission price).

EGROY/SHUTTERSTOCK ©

ℹ️ Need to Know

Map p256; ☎01 85 56 00 36; www.musee picassoparis.fr; 5 rue de Thorigny, 3e; adult/ child €12.50/free; ⏰10.30am-6pm Tue-Fri, from 9.30am Sat & Sun; Ⓜ️Chemin Vert, St-Paul

✕ Take a Break

Stop by the museum's 'rooftop cafe', overlooked by an ancient stone sphinx.

★ Top Tip

To best appreciate the artworks and building's history, rent an audioguide (€5).

Jewish communities from the Middle Ages to the present, including French Jewish history. Highlights include documents relating to the Dreyfus Affair, and artworks by Chagall, Modigliani and Soutine. Creative workshops for children, adults and families complement excellent temporary exhibitions. To learn more about Le Marais' Jewish history, take a guided walking tour of the neighbourhood (including museum entrance adult/youth €25/16; English available).

What's Nearby?

Musée Carnavalet   Museum
(Map p256; ☎01 44 59 58 58; www.carnavalet. paris.fr; 23 rue de Sévigné, 3e; Ⓜ️St-Paul, Chemin Vert) **FREE** Paris' history museum, spanning Gallo-Roman times onwards, rambles over a pair of remarkable *hôtels particuliers* (private mansions), the 1560-built **Hôtel Carnavalet** and 1688-built **Hôtel Le Peletier de St-Fargeau**. In early 2020, the museum will reopen after a four-year renovation that will give it better accessibility.

Musée d'Art et d'Histoire du Judaïsme   Museum
(Map p256; ☎01 53 01 86 60; www.mahj.org; 71 rue du Temple, 3e; adult/youth €10/free; ⏰11am-6pm Tue-Fri, from 10am Sat & Sun; Ⓜ️Rambuteau) Inside the Hôtel de St-Aignan, dating from 1650, this museum traces the evolution of

Pavillon de l'Arsenal   Museum
(Map p256; www.pavillon-arsenal.com; 21 bd Morland, 4e; ⏰11am-7pm Tue-Sun; Ⓜ️Sully–Morland) **FREE** Built in 1879 as a museum, this magnificent glass-roofed building with arched wrought-iron girders wasn't actually used as one until over a century later, when it opened as a centre for Parisian urbanism and architecture. Exhibitions showcase the city's past, present and future. Interpretative information is in French but it's fascinating for anyone with an interest in the evolution of Paris. There's a small but excellent architectural bookshop.

Chef at Le Cordon Bleu

OWEN FRANKEN/GETTY IMAGES ©

Cooking & Wine-Tasting Courses

If dining in the city's restaurants whets your appetite, Paris has some outstanding cookery schools. And where there's food in Paris, wine is never more than an arm's length away.

Great For

☑ Don't Miss

Myriad short-course options, even during a lightning-quick trip, but book ahead.

Top Choices

Le Cordon Bleu (Map p262; ☎01 85 65 15 00; www.cordonbleu.edu/paris; 13-15 quai André Citroën, 15e; Ⓜ Javel–André Citroën or RER Javel) One of the world's foremost culinary arts schools, Le Cordon Bleu's campus overlooks the Seine and Statue of Liberty, with views of the nearby Eiffel Tower from its terrace. Prices start at €120 for themed three-hour classes (food and wine pairing, vegetarian cuisine, éclairs, choux pastry etc) and €470 for two-day courses. There are also evening wine tastings (€105), chef demonstrations (€50) and classes for kids (eight to 12 years, €90). Its on-site cafe serves pastries, artisan breads, gourmet sandwiches and salads incorporating produce grown in the school's rooftop garden.

La Cuisine Paris (Map p256; ☎01 40 51 78 18; www.lacuisineparis.com; 80 quai de l'Hôtel de Ville, 4e; 2hr cooking class/walking tour & class

Preparing macarons, La Cuisine Paris

MATT MUNRO/LONELY PLANET ©

from €69/165; M Pont Marie, Hôtel de Ville) English-language classes range from how to make bread and croissants to macarons as well as market classes and gourmet 'foodie walks'.

Le Foodist (Map p260; ☏ 06 71 70 95 22; www. lefoodist.com; 59 rue du Cardinal Lemoine, 5e; M Cardinal Lemoine) Classes at this culinary school include classic French cookery and patisserie courses, allowing you to create your own eclairs and choux pastry, macarons or croissants. Market tours and wine and cheese tastings and pairings are also available. Instruction is in English. Three-hour classes start at €99.

Wine Tasting in Paris (Map p260; ☏ 06 76 93 32 88; www.wine-tasting-in-paris.com; 14 rue des Boulangers, 5e; tastings from €46; ◷ tastings 5-7.30pm Tue, Thu & Sat; M Jussieu) Find this wine-tasting school on a winding cobblestone backstreet. With the knowledgeable Thierry from wine-rich Burgundy at the helm, themed tastings

and tours do not disappoint. The comprehensive French Wine Tour (€62, 2½ hours, six wines) covers tasting methodology, wine vocabulary and French winegrowing regions. Foodies will adore the tasty lunchtime cheese-wine pairing (€46, 1½ hours, four wines). All are in English.

Cook'n With Class (☏ 01 42 57 22 84; www. cooknwithclass.com; 6 rue Baudelique, 18e; ◷ 2hr classes adult/child from €109/95; M Simplon, Jules Joffrin) A bevy of international chefs, small classes and an enchanting Montmartre location are ingredients for success at this informal cooking school, which organises dessert classes for kids, cheese and wine courses, market visits, gourmet food tours and six-course dinners with the chef and sommelier as well as regular cookery classes. Classes are taught in English.

Ô Chateau (Map p254; ☏ 01 44 73 97 80; www. o-chateau.com; 68 rue Jean-Jacques Rousseau, 1er; ◷ 4pm-midnight Mon-Sat; 🛜; M Les Halles or RER Châtelet–Les Halles) Wine aficionados can thank this young, fun, cosmopolitan wine bar for bringing affordable tasting to Paris. Choose from 50 grands vins served by the glass (or 1000-plus by the bottle!). Or sign up in advance for a 'tour de France' of French wines (€59) or a guided cellar tasting in English over lunch (€75) or dinner (€99).

Meeting the French (☏ 01 42 51 19 80; www. meetingthefrench.com; tours & courses from €12) French table decoration, market tours and baking with a Parisian baker are among Meeting the French's repertoire of English-language cultural and gourmet tours.

DINING OUT

Produce-laden markets, intimate bistros, gastronomic temples and more

Dining Out

The inhabitants of some cities rally around local sports teams, but in Paris they rally around la table. Pistachio macarons, shots of tomato consommé, decadent bœuf bourguignon, a gooey wedge of Camembert running onto the cheese plate... Food is not fuel here, it's the reason you get up in the morning.

Paris doesn't have its own 'local' cuisine, but is the crossroads for the regional flavours of France. Dishes from the hot south favour olive oil, garlic and tomatoes; the cooler, pastoral northern regions turn to cream and butter; and coastal areas concentrate on seafood. The freshness of ingredients and reliance on natural flavours, combined with refined, often very complex cooking methods (and, of course, wine), means you're in a gourmet's paradise.

In This Section

Price Ranges/Tipping

The following price ranges refer to the cost of a two-course meal.

€ Less than €20

€€ €20 to €40

€€€ More than €40

A *pourboire* (tip) is unnecessary, as service is always included in the bill. It's not uncommon to round up the bill for good service.

Previous page: Picnics on the Pont des Arts
YANN ARTHUS-BERTRAND/GETTY IMAGES ©

Montmartre & Northern Paris
Neo-bistros, wine bars and world cuisine (p128)

Champs-Élysées & Grands Boulevards
Big-name chefs, backstreet bistros (p124)

Louvre & Les Halles
Trendy restaurants on the rise (p126)

Le Marais, Ménilmontant & Belleville
Premier foodie destination (p130)

Seine

Eiffel Tower & Western Paris
Gastronomic palaces and museum restaurants (p124)

St-Germain & Les Invalides
Chic cafes, *haute cuisine* (p140)

The Islands
Romantic setting but limited options (p137)

Bastille & Eastern Paris
Balances tradition and innovation (p135)

Latin Quarter
Cheap eats and Left Bank treasures (p139)

Seine

Montparnasse & Southern Paris
Historic brasseries, neighbourhood favourites (p144)

Useful Phrases

I'd like to reserve a table for...
Je voudrais réserver une table pour...

...(eight) o'clock (*vingt*) *heures*

...two/three people *deux/trois personnes*

I don't eat... *Je ne mange pas...*

The bill, please. *L'addition, s'il vous plaît.*

Classic dishes

Bœuf bourguignon Beef marinated and cooked in young red wine with mushrooms, onions, carrots and bacon.

Confit de canard Duck cooked slowly in its own fat.

Entrecôte Thin, boneless rib-eye steak.

Tarte Tatin Upside-down apple tart.

The Best...

Experience Paris' top
restaurants and cafes

Classic Bistros

Le Bistrot Paul Bert (p136) Legendary
address with vintage decor.

Chez Paul (p136) Paris as your grandmother
knew it.

Chez Dumonet (p143) The quintessential
Parisian bistro experience.

Wine-Bar Dining

Le Verre Volé (p128; pictured) Excellent
wines, expert advice and hearty *plats du jour*
(daily specials).

Café de la Nouvelle Mairie (p139) Latin
Quarter favourite for by-the-glass wines and
seasonal bistro dishes.

Neobistros

Marrow (p130) Inventive ingredients and
knock-out paired cocktails.

Richer (p124) Brilliant-value bistro fare.

Le Beurre Noisette (p145) Creative, locally
loved cooking.

Clover (p143) Watch the chefs at work in the
combined dining space/kitchen.

Le Servan (p133; pictured) Daily changing
creations near Père Lachaise.

Crêpes

Breizh Café (p132) Among the most authentic Breton crêpes in town.

Crêperie Pen-Ty (p129) Northern Paris' best
crêperie, with traditional Breton aperitifs.

Little Breizh (p142) Innovative twists such
as Breton sardines.

Seafood

Le Dôme (p145) Magnificent shellfish platters in a timeless art deco brasserie.
Huîtrerie Regis (p143) Oyster heaven.
Le Vent d'Armor (p140) Seafood by the Seine.

Traditional French

Bouillon Racine (p141; pictured) Traditional fare inspired by age-old recipes.
Chez La Vieille (p127) Homage to the former wholesale markets Les Halles.
Le Coupe-Chou (p139) French classics in a romantic, candlelit setting.

Vegetarian & Vegan

Abattoir Végétal (p128) Plant-filled vegan cafe in Montmartre.
Soul Kitchen (p130) Market-driven vegetarian dishes.
Raw Cakes (p145) Not only cakes but yes, it's all raw.

Lonely Planet's Top Choices

Tomy & Co (p140) Tomy Gousset uses organic produce from his own garden.
Restaurant AT (p140) Abstract-art-like masterpieces made from rare ingredients.
Restaurant Guy Savoy (p141) Resplendent triple-Michelin-starred flagship.
Berthillon (p137) Sublime ice creams and sorbets on the Île Saint-Louis.

⊗ Eiffel Tower & Western Paris

Arnaud Nicolas   French €€

(Map p262; ☑01 45 55 59 59; www.arnaud
nicolas.paris; 46 ave de la Bourdonnais, 7e; mains
€23-34; ☺restaurant 7-9.45pm Mon, noon-
1.45pm & 7-9.45pm Tue-Sat, boutique 5-9pm Mon,
10am-3pm & 5-9pm Tue-Sat; Ⓜ École Militaire)
The upmarket restaurant and boutique of
chef Arnaud Nicolas combines two natural
French loves: gastronomy and charcuterie.
Be it a posh pie (such as pork flavoured
with herbs, or foie gras and quail with pear
and pistachio), fancy terrine or a simple
plate of cold cuts, this sleek address serves
it to astonishing effect. End with a sublime
dark-chocolate soufflé.

L'Astrance   Gastronomy €€€

(Map p262; ☑01 40 50 84 40; www.astrance
restaurant.com; 4 rue Beethoven, 16e;
3-/5-course lunch menus €95/170, 7-course
dinner menu €250; ☺12.15-1.15pm & 8.15-9.15pm
Tue-Fri, closed Aug; Ⓜ Passy) It's almost two
decades since Pascal Barbot's dazzling cuisine at the twin-Michelin-starred L'Astrance
made its debut, but it's shown no signs of
losing its cutting edge. Look beyond the
complicated descriptions on the menu and
expect exquisite elements making up intricate plates that are as spectacular as the
artworks adorning Paris' grand galleries.
Reserve one to two months in advance.

Ducasse sur Seine   Gastronomy €€€

(Map p262; ☑01 58 00 22 08; www.ducasse-
seine.com; Port Debilly, 16e; 3-course lunch
menus from €100, 4-course dinner menus from
€150, afternoon tea €35; ☺12.45-2.30pm,
4-5.30pm & 8.30-10.30pm; Ⓜ Trocadéro) ✿
Launched by multi-Michelin-starred chef
Alain Ducasse, 'floating restaurant' Ducasse
sur Seine sails through the city past icons
like Notre Dame at lunch and dinner, served
at white-clothed tables. Pricier menus
for both services include wine pairings.
At 4pm, 4.30pm and 5pm, you can order
a sweet and savoury dish while the boat
remains docked opposite the Eiffel Tower.

⊗ Champs-Élysées & Grands Boulevards

Richer   Bistro €

(Map p254; www.lericher.com; 2 rue Richer, 9e;
mains €17-28; ☺noon-2.30pm & 7.30-10.30pm;
Ⓜ Poissonnière, Bonne Nouvelle) Run by the
same team as across-the-street neighbour
L'Office (☑01 47 70 67 31; www.office-resto.
com; 3 rue Richer; 2-/3-course lunch menus
€22/27), Richer's pared-back, exposed-
brick decor is a smart setting for genius
creations including smoked-duck-breast
ravioli in miso broth, and quince-and-lime
cheesecake for dessert. It doesn't take
reservations, but does serve snacks and
Chinese tea, and has a full bar (open until
midnight). Fantastic value.

Ladurée   Pastries €€

(Map p252; ☑01 40 75 08 75; www.laduree.fr; 75
av des Champs-Élysées, 8e; pastries €2.60-13,
mains €20-45, 2-/3-course lunch menu €35/42;
☺7.30am-11.30pm Mon-Thu, 7.30am-12.30am
Fri, 8.30am-12.30am Sat, 8.30am-11.30pm
Sun; ☏ ♨; Ⓜ George V) One of Paris' oldest
patisseries, Ladurée has been around
since 1862 and first created the lighter-
than-air, ganache-filled macaron in the
1930s. Its tearoom is the classiest spot to
indulge on the Champs. Alternatively, pick
up some pastries to go – from croissants
to its trademark macarons, they're all quite
heavenly.

Détour   French €€

(Map p252; ☑01 45 26 21 48; www.facebook.
com/detourrestaurant; 15 rue de la Tour des
Dames, 9e; lunch menu €28, dinner menu €35-
50; ☺noon-1.30pm Wed-Sat, 7.30-10.30pm
Tue-Sat; Ⓜ Trinité) As the name suggests,
Adrien Cachot's 16-seat neobistro is off the
beaten track, both literally and figuratively.
Diners choose between just two options
(meat or fish), leaving the rest in the hands
of the highly original chef. Expect dishes
like sweet carrots puréed with miso and
topped with shaved Mimolette, or veal
tartare with coffee vinaigrette and truffled
egg cream.

86 Champs   Pastries €

(Map p252; ☎01 70 38 77 38; www.86champs. com; 86 av Champs-Élysées, 8e; pastries €13-17; ☺8.30am-11.30pm Sun-Thu, to 12.30am Fri & Sat; Ⓜ George V) A swirling fantasy of floral aromas – vervain, rose, lavender – lures visitors into this opulent shrine to French pastries. It's half Pierre Hermé (of macaron fame), half L'Occitane (Provençe-themed beauty products); after you're done browsing the boutique, head to the horseshoe-shaped dessert bar in the back, where you can dine on whimsical creations prepared in front of you.

Le Hide   French €€

(Map p252; ☎01 45 74 15 81; www.lehide.fr; 10 rue du Général Lanrezac, 17e; 2-/3-course menus €32/38, mains €24-31; ☺6-11pm Mon-Sat; Ⓜ Charles de Gaulle–Étoile) A perpetual favourite, Le Hide is a tiny neighbourhood bistro serving scrumptious traditional French fare: snails; seared duck breast with celery purée and truffle oil; baked shoulder of lamb, and monkfish with *beurre blanc* (white sauce). Unsurprisingly, this place fills up faster than you can scamper down the steps of the nearby Arc de Triomphe – reserve well in advance.

Lasserre   Gastronomy €€€

(Map p252; ☎01 43 59 53 43; www.restaurant-lasserre.com; 17 av Franklin D Roosevelt, 8e; 3-course lunch menu €90, tasting menu €190, mains €67-110; ☺noon-2pm Thu & Fri, 7-10pm Tue-Sat; Ⓜ Franklin D Roosevelt) Since 1942, this exceedingly elegant restaurant in the Triangle d'Or has hosted style icons, including Audrey Hepburn, and is still a superlative choice for a Michelin-starred meal to remember. A bellhop-attended lift, white-and-gold chandeliered decor, extraordinary retractable roof and flawless service set the stage for inspired creations such as roast blue lobster *à la Parisienne*. Smart clothing is required (jackets for men).

Marxito   Cafe €

(Map p252; www.marxito.com; 1bis rue Jean Mermoz, 8e; dishes €10-13; ☺8am-5.30pm Mon-Fri; ☑; Ⓜ Franklin D Roosevelt) ✎

🚌 Mobile Gastronomy: Bustronome

A true moveable feast, **Bustronome** (Map p252; ☎09 54 44 45 55; www.bustronome.com; 2 av Kléber, 16e; 4-course lunch €65, 6-course dinner €100; ☺by reservation 12.15pm, 12.45pm, 7.45pm & 8.45pm; ☑; Ⓜ Kléber, Charles de Gaulle–Étoile) is a voyage into French gastronomy aboard a glass-roofed bus. Paris' famous monuments – the Arc de Triomphe, Grand Palais, Palais Garnier, Notre Dame and Eiffel Tower – glide by as you dine on seasonal creations prepared in the purpose-built vehicle's lower-deck galley. Children's menus for lunch/dinner cost €40/50; vegetarian, vegan and gluten-free menus are available.

Exquisite dishes might include escabeche of shrimp with candied lemon, roast pigeon and artichokes with apricot and rosemary jus, melon meringue with vanilla-bean syrup and mint-and-lime sorbet, and the finest French cheeses. Wine-pairing menus are available.

Two-Michelin-starred chef Thierry Marx opened his 'gourmet fast food' restaurant with a striking coral-coloured, neo-retro interior in 2018. Its speciality is the 'Marxito', a variation on the Japanese *doryaki* (filled pancakes), made with buckwheat flour and organic ingredients, both savoury (eg smoked salmon, Japanese radish, avocado and miso) and sweet (like zesty pomelo and yuzu jam). Expect lunchtime queues.

⊗ Louvre & Les Halles

Fou de Pâtisserie   Patisserie €

(Map p254; www.foudepatisserieboutique.fr;
45 rue Montorgueil, 2e; ⊙11am-8pm Mon-Fri,
10am-8pm Sat, 10am-6pm Sun; Ⓜ Les Halles,
Sentier or RER Châtelet–Les Halles) Single-
name patisseries scatter across the city,
but for a greatest-hits range from its finest
pastry chefs – Cyril Lignac, Christophe
Adam (L'Éclair de Génie), Jacques Genin,
Pierre Hermé and Philippe Conticini
included – head to this one-stop concept
shop. A Paris first, it's the brainchild of
the publishers of pastry magazine *Fou de
Pâtisserie* (also sold here).

Stohrer   Patisserie €

(Map p254; www.stohrer.fr; 51 rue Montorgueil,
2e; ⊙7.30am-8.30pm; Ⓜ Étienne Marcel, Sentier)
Opened in 1730 by Nicolas Stohrer, the
Polish pastry chef of queen consort Marie
Leszczyńska (wife of Louis XV), Stohrer's
house-made specialities include its own
inventions, the *baba au rhum* (rum-soaked
sponge cake) and *puits d'amour* (caramel-
topped, vanilla cream–filled puff pastry).

The beautiful pastel murals were added
in 1864 by Paul-Jacques-Aimé Baudry, who
also decorated the Palais Garnier's Grand
Foyer.

Maison Maison   Mediterranean €€

(Map p254; ☏09 67 82 07 32; www.restaurant-
maisonmaison.com; 63 Parc Rives de Seine,
1er; 2-/3-course lunch menu €20/25, small
plates €7-16; ⊙kitchen 7-10pm Mon, noon-3pm
& 7-10pm Tue-Sun, bar to 2am; Ⓜ Pont Neuf)
Halfway down the stairs by Pont Neuf is
this wonderfully secret space beneath the
bouquinistes (used-book sellers), where
you can watch the *bateaux-mouches*
(river-cruise boats) float by as you dine
on creations such as beetroot and pink-
grapefruit-cured bonito or gnocchi with
white asparagus and broccoli pesto. In nice
weather, cocktails on the glorious riverside
terrace are not to be missed.

Balagan   Israeli €€

(Map p252; ☏01 40 20 72 14; www.balagan-
paris.com; 9 rue d'Alger, 1er; mains €24-34;
⊙7-10.30pm; Ⓜ Tuileries) Cool navy blues and
creamy diamond tiling contrast with the

Berthillon (p137)

LAUTARO/ALAMY STOCK PHOTO ©

chic vibe at this Israeli hotspot. Come here to sample delectable starters – deconstructed kebabs, crispy halloumi cheese with dates, onion confit Ashkenazi chicken liver or a spicy, succulent tuna tartare with fennel, cilantro, capers and pistachios – followed by praiseworthy mains such as the sea bream black pasta.

Chez La Vieille   French €€

(Map p254; ☎01 42 60 15 78; www.chezlavieille. fr; 1 rue Bailleul, 1er; mains €24-26; ☺noon-2pm & 6-10.30pm Tue-Sat, closed Aug; MLouvre Rivoli) In salvaging this history-steeped spot within a 16th-century building, star chef Daniel Rose pays homage to the former wholesale markets, erstwhile legendary owner Adrienne Biasin (many of her timeless dishes have been updated, from terrines and rillettes to veal blanquette), and the soul of Parisian bistro cooking itself. Dine at the street-level bar or upstairs in the peacock-blue dining room.

Jòia   French €€

(Map p254; ☎01 40 20 06 06; www.joia helenedarroze.com; 39 rue des Jeuneurs, 2e; 2-/3-course lunch menu €24/29, mains €21-32, Sunday brunch €42; ☺noon-2.30pm & 7-11pm; MGrands Boulevards) Twin-Michelin-starred chef Hélène Darroze, whose flagship Parisian restaurant is on the Left Bank, is behind this spacious, airy Right Bank restaurant. Flavours of her native southwestern France are at the fore of dishes like spiced suckling lamb confit, and brioche- and foie gras–stuffed chicken with roast garlic. Upstairs the cocktail bar revisits classic French recipes.

Frenchie   Bistro €€€

(Map p254; ☎01 40 39 96 19; www.frenchie-ruedunil.com; 5 rue du Nil, 2e; 3-course lunch menu €48, 5-course dinner menu €65, with wine €175; ☺6.30-10pm Mon-Wed, noon-2.30pm & 6.30-10pm Thu & Fri; MSentier) Tucked down an inconspicuous alley, this tiny bistro with wooden tables and old stone walls is always packed and for good reason: French chef Gregory Marchand's modern, market-driven dishes prepared with

unpretentious flair have earned him a Michelin star. Reserve well in advance or arrive early and pray for a cancellation (it does happen). Alternatively, head to neighbouring **Frenchie Bar à Vins** (www. frenchie-bav.com; 6 rue du Nil, 2e; dishes €8-28; ☺6.30-11pm).

Au Pied de Cochon   Brasserie €€

(Map p254; ☎01 40 13 77 00; www.piedde cochon.com; 6 rue Coquillière, 1er; mains €20-41, seafood platters per person €30-80; ☺24hr; MLes Halles or RER Châtelet–Les Halles) Enduring brasserie Au Pied de Cochon, with huge mirrors, crimson banquettes and frosted-glass lamps, opens around the clock, just as it did when workers at the former Les Halles wholesale markets started and ended their day here. Specialities include superb onion soup topped with melted Emmental cheese, pigs' trotters, tails, ears and snouts, and spectacular shellfish platters.

Verjus   Modern American €€€

(Map p254; ☎01 42 97 54 40; www.verjusparis. com; 52 rue de Richelieu, 1er; menu €78, with wine €133; ☺7-11pm Mon-Fri; MBourse, Pyramides) Opened by American duo Braden Perkins and Laura Adrian, Verjus was born out of their former clandestine supper club, the Hidden Kitchen. The restaurant builds on that tradition, offering a chance to sample some excellent, creative cuisine in a casual space. The tasting menu is a series of small plates, using ingredients sourced straight from producers. Reserve well in advance.

Le Grand Véfour   Gastronomy €€€

(Map p254; ☎01 42 96 56 27; www.grand-vefour. com; 17 rue de Beaujolais, 1er; lunch/dinner menu €115/315, mains €98-128; ☺noon-2.30pm & 7.30-10.30pm Mon-Fri; MPyramides) Holding two Michelin stars, this 18th-century jewel on the northern edge of the Jardin du Palais Royal has been a dining favourite since 1784; names ascribed to each table include Napoléon, Victor Hugo and Colette (who lived next door). Expect a voyage of discovery from chef Guy Martin in one of the most beautiful restaurants in the world.

🍴 Foodie Hotspot: Beaupassage

Some of France's finest chefs, artisans and purveyors – with a combined 17 Michelin stars – occupy the open-air 'mini district' **Beaupassage** (Map p262; www.beaupassage.fr; 53-57 rue de Grenelle, 7e; ☺passage 7am-midnight, individual hours vary; ⓜSèvres–Babylone). Look out for Yannick Alléno (with a restaurant, wine cellar and art gallery), Anne-Sophie Pic (gastronomy), Alexandre Polmard (meats), Olivier Bellin (seafood), Thierry Marx (bakery/patisserie) and Pierre Hermé (pastries, including his signature macarons; Beaupassage incorporates his inaugural sit-down cafe).

CLAUDE THIBAULT/ALAMY STOCK PHOTO ©

🛇 Montmartre & Northern Paris

Du Pain et des Idées   Bakery €
(Map p256; www.dupainetdesidees.com; 34 rue Yves Toudic, 10e; breads €1.20-7, pastries €2.50-6.50; ☺6.45am-8pm Mon-Fri, closed Aug; ⓜJacques Bonsergent) This traditional bakery with an exquisite interior from 1889 is famed for its naturally leavened bread, orange-blossom brioche and *escargots* (scroll-like 'snails') in four sweet flavours. Its mini savoury *pavés* (breads) flavoured with Reblochon cheese and fig, or goat's cheese, sesame and honey, are perfect for lunch on the run. A wooden picnic table sits on the pavement outside.

Abattoir Végétal   Vegan €
(Map p250; www.abattoirvegetal.fr; 61 rue Ramey, 18e; 2-/3-course lunch menu €16.50/19, mains €10-16.50; ☺9am-6pm Tue, 9am-10.30pm Wed-Fri, 10am-10.30pm Sat, 11am-4.30pm Sun; 🛜🍽; ⓜJules Joffrin) Mint-green wrought-iron chairs and tables line the pavement outside the 'plant slaughterhouse' (it occupies a former butcher shop), while the light, bright interior has bare-bulb downlights, distempered walls and greenery-filled hanging baskets. Each day there's a choice of three raw and cooked organic dishes per course, cold-pressed juices and craft beers from Parisian brewery BapBap.

Le Verre Volé   Bistro €
(Map p256; ☏01 48 03 17 34; www.leverrevole.fr; 67 rue de Lancry, 10e; mains €11-22, sandwiches €7.90; ☺bistro 12.30-2.30pm & 7.30-11.30pm, wine bar 10am-2am; 🛜; ⓜJacques Bonsergent) The tiny 'Stolen Glass' – a wine shop with a few tables – is one of Paris' most popular wine bar–restaurants, with outstanding natural and unfiltered wines and expert advice. Unpretentious, hearty *plats du jour* are excellent. Reserve in advance for meals, or stop by to pick up a gourmet sandwich (such as mustard-smoked burrata with garlic-pork sausage) and a bottle.

Holybelly 5   Cafe €
(Map p256; www.holybellycafe.com; 5 rue Lucien Sampaix, 10e; dishes €3.50-13.50; ☺9am-4pm; 🛜🍽; ⓜJacques Bonsergent) Light-filled Holybelly's regulars never tire of its outstanding coffee, cuisine and service. Sarah Mouchot's breakfast pancakes (with eggs, bacon, bourbon butter and maple syrup) and black rice porridge are legendary, as are dishes like fennel sausage patties, and crunchy hash browns. Wash them down with a Bloody Mary or Deck & Donohue beer. No reservations.

Le Petit Château d'Eau   French €
(Map p256; ☏01 42 08 72 81; 34 rue du Château d'Eau, 10e; mains €11-16; ☺kitchen noon-3pm Mon, noon-3pm & 7-11.30pm Tue-Sat, bar 8am-3.30pm Mon, to 2am Tue-Fri, 9am-2am Sat; ⓜJacques Bonsergent) Scarcely changed in

a century, with lemon- and lime-tiled walls, horseshoe-shaped zinc bar and burgundy banquettes, this neighbourhood treasure endures in defiance of the post-industrial co-working cafes that have sprung up around it. Classical cooking ranges from duck with honey sauce to beef entrecôte with roast garlic potatoes; you can just stop by for a morning coffee or afternoon Kir.

Crêperie Pen-Ty   Crêpes €

(Map p250; ☑01 48 74 18 49; www.creperiepenty. com; 65 rue de Douai, 9e; galettes €4-15, crêpes €4.90-10.40; ☺noon-2.30pm & 7.30-11.15pm Mon-Fri, 12.30-4pm & 6.30-11.30pm Sat, to 10.30pm Sun; Ⓜ Place de Clichy) Hailed as the best crêperie in northern Paris, Pen-Ty is well worth the detour. Book ahead, and don't miss the selection of authentic Breton aperitifs like *chouchen* (a type of mead) and *pastis marin* (an aniseed and seaweed liquor), along with superb savoury *galettes* (buckwheat-flour crêpes) and sweet crêpes. There is a takeaway window too.

Fric-Frac   Sandwiches €

(Map p256; ☑01 42 85 87 34; www.fricfrac.fr; 79 quai de Valmy, 10e; sandwiches €11.50-15; ☺noon-3pm & 7.30-11pm Tue-Fri, noon-11pm Sat & Sun; Ⓜ Jacques Bonsergent) Traditional snack croque monsieur (toasted cheese-and-ham sandwich) gets a contemporary makeover at this quayside space. Gourmet Winnie (Crottin de Chavignol cheese, dried fruit, chestnut honey, chives and rosemary) and exotic Shaolin (king prawns, lemon-grass paste, shiitake mushrooms and Thai basil) are among the creative combos served with salad and fries. Eat in or head to the canal.

L'affineur Affiné   Cheese €

(Map p250; ☑09 66 94 22 15; www.laffineur affine.com; 51 rue Notre Dame de Lorette, 9e; cheese platters €6.50-39, weekend brunch €21; ☺kitchen noon-2pm & 5.30-8.45pm Wed-Sat, 11.30am-2pm & 5.30-6.45pm Sun, shop 10.30am-9pm Wed-Sat, to 7pm Sun; Ⓜ St-Georges) With 120 French cheeses, this *fro-magerie* (cheese shop) is a fabulous place to stock up and taste them at its on-site *bar*

à fromages (cheese bar). Let the staff know your preferences and they'll prepare platters of two to 15 varieties, with charcuterie available as well as paired wines. Weekend brunch is a multicourse feast.

Le Grenier à Pain   Bakery €

(Map p250; www.legrenierapain.com; 38 rue des Abbesses, 18e; pastries €1.10-4.50; ☺7.30am-8pm Thu-Mon; Ⓜ Abbesses) A past winner of Paris' annual 'best baguette' prize, this enchanting bakery with a semi-open kitchen is an ideal place to pick up picnic fare. Join the queue for a crusty baguette sandwich, Provence-style *fougasse* bread and alluring mini breads topped with fig and goat's cheese or bacon and olives. End on a sweet high with a fruit-bejewelled loaf cake.

Mesdemoiselles Madeleines   Pastries €

(Map p250; www.mllesmadeleines.com; 37 rue des Martyrs, 9e; madeleines small €0.70, large €2.50-4.50; ☺10.30am-7pm Tue-Sat, 10.30am-2pm & 3.30-6.30pm Sun; Ⓜ St-Georges) Shell-shaped French madeleine cakes, immortalised by Marcel Proust, are the sole product of this ingenious spot, in a dazzling array of flavours: 'simple' (Tahitian vanilla; Ethiopian coffee), 'savoury' (red onion, chives and crème fraîche; basil, feta and pine nuts), and 'gourmet' (Rhône valley raspberries with raspberry coulis; cara-melised hazelnuts, salted caramel mousse and a caramel shell), along with bite-sized mini-madeleines.

Pain Pain   Bakery €

(Map p250; www.pain-pain.fr; 88 rue des Martyrs, 18e; sandwiches & pastries €2.20-5.50; ☺7am-8pm Tue-Sat, 7.30am-7.30pm Sun; Ⓜ Abbesses) Sébastien Mauvieux is famed for his baguettes (his accolades include Paris' 'best baguette' prize) and bakes delicious corn bread, rye and chestnut loaves and other varieties of *pain* (bread). Pick up a sandwich and an exquisite pastry, such as a layered Opéra cake with yuzu and rasp-berries or signature Zéphyr tart with white chocolate and sweetened Chantilly cream.

Soul Kitchen
Vegetarian €

(Map p250; ☑01 71 37 99 95; www.facebook.com/
soulkitchenparis; 33 rue Lamarck, 18e; 3-course
lunch menus €14, snacks €3-5.75; ☺8.45am-
6pm Mon-Fri, 10am-6.30pm Sat & Sun; ☏☑♿;
ⓂLamarck–Caulaincourt) This vegetarian
eatery with a shabby-chic vintage interior
and tiny open kitchen serves market-driven
dishes including creative salads, homemade
soups, savoury tarts, burritos and wraps –
all gargantuan in size and packed with
seasonal veggies. Round off lunch or snack
between meals with muffins, cakes and
mint-laced *citronnade maison* (homemade
lemonade). Families should check out the
sage-green 'games' cupboard.

Marrow
Bistro €€

(Map p256; ☑09 81 34 57 00; 128 rue du Faubourg
St-Martin, 10e; mains €13-22; ☺6-10pm Tue-Sat,
bar to 2am, closed Aug; ⓂGare de l'Est) Hay-
smoked quail with peat vinaigrette, grilled
octopus and fennel confit, and breaded roast
bone marrow are among the adventurous
flavour combinations from Hugo Blanchet,
who partnered with mixologist Arthur
Combe to open this neobistro that's taking
Paris' foodie scene by storm. Rough stone
walls, blonde wood tables and a small pavement terrace create a relaxed backdrop.

Le Bistrot de la Galette
Bistro €

(Map p250; ☑01 46 06 19 65; www.bistrot
delagalette.fr; 102ter rue Lepic, 18e; mains €14-17;
☺11am-10pm Tue-Sun; ⓂAbbesses, Lamarck–
Caulaincourt) ✐ In the shadow of Montmartre
windmill Moulin de la Galette, this vintage-
fitted bistro is the creation of pastry chef
Gilles Marchal, who uses locally hand-milled
flour in *feuilletés* (delicately laminated
pastry puffs) that accompany most dishes,
such as *galette parisienne* (roast ham, sau-
téed mushrooms and Comté) and *galette
provençale* (shredded roast lamb, aubergine,
garlic and sun-dried tomatoes).

Le Bel Ordinaire
Mediterranean €

(Map p254; ☑01 46 27 46 67; www.lebelordinaire.
com; 54 rue de Paradis, 10e; dishes €5-18;
☺kitchen 12.30-10.30pm Tue-Fri, 4-10.30pm Sat,

bar 11am-11.30pm Tue-Sat; ☏; ⓂPoissonnière)
Floor-to-ceiling, wall-to-wall open shelves
lined with bottles and gourmet products
(hams, cheeses, shellfish, preserves, straw
baskets of farm eggs and fresh fruit and
vegetables) fire up your appetite for tapas-
style small plates, such as tuna gravlax with
grated apple; smoked burrata with sesame
pesto, or cuttlefish-ink risotto with blue
cheese, at this contemporary wine bar. Over
300 winemakers are represented.

⊗ Le Marais, Ménilmontant & Belleville

La Maison Plisson
Cafe, Deli €

(Map p256; www.lamaisonplisson.com; 93 bd
Beaumarchais, 3e; dishes €7-22, platters €15-29;
☺9.30am-9pm Mon, 8.30am-9pm Tue-Sat,
9am-8pm Sun; ⓂSt-Sébastien–Froissart)
Framed by glass-canopied wrought-iron
girders, this gourmand's dream incorporates a covered-market-style, terrazzo-
floored food hall filled with exquisite, mostly
French produce: meat, vegetables, cheese,
wine, chocolate, jams, freshly baked breads
and much more. If your appetite's whetted,
its cafe, opening to twin terraces, serves
charcuterie, foie gras and cheese planks,
bountiful salads and delicacies such as
olive-oil-marinated, Noilly Prat–flambéed
sardines.

Jacques Genin
Pastries, Chocolate €

(Map p256; ☑01 45 77 29 01; www.jacquesgenin.
fr; 133 rue de Turenne, 3e; pastries €9; ☺11am-
7pm Tue-Fri & Sun, to 7.30pm Sat; ⓂOberkampf,
Filles du Calvaire) Wildly creative chocolatier
Jacques Genin is famed for his flavoured
caramels, *pâtes de fruits* (fruit jellies) and
exquisitely embossed *bonbons de chocolat*
(chocolate sweets). But what completely
steals the show at his elegant chocolate
showroom is the *salon de dégustation* (aka
tearoom), where you can order a pot of out-
rageously thick hot chocolate and legendary
Genin *millefeuille*, assembled to order.

Clockwise from bottom left: Typical French breakfast pastries and coffee; Bistrot dining; Cheeses for sale at Marché d'Aligre (p83)

Bonbons de chocolat (chocolate sweets), Jacques Genin (p130)

Breizh Café
Crêpes €

(Map p256; ☑01 42 72 13 77; www.breizhcafe.com; 109 rue Vieille du Temple, 3e; crêpes & galettes €6.80-18.80; ⊙10am-11pm; ⓂSt-Sébastien–Froissart) Everything at the Breizh ('Breton' in Breton) is 100% authentic, including its organic-flour crêpes and *galettes* that top many Parisians' lists for the best in the city. Other specialities include Cancale oysters and 20 types of cider. Tables are limited and there's often a wait; book ahead or try its deli, **L'Épicerie** (Map p256; ☑01 42 71 39 44; 111 rue Vieille du Temple, 3es), next door.

Café Méricourt
Cafe €

(Map p256; www.cafemericourt.com; 22 rue de la Folie Méricourt, 11e; 2-course midweek lunch menus €15, mains €9.50-16; ⊙9am-6pm; 🖥📍; ⓂSt-Ambroise) With a pretty peppermint-green facade and airy, plant-filled interior, Méricourt is a delightful backstreet find. Breakfast (honey-ricotta pancakes with roasted pineapple, spinach-wrapped eggs with feta, congee rice porridge) is served until 3pm, with lunch options from 11am. Parisian-roasted coffee, homemade ginger

beer and lemonade, natural wines and Bloody Marys and Mimosas make it easy to while away a few hours.

Chambelland
Bakery €

(Map p256; ☑01 43 55 07 30; www.chambelland.com; 14 rue Ternaux, 11e; lunch menus €10-12, pastries €2.50-5.50; ⊙8am-8pm Tue-Sat, to 6pm Sun; ⓂParmentier) Using rice and buckwheat flour from its own mill in southern France, this pioneering 100% gluten-free bakery creates exquisite cakes and pastries as well as sourdough loaves and brioches peppered with nuts, seeds, chocolate and fruit. Stop for lunch at one of the handful of formica tables in this relaxed space, strewn with sacks of flour and books.

L'As du Fallafel
Felafel €

(Map p256; 34 rue des Rosiers, 4e; takeaway €5.50-8.50, mains €12-18; ⊙noon-midnight Sun-Thu, to 4pm Fri; 📍; ⓂSt-Paul) The lunchtime queue stretching halfway down the street from this place says it all. This Parisian favourite, 100% worth the inevitable wait, is the address for kosher, perfectly deep-fried falafel (chickpea balls) and turkey or lamb shawarma sandwiches. Do as every Parisian does and get them to take away.

Miznon
Israeli €

(Map p256; 01 42 74 83 58; www.facebook.com/miznonparis; 22 rue des Écouffes, 4e; pita sandwiches €6-12.50; noon-11pm Sun-Thu, to 4pm Fri; ; St-Paul, Hôtel de Ville) Parisians can't get enough of this hip outpost of celebrity chef Eyal Shani's famed Tel Aviv restaurant. Head past the grocery crates to the bar to order a warm, fluffy pita (such as lamb, fish or roasted cauliflower) and phenomenal house-made hummus. Don't miss the sweet *banane au chocolat* pita to finish. Takeaway's available if you can't get a seat.

Pastelli
Gelato €

(Mary; Map p256; www.facebook.com/pastelli marygelateria; 60 rue du Temple, 3e; gelato 1/2/3/4 scoops €3.50/5/6.50/7.50; 11am-10pm; Rambuteau) The youngest winner of Milan's prestigious Cone d'Oro (Golden Cone), artisan gelato maker Mary Quarta has more than 100 different flavours in her all-natural repertoire, and serves around a dozen different freshly made small batches each day at her light, white-painted Haut Marais shop. Standouts include avocado, black sesame, peach Champagne bellini and coffee-laced tiramisu.

Au Passage
Bistro €€

(Map p256; 01 43 55 07 52; www.restaurant-aupassage.fr; 1bis passage St-Sébastien, 11e; small plates €8-18, meats to share €25-70; 7-11pm Tue-Sat, bar to 1.30am Tue-Sat; St-Sébastien–Froissart) Rising-star chefs continue to make their name at this *petit bar de quartier* (little neighbourhood bar). Choose from a good-value, uncomplicated selection *of petites assiettes* (small tapas-style plates) of cold meats, raw or cooked fish, vegetables and so on, and larger meat dishes such as slow-roasted lamb shoulder or *côte de bœuf* (rib steak) to share. Reservations are essential.

The Five Basic Cheese Types

The choices on offer at a *fromagerie* (cheese shop) can be overwhelming, but vendors are usually very generous with their guidance and pairing advice.

Fromage à pâte demi-dure 'Semi-hard cheese' means uncooked, pressed cheese. Among the finest are Tomme de Savoie, Cantal, St-Nectaire and Ossau-Iraty.

Fromage à pâte dure 'Hard cheese' is always cooked and then pressed. Popular varieties are Beaufort, Comté, Emmental and Mimolette.

Fromage à pâte molle 'Soft cheese' is moulded or rind-washed. Camembert and Brie de Meaux are both made from raw cow's milk. Munster, Chaource, Langres and Époisses de Bourgogne are rind-washed, fine-textured cheeses.

Fromage à pâte persillée This French term for marbled or blue cheese comes from the pattern of veins that resembles *persille* (parsley). Roquefort is a ewe's-milk veined cheese that is to many the king of French cheeses. Fourme d'Ambert is a mild cow's-milk cheese from Rhône-Alpes. Bleu du Haut Jura is a mild, blue-veined mountain cheese.

Fromage de chèvre 'Goat's-milk cheese' is usually creamy and both sweet and slightly salty when fresh, but hardens and gets much saltier as it matures. Among the best varieties are Ste-Maure de Touraine, Crottin de Chavignol, Cabécou de Rocamadour and soft, slightly aged Chabichou.

Le Servan
Bistro €€

(Map p256; 01 55 28 51 82; www.leservan.com; 32 rue St-Maur, 11e; 3-course lunch menu €27, mains €25-38; 7.30-10.30pm Mon, noon-2.30pm & 7.30-10.30pm Tue-Fri; Voltaire, Rue St-Maur, Père Lachaise) Ornate cream-coloured ceilings with moulded cornices and pastel murals, huge windows and wooden floors give this neighbourhood neobistro near Père Lachaise a light, airy feel on even the greyest Parisian day. Sweetbread wontons, cockles with chilli and sweet basil, and roast pigeon with tamarind jus are among the inventive creations on the daily changing menu. Reserve to avoid missing out.

Robert et Louise   French €€

(Map p256; ✏01 42 78 55 89; www.robertet louise.com; 64 rue Vieille du Temple, 3e; 2-course lunch menus €14, mains €13-26; ☺7-11pm Tue & Wed, noon-3pm & 7-11pm Thu & Fri, noon-11pm Sat & Sun; Ⓜ Rambuteau) Going strong since 1958, this wonderfully convivial 'country inn' with red gingham curtains and rustic timber beams offers simple and inexpensive French food, including *côte de bœuf* (side of beef for two or three people) cooked on an open fire. Arrive early to snag the farmhouse table next to the fireplace – the makings of a real jolly Rabelaisian evening.

Le Rigmarole   Bistro €€

(Map p256; ✏01 71 24 58 44; www.lerigmarole. com; 10 rue du Grand Prieuré, 11e; small plates €8-16, tasting menu €69; ☺7.30-10.30pm Wed-Sun; Ⓜ Oberkampf) Old and new timbers create a warm environment at this hotspot, which specialises in meat, fish and vegetable skewers cooked over Japanese *binchōtan* (aka white charcoal), which burns at a lower temperature than traditional grills and doesn't release odours, resulting in a cleaner, purer taste. Skewer combinations might include turbot and radish, or chicken with pickled lemon and basil leaves.

Les Enfants du Marché   French €€

(Map p256; www.lesenfantsdumarche.fr; 39 rue de Bretagne, 3e; mains €18-32, platters €14-22; ☺9am-5pm Tue, Wed & Sun, to 9pm Thu-Sat; Ⓜ Filles du Calvaire) Tucked down the rear right-hand side of covered market **Marché des Enfants Rouges** (☺8.30am-1pm & 4-7.30pm Tue-Sat, 8.30am-2pm Sun, individual

stall hours vary), this sizzling-hot *comptoir* (counter) has bamboo stools where you can pair natural wines, artisan French spirits, craft beers and cocktails with charcuterie, cheese and seafood platters or mains like herb-roasted Gascon pig, Loire Valley hare with foie gras and Burgundy truffles or wild abalone bouillabaisse. No reservations.

Istr   Seafood, Breton €€

(Map p256; ✏01 43 56 81 25; www.facebook. com/istr.paris; 41 rue Notre Dame de Nazareth, 3e; half-dozen oysters €12-21, mains €13-26, 2-/3-course lunch menus €19/25; ☺kitchen noon-2.30pm & 6-10pm Tue-Fri, 6-11pm Sat, bar to 2am Tue-Sat; Ⓜ Temple) Fabulously patterned wallpaper and a gleaming zinc bar set the stage for innovative Breton-inspired cuisine. The region's famed *istr* ('oyster' in Breton) is the star of the show here, served plain, as a Bloody Mary–style shot, or with sauces such as soy and ginger. Other creations include buckwheat chips with smoked haddock fishcakes. It doubles as a rocking bar.

La Cave de l'Insolite   Bistro €€

(Map p256; ✏01 53 36 08 33; www.lacave delinsolite.fr; 30 rue de la Folie Méricourt, 11e; 2-/3-course midweek lunch menus €18/20, mains €20-36; ☺12.15-2.30pm & 7.30-10.30pm Tue-Sat; 🐾; Ⓜ St-Ambroise, Parmentier) Brothers Axel and Arnaud, who have worked at some of Paris' top addresses, run this rustic-chic wine bar with barrels, timber tables and a wood-burning stove. Duck pâté with cider jelly, haddock rillettes with lime and endive confit, and beef with mushroom and sweetbread sauce are among the seasonal dishes; its 100-plus hand-harvested wines come from small-scale French vineyards.

Le Clown Bar   French €€

(Map p256; ✏01 43 55 87 35; www.clown-bar-paris.com; 114 rue Amelot, 11e; mains €28-34; ☺kitchen noon-2.30pm & 7-10.30pm Wed-Sun, bar 9am-2am Wed-Sat, noon-2am Sun; Ⓜ Filles du Calvaire) The former staff dining room of the city's winter circus, the 1852-built Cirque d'Hiver, is a historic monument with colourful clown-themed ceramics and mosaics, painted glass ceilings and its original zinc bar. Modern French cuisine ranges from line-caught whiting with whelks to Mesquer pigeon stuffed with anchovies. The pavement terrace gets packed out on sunny days.

Double Dragon   Asian €

(Map p256; 52 rue St-Maur, 11e; 3-course lunch menu €18, mains €7.50-17.50; ⊙noon-2.30pm Wed, noon-2.30pm & 7.30-10.30pm Thu-Sun; ✏; MRue St-Maur) Sisters Tatiana and Katia Levha, who run nearby bistro Le Servan (p133), fire up the spice at Double Dragon. Pig's-ear dumplings, beef and purple shiso-leaf spring rolls, peanut- and chilli-crusted corn on the cob, and stone-crab claws with *nam chim* (sweet chili) dipping sauce are among the dishes you might find on the frequently changing menu. No reservations (expect to wait).

✖ Bastille & Eastern Paris

Mokonuts   Cafe €

(Map p259; ☏09 80 81 82 85; www.facebook.com/mokonuts; 5 rue St-Bernard, 11e; pastries €2-7, mains €8-21; ⊙8.45am-6pm Mon-Fri, closed Aug; ☎; MFaidherbe-Chaligny) ✐ Much-loved hole-in-the-wall Mokonuts, with a beautiful mosaic-tiled floor, makes a cosy refuge for snacks like flourless chocolate layer cake, clementine almond cake and white-chocolate and roasted-almond cookies. Sea bream with chickpeas and capers, and lamb shoulder with hummus are among the all-organic lunchtime mains (book well ahead). Natural wines and craft beers feature on the drinks list.

CheZaline   Sandwiches €

(Map p259; 85 rue de la Roquette, 11e; sandwiches €5.50-8.50; ⊙11am-5.30pm Mon-Fri; MVoltaire) A former horsemeat butcher's shop (*chevaline,* hence the spin on the name; look for the gold horse head above the door) is now a fabulous deli for baguettes filled with ingredients such

Le Bistrot Paul Bert (p136)

as Prince de Paris ham and house-made garlic pesto, salads and terrines. There's a handful of seats (and plenty of parks nearby). Prepare to queue at lunchtime.

Buffet   Bistro €€

(Map p259; ✆01 83 89 63 82; www.restaurant buffet.fr; 8 rue de la Main d'Or, 11e; 2-/3-course lunch menu €16.50/19, small plates €6-20; ⏱7.30-11pm Tue-Fri, noon-2.30pm & 7.30-11pm Sat; Ⓜ Ledru-Rollin) Tucked away on a charming Bastille backstreet behind a mulberry-coloured facade, Buffet has burgundy leather seating, wooden tables, mirrors and terrazzo floors. Despite its name, there's no smorgasbord but a short daily changing blackboard menu of bistro dishes like lemon sole with hand-cut chips, lamb shoulder with prunes, and chestnut and chocolate mousse that belies the complexity of the cooking.

Virtus   Bistro €€

(Map p259; ✆09 80 68 08 08; www.virtus-paris. com; 29 rue de Cotte, 12e; mains €18-29, 3-course weekday lunch menu €35, 6-course tasting menu €64.50; ⏱noon-2pm & 7-10pm Tue-Sat; Ⓜ Ledru-Rollin) Occupying stunning premises with a kingfisher-blue facade and traditional mosaic-tiled floors, Virtus' market-sourced, daily changing menu is at the cutting edge, with dishes such as black mullet tartare with avocado, radish and chive cream; pan-fried scallops with lemon confit; and squid with Chinese cabbage in eel sauce.

Passerini   Italian €€

(Map p259; ✆01 43 42 27 56; www.passerini. paris; 65 rue Traversière, 12e; lunch menus €26-48, dinner mains €18-32; ⏱7-10pm Tue, 12.30-3pm & 7-10pm Wed-Sat, closed early May & Aug; Ⓜ Ledru-Rollin) Rome native Giovanni Passerini is one of the finest Italian chefs cooking in Europe today. Delectable specialities include roast pigeon with smoked ricotta, and *tagliolini* (long pasta) with red Sicilian shrimp, and are complemented by natural wines sourced from small vineyards. Pastas are made fresh and are also sold at its adjoining deli, Pastificio Passerini.

Le Bistrot Paul Bert   Bistro €€

(Map p259; ✆01 43 72 24 01; 18 rue Paul Bert, 11e; 3-course menu €41, mains €29; ⏱noon-2pm & 7.30-11pm Tue-Thu, 7.30-11pm Fri, noon-2.30pm Sat, closed Aug; Ⓜ Faidherbe-Chaligny) When food writers list Paris' best bistros, Paul Bert's name consistently pops up. The timeless decor and classic dishes such as *steak-frites* (steak and chips) and hazelnut-cream Paris-Brest pastry reward those booking ahead. Siblings in the same street: **L'Écailler du Bistrot** (✆01 43 72 76 77; 22 rue Paul Bert; oysters per half-dozen €9-22, mains €32-48, seafood platters per person from €40; ⏱noon-2.30pm & 7.30-11pm Tue-Sat) for seafood; **La Cave Paul Bert** (✆01 58 53 50 92; 16 rue Paul Bert; ⏱noon-midnight, kitchen noon-2pm & 7.30-11.30pm), a wine bar with small plates; and **Le 6 Paul Bert** (✆01 43 79 14 32; www.le6paulbert.com; 6 rue Paul Bert; mains €24-34; ⏱noon-2pm & 7.30-11pm Tue-Fri, 7.30-11pm Sat) for modern cuisine.

Chez Paul   Bistro €€

(Map p259; ✆01 47 00 34 57; www.chezpaul.com; 13 rue de Charonne, 11e; 2-/3-course weekday lunch menu €18/21, mains €17-22; ⏱noon-12.30am; Ⓜ Ledru-Rollin) This is Paris as your grandmother knew it: chequered red-and-white napkins, faded photographs on the walls, old red banquettes and traditional French dishes such as pig trotters, *andouil-lette* (a feisty tripe sausage) and *tête de veau et cervelle* (calf head and brains). If offal isn't for you, alternatives include a steaming bowl of *pot au feu* (beef stew).

Septime   Gastronomy €€€

(Map p259; ✆01 43 67 38 29; www.septime-charonne.fr; 80 rue de Charonne, 11e; 4-course lunch menu with/without wine €80/42, 7-course dinner menu with/without wine €135/80; ⏱7.30-10pm Mon, 12.15-2pm & 7.30-10pm Tue-Fri; Ⓜ Charonne) The alchemists in Bertrand Grébaut's Michelin-starred kitchen produce truly beautiful creations, served by blue-aproned waitstaff. The menu reads like an obscure shopping list: each dish is a mere listing of three ingredients, while the mystery *carte blanche* dinner *menu* puts you in the hands of the innovative chef. Reservations require planning and perseverance – book at least three weeks in advance.

Café du Coin
Bistro €€

(Map p256; ☑01 48 04 82 46; 9 rue Camille Desmoulins, 11e; 3-course lunch menu €20, small plates dinner €7-16; ☺kitchen 12.15-2.30pm & 6-10.30pm Mon-Fri, 6-10.30pm Sat, bar 8am-midnight Mon-Fri, 6pm-midnight Sat; Ⓜ Voltaire) This 'corner cafe', with big picture windows, high ceilings, original floor tiles and pot plants lining the staircase, is a neighbourhood favourite for its adventurous bistro cooking (pickled pumpkin, broccoli leaf and Hungarian blue squash salad; sourdough-crumbed red mullet with basil-sautéed cockles) and fantastic selection of all-natural wines.

La Chocolaterie Cyril Lignac
Sweets, Pastries €

(Map p259; www.cyrillignac.com; 25 rue Chanzy, 11e; pastries €1.40-6; ☺8am-7pm; Ⓜ Charonne) At this navy-blue-fronted boutique/tearoom, celebrity chef Cyril Lignac sells his superb range of chocolate bars – over 25 different varieties, in flavours such as green tea and sesame or coconut and raspberry, plus his chocolate-hazelnut spread – along with pastries, cakes and biscuits to eat in or take away. When it's chilly, warm up with a wonderfully rich, thick hot chocolate.

⊗ The Islands

Berthillon
Ice Cream €

(Map p256; www.berthillon.fr; 29-31 & 46 rue St-Louis en l'Île, 4e; 1/2/3/4 scoops takeaway €3/4.50/6/7.50; ☺10am-8pm Wed-Sun, closed mid-Feb–early Mar & Aug; Ⓜ Pont Marie) Founded here in 1954, this esteemed *glacier* (ice-cream maker) is still run by the same family today. Its 70-plus all-natural, chemical-free flavours include fruit sorbets (pink grapefruit, raspberry and rose) and richer ice creams made from fresh milk and eggs (salted caramel, candied Ardèche chestnuts, Armagnac and prunes, gingerbread, liquorice, praline and pine kernels). Watch for tempting new seasonal flavours.

🍽 Menu Advice

Carte Menu, as in the written list of what's cooking, listed in the order you'd eat it: starter, main course, cheese, then dessert. Note that an *entrée* is a starter, not the main course (as in the US).

Menu Not at all what it means in English, *le menu* in French is a *prix-fixe* menu: a multicourse meal at a fixed price. It's by far the best-value dining there is and most restaurants chalk one on the board. In some cases, particularly at neobistros, there is no *carte* – only a stripped-down *menu* with one or two choices.

À la carte Order whatever you fancy from the menu (as opposed to opting for a *prix-fixe* menu).

Formule Similar to a *menu*, *une formule* is a cheaper lunchtime option comprising a main plus starter or dessert. Wine or coffee is sometimes included.

Plat du jour Dish of the day, invariably good value.

Menu enfant Two- or three-course meal for kids (generally up to the age of 12) at a fixed price; usually includes a drink.

Menu dégustation Fixed-price tasting menu served in many top-end restaurants, consisting of at least five modestly sized courses.

Café Saint Régis
Cafe €

(Map p256; ☑01 43 54 59 41; www.cafesaint regisparis.com; 6 rue Jean du Bellay, 4e; breakfast & snacks €3.50-15.50, mains €18-33.50;

Paris on a Plate

Two ground-almond meringues with a smooth, eggshell-like surface.

Pistachio, raspberry, chocolate, coffee and vanilla flavours are classics.

Ganache filling, with a ruffled *pied* ('foot'; circumference).

Best eaten within three days of purchase (maximum five days).

Macaron Essentials

BUTSAYA-SHUTTERSTOCK ©

Brought to Paris in the 1600s by Catherine de Medici's Italian chefs, today's ganache-filled Parisian macarons were created by patisserie Ladurée in the 1930s, and updated in the 1990s by its then-pastry chef Pierre Hermé (who now helms his own empire). Exquisite tearooms and patisseries citywide sell these rainbow-coloured delicacies (beautifully boxed to take away). Macaron Day (20 March) sees free samples, workshops and more.

Pierre Hermé macarons
MING TANG-EVANS/LONELY PLANET ©

★ Best Macarons

Ladurée (p124) Creator of the macaron, with a beautiful Champs-Élysées tearoom.

Beaupassage (p128) Home to macaron maestro Pierre Hermé's inaugural cafe.

Fou de Pâtisserie (p126) Pastries from Paris' masters of their craft.

⊘6.30am-2am, kitchen 8am-midnight; 🛜;
Ⓜ Pont Marie) Waiters in long white aprons,
a ceramic-tiled interior and retro vintage
decor make the hip Saint Régis a deliciously
Parisian hang-out any time of day – for
eating or drinking. From breakfast pastries,
organic eggs and bowls of fruit-peppered
granola to mid-morning pancakes or waffles, lunchtime salads, burgers, dusk-time
oysters and late-night cocktails, it is the
hobnobbing hotspot on the islands.

Le Caveau du Palais   Modern French €€

(Map p254; 📞01 43 26 04 28; www.caveaudu
palais.fr; 19 place Dauphine, 1er; mains €18-27.50;
⊘noon-2.30pm & 7-10pm; Ⓜ Pont Neuf) Even
when the western Île de la Cité shows few
other signs of life, the Caveau's half-timbered
dining areas and (weather permitting)
alfresco terrace are packed with diners
tucking into bountiful fresh fare: pan-seared
scallops with artichokes, grilled codfish with
smoked haddock cream and coriander-
spiced cauliflower, or vegetable risotto.

Sequana   Modern French €€€

(Map p254; 📞01 43 29 78 81; www.sequana.
paris; 72 quai des Orfèvres, 1er; 2-/3-course
lunch menu €24/32, 4-/6-course dinner menu
€55/75; ⊘noon-2pm & 7.30-10pm Tue-Fri, 7.30-
10pm Sat; 🖥; Ⓜ Pont Neuf) At home in a chic
steel-grey dining room with 1950s-style
banquette-seating on Île de la Cité's southwestern tip, sleek Sequana evokes the
Gallo-Roman goddess of the River Seine. In
the kitchen are well-travelled Philippe and
Eugénie, whose childhood in Senegal finds
its way into colourful combos such as wild
turbot with spinach; mallard and butternut
pumpkin, and mango and chocolate.

⊗ Latin Quarter

Café de la Nouvelle Mairie   Cafe €

(Map p260; 📞01 44 07 04 41; 19 rue des Fossés
St-Jacques, 5e; mains €11-17; ⊘8am-12.30am
Mon-Fri, kitchen noon-2.30pm & 8-10.30pm Mon-
Thu, 8-10pm Fri; Ⓜ Cardinal Lemoine) Shhhh...
just around the corner from the Panthéon
but hidden away on a small, fountained

square, this hybrid cafe-restaurant and
wine bar is a tip-top neighbourhood
secret, serving natural wines and delicious
seasonal bistro fare from oysters and ribs
(à la française) to grilled lamb sausage over
lentils. It takes reservations for dinner but
not lunch – arrive early.

Baieta   French €€

(Map p260; 📞01 42 02 59 19; www.restaurant-
baieta-paris.fr; 5 rue de Pontoise, 5e; 2-/4-course
weekday lunch menu €29/45, 7-course dinner
menu €85, mains €28-36; ⊘noon-2.30pm
& 7-10.30pm Tue-Sat; Ⓜ Maubert-Mutualité)
Baieta means 'little kiss' in the patois of
Nice, the home town of culinary sensation Julia Sedefdjian, who was France's
youngest Michelin-starred chef aged 21
when she helmed Paris' Les Fables de La
Fontaine. Opened in 2018, her timber- and
charcoal-toned Latin Quarter premises
showcase her Niçoise roots in creations
like confit octopus with crab gnocchi, and
smoked-quail *barbajuan* (ricotta-filled
pastry).

Le Coupe-Chou   French €€

(Map p260; 📞01 46 33 68 69; www.lecoupechou.
com; 9 & 11 rue de Lanneau, 5e; menu lunch €15,
2-/3-course dinner €27/33, mains €20.50-34;
⊘noon-1.30pm & 7-10.30pm Mon-Sat, 7-10.30pm
Sun Sep-Jun, 7-10.30pm Jul & Aug; Ⓜ Maubert-
Mutualité) This maze of candlelit rooms
inside a vine-clad 17th-century townhouse
is overwhelmingly romantic. Ceilings have
beams, furnishings are antique, open
fireplaces crackle and background classical
music mingles with the intimate chatter of
diners. As in the days when Marlene Diet-
rich dined here, reservations are essential.
Timeless French dishes include Burgundy
snails, steak tartare and bœuf bourguignon.

Circus Bakery   Bakery €

(Map p260; 63 rue Galande, 5e; breads & pastries
€4-8.50; ⊘9am-6pm Fri-Mon; Ⓜ Maubert-
Mutualité) Spectacular sourdough cinnamon
scrolls are the showstoppers at this bakery
with a rustic dark-timber exterior and
exposed stone and brick interior. Other
treats include apple tarts and breads

🍴 Historic Bakery: Poilâne

Pierre Poilâne opened his *boulangerie* (bakery) **Poilâne** (Map p262; 📞01 45 48 42 59; www.poilane.com; 8 rue du Cherche Midi, 6e; ⏰7am-8.30pm Mon-Sat; Ⓜ Sèvres-Babylone) upon arriving from Normandy in 1932. Today his granddaughter Apollonia runs the company, which still turns out wood-fired, rounded sourdough loaves made with stone-milled flour and Guérande sea salt. A clutch of other outlets include one in the **15e** (Map p262; 49 bd de Grenelle, 15e; ⏰7am-8.30pm Tue-Sun; Ⓜ Dupleix).

Loaves at Poilâne
EQROY/SHUTTERSTOCK ©

including chocolate-marbled varieties (though no baguettes), and Parisian-roasted Hexagone coffee to take away.

Les Papilles
Bistro €€

(Map p260; 📞01 43 25 20 79; www.les papillesparis.fr; 30 rue Gay Lussac, 5e; 2-/4-course menus €26/37; ⏰noon-2pm & 7-10.30pm Tue-Sat; Ⓜ Raspail or RER Luxembourg) This hybrid bistro, wine cellar and *épicerie* (specialist grocer) with a sunflower-yellow facade is one of those fabulous Parisian dining experiences. Meals are served at simply dressed tables wedged beneath bottle-lined walls, and fare is market driven: each weekday cooks up a different *marmite du marché* (market casserole). But what really sets it apart is its exceptional wine list.

Restaurant AT
Gastronomy €€€

(Map p260; 📞01 56 81 94 08; www.atsushi tanaka.com; 4 rue du Cardinal Lemoine, 5e; 6-course lunch menu €55, 12-course dinner tasting menu €95, with paired wines €170; ⏰12.15-2pm & 8-9.30pm Mon-Sat; Ⓜ Cardinal Lemoine) Trained by some of the biggest names in gastronomy (Pierre Gagnaire included), chef Atsushi Tanaka showcases abstract artlike masterpieces incorporating rare ingredients (charred bamboo, kohlrabi turnip cabbage, juniper berry powder, wild purple fennel, Nepalese Timut pepper) in a blank-canvas-style dining space on stunning outsized plates. Reservations essential.

Le Vent d'Armor
Seafood €€€

(Map p260; 📞01 46 34 50 99; www.le-vent-darmor.com; 25 quai de la Tournelle, 5e; 2-/3-course weekday lunch menu €30/36, 4-course dinner menu €67, mains €34-50; ⏰7.30-10pm Mon, noon-2pm & 7.30-10pm Tue-Sat; Ⓜ Maubert-Mutualité) Porthole- and lantern-style light fittings are among the contemporary nautical design elements at this sleek Seine-side restaurant. Premium seafood dishes include Marennes Oléron oysters with Pernod foam, grilled Brittany sole with truffle-butter sauce, Normandy St-Pierre (John Dory) with roasted black garlic crème, and scallop tartare with smoked haddock hearts.

⊗ St-Germain & Les Invalides

Tomy & Co
Gastronomy €€

(Map p262; 📞01 45 51 46 93; www.tomygousset.com; 22 rue Surcouf, 7e; 2-course lunch menu €27, 3-course/tasting dinner menu €48/69, mains €29-36; ⏰noon-2pm & 7.30-9.30pm Mon-Fri; Ⓜ Invalides) Tomy Gousset's restaurant near the Eiffel Tower has been a sensation since day one. The French-Cambodian chef works his magic on inspired seasonal dishes using produce from his organic garden. Winter ushers in aromatic black truffles. The spectacular desserts – chocolate tart with fresh figs, Cambodian palm sugar

MATT MUNRO/LONELY PLANET ©

Les Papilles

and fig ice cream, anyone? – are equally seasonal. Reservations essential.

Bouillon Racine
Brasserie €€

(Map p260; ☑01 44 32 15 60; www.bouillon racine.fr; 3 rue Racine, 6e; 2-course weekday lunch menu €17.50, 3-course menu €35, mains €17-24.50; ⊗noon-11pm; 🍴; MCluny–La Sorbonne) Inconspicuously situated in a quiet street, this heritage-listed art nouveau 'soup kitchen', with mirrored walls, floral motifs and ceramic tiling, was built in 1906 to feed market workers. Despite the magnificent interior, the food – inspired by age-old recipes – is no afterthought but superbly executed (stuffed, spit-roasted suckling pig, pork shank in Rodenbach red beer, scallops and shrimps with lobster coulis).

Restaurant Guy Savoy
Gastronomy €€€

(Map p254; ☑01 43 80 40 61; www.guysavoy. com; 11 quai de Conti, 6e, Monnaie de Paris; lunch menu via online booking €250, 12-course tasting menu €445; ⊗noon-2pm & 7-10.30pm Tue-Fri, 7-10.30pm Sat; MPont Neuf) If you're considering visiting a three-Michelin-star temple to gastronomy, this should certainly be on your list. The world-famous chef needs no introduction (he trained Gordon Ramsay, among others); his flagship, entered via a red-carpeted staircase, is ensconced in the neoclassical **Monnaie de Paris** (☑01 40 46 56 66; www. monnaiedeparis.fr; adult/child €10/free; ⊗11am-7pm Tue & Thu-Sun, to 9pm Wed). Monumental cuisine to match includes Savoy icons such as artichoke and black-truffle soup with layered brioche.

Au Pied de Fouet
Bistro €

(Map p262; ☑01 42 96 59 10; 3 rue St-Benoît, 6e; mains €9-12.50; ⊗noon-2.30pm & 7-11pm Mon-Sat; MSt-Germain des Prés) At this tiny, lively bistro, wholly classic dishes such as entrecôte (steak), confit de canard (duck cooked slowly in its own fat) with creamy potatoes, and foie de volailles sauté (pan-fried chicken livers) are astonishingly good value. Round off your meal with a tarte Tatin (upside-down apple tart), wine-soaked prunes, or deliciously rich fondant au chocolat.

Little Breizh
Crêpes €

(Map p254; ☑01 43 54 60 74; www.facebook. com/littlebreizhcreperie; 11 rue Grégoire de Tours, 6e; crêpes €5-15; ⓧnoon-2.15pm & 7-10.30pm Tue-Sat, closed Aug; ☑; ⓜOdéon) As authentic as you'd find in Brittany, but with some innovative twists (such as Breton sardines, olive oil and sundried tomatoes; goat's cheese, stewed apple, hazelnuts, rosemary and honey; smoked salmon, dill cream, pink peppercorns and lemon), the crêpes at this sweet spot are infinitely more enticing than those sold on nearby street corners. Hours can fluctuate; book ahead.

L'Avant Comptoir de la Terre
French €

(Map p260; www.hotel-paris-relais-saint-germain. com; 3 Carrefour de l'Odéon, 6e; tapas €5.50-13.50; ⓧnoon-11pm; ⓜOdéon) Squeeze in around the zinc bar (there are no seats and it's tiny) and feast on amazing tapas (crab custard tarts with Pernod foam, Iberian ham or salmon tartare croquettes, duck confit hot dogs, blood-sausage macarons,

and prosciutto and artichoke waffles), with wines by the glass, in a chaotically sociable atmosphere.

La Crèmerie
French €

(Map p260; ☑01 43 54 99 30; www.facebook. com/lacremerieparis; 9 rue des Quatre-Vents, 6e; small plates €7-21; ⓧ11am-10.30pm Mon-Sat; ⓜOdéon) Beneath an original glass-covered ceiling, this marble-walled *caviste* (wine cellar) is a delicious flashback to 1880s Paris. With a stock of 400-odd wines and an exquisite array of France's finest gourmet goods, it is a delightful spot for an early-evening *apéro* (pre-dinner drink) accompanied by tapas-style dishes (smoked-trout terrine, goat's cheese and olives, black-pudding-topped toast) or a fully-fledged meal.

Clover
Bistro €€€

(Map p262; ☑01 75 50 00 05; www.clover-paris. com; 5 rue Perronet, 7e; 2-/3-course lunch menu €37/48, 3-/5-course dinner menu €62/74; ⓧ12.30-2pm & 7-10pm Tue-Fri, 12.30-2.30pm & 7-10pm Sat; ⓜSt-Germain des Prés) Dining at

Chez Dumonet

hot-shot chef Jean-François Piège's casual bistro is like attending a private party: the galley-style open kitchen adjoining the 20 seats is part of the dining-room decor, putting customers at the front and centre of the culinary action. Light, luscious dishes range from tomato gazpacho with pea sorbet to cabbage leaves with smoked herring crème and chestnuts.

Anicia   French €€
(Map p262; ☑01 43 35 41 50; www.facebook. com/aniciabistrot; 97 rue du Cherche Midi, 6e; 2-/3-course weekday lunch menu €24/29, 3-/5-course dinner menu €49/58, mains €27-34; ⊙noon-10.30pm Tue-Sat; MDuroc, Vaneau) An advance online booking is essential at this glorious 'bistro nature', showcase for the earthy but refined cuisine of chef François Gagnaire who ran a Michelin-starred restaurant in Puy-en-Velay in the Auvergne before uprooting to the French capital. He still sources dozens of regional products – Puy lentils, Velay snails, St-Nectaire cheese – from small-time producers in central France, to stunning effect.

Huîtrerie Regis   Seafood €€
(Map p254; www.huitrerie-regis.com; 3 rue de Montfaucon, 6e; dozen oysters from €26; ⊙noon-2.30pm & 6.30-10.30pm Mon-Fri, noon-10.45pm Sat, noon-10pm Sun; MMabillon) Hip, trendy, tiny and white, this is the spot for slurping oysters on crisp winter days – inside or on the tiny pavement terrace sporting sage-green Fermob chairs. Oysters arrive live from the Bassin de Marennes-Oléron and come only by the dozen. Wash them down with a glass of chilled Muscadet. No reservations, so arrive early.

Cuppa   Cafe, Vegetarian €
(Map p262; 86 rue de l'Université, 7e; dishes €4-12.50; ⊙9am-5pm Tue-Fri, 10am-5pm Sat; 🛜🍴; MSolférino) 🍃 Footsteps from the Musée d'Orsay, behind a dark-green facade framing original glass window panes, teensy Cuppa is a fabulous find for all-organic breakfasts (eg caramelised grapefruit or granola with cardamom,

pistachios and yuzu zest), lunches (like avocado and hummus tartines), homemade cakes, and expertly brewed coffee using ethically sourced beans. Everything is vegetarian; many dishes are vegan and/or gluten-free.

Semilla   Neobistro €€
(Map p254; ☑01 43 54 34 50; www.semillaparis. com; 54 rue de Seine, 6e; 2-/3-course weekday lunch menu €36/40, mains €28-42; ⊙12.30-2.30pm & 7-11pm Mon-Sat, to 10pm Sun, closed early–mid-Aug; MMabillon) Stark concrete floor, beams and an open kitchen (in front of which you can book front-row 'chef seats') set the factory-style scene for edgy, modern, daily changing dishes such as scallops cooked in vin jaune wine with crunchy endives, or trout with passionfruit and ginger. Desserts are equally creative and irresistible. Be sure to book.

Chez Dumonet   Bistro €€
(Joséphine; Map p262; ☑01 45 48 52 40; www. facebook.com/chezdumonetjosephine; 117 rue du Cherche Midi, 6e; mains €24-56; ⊙noon-2.30pm & 7.30-9.30pm Tue-Sat; MDuroc) Fondly known by its former name, Joséphine, this lace-curtained, mosaic-tiled place with white-cloth tables inside and out is the Parisian bistro of many people's dreams, serving timeless standards such as confit duck and grilled châteaubriand steak with Béarnaise sauce. Order the enormous signature Grand Marnier soufflé at the start of your meal. Mains, unusually, come in full or half-portion size.

Restaurant Cinq-Mars   Bistro €€
(Map p262; ☑01 45 44 69 13; www.cinq-mars-restaurant.com; 51 rue de Verneuil, 7e; mains €17-32; ⊙noon-2.30pm & 7.30-10.30pm Mon-Thu, noon-2.30pm & 7.30-11pm Fri, 12.30-3pm & 7.30-11pm Sat, 12.30-3pm & 7.30-10.30pm Sun; MSolférino, RER Musée d'Orsay) A huge dining room partition with blackboard paint chalks up Cinq-Mars' vast array of wines, while the seasonal menu is scrawled on one side. Traditional bistro dishes are given a contemporary spin (*œufs mayonnaise* with trout

🍽️ Dining Tips

Bread Order a meal and within seconds a basket of fresh bread will be brought to the table. Butter is rarely an accompaniment. Except in the most upmarket of places, don't expect a side plate – simply put it on the table.

Water Asking for *une carafe d'eau* (jug of tap water) is perfectly acceptable, although some waiters will presume you don't know this and only offer mineral water, which you have to pay for. Should you prefer bubbles, ask for *de l'eau gazeuze* (fizzy mineral water). Ice (*glaçons*) can be hard to come by.

Service To state the obvious, France is not a service-oriented country. No one is working for tips here, so to get around this, think like a Parisian – acknowledge the expertise of your *serveur* by asking for advice (even if you don't really want it) and don't be afraid to flirt. In France flirtation is not the same as picking someone up; it is both a game that makes the mundane more enjoyable and a vital life skill to help you get what you want (such as the bill). Being witty and speaking French with an accent will often help your cause.

Dress Smart casual is best. How you look is very important, and Parisians favour personal style above all else. But if you're going somewhere dressy, don't assume this means a formal suit – that's more business-meal attire. At the other end of the spectrum, running shoes may be too casual, unless, of course, they are more hip than functional, in which case you may fit right in.

roe, seared fennel with lemon-marinated squid, or Normandy veal cutlet with pepper-crusted, lavender-coloured Violetta potatoes). Finish with desserts like chestnut crème caramel.

Les Climats   French €€€

(Map p262; ☎01 58 62 10 08; www.lesclimats. fr; 41 rue de Lille, 7e; 3-course lunch menu €49, 5-course dinner menu €130, mains €52-88; ⊙12.15-2.15pm & 7-9pm Tue-Sat; MSolférino) Like the neighbouring Musée d'Orsay, this is a magnificent art nouveau treasure. Once a 1905-built former home for female telephone, telegram and postal workers, it features soaring vaulted ceilings and original stained glass, along with a lunchtime summer garden and glassed-in winter garden. Exquisite Michelin-starred dishes complement its 150-page list of wines, sparkling wines and whiskies purely from the Burgundy region.

✪ Montparnasse & Southern Paris

Le Cassenoix   Modern French €€

(Map p262; ☎01 45 66 09 01; www.le-cassenoix. fr; 56 rue de la Fédération, 15e; 3-course menu €34; ⊙noon-2pm & 7-10.30pm Mon-Fri; MBir Hakeim) The Nutcracker is everything a self-respecting neighbourhood bistro should be. *'Tradition et terroir'* (tradition and provenance) dictate the menu that inspires owner-chef Pierre Olivier Lenormand to deliver feisty dishes such as braised veal chuck with mashed potato and caramelised onions or grilled hake with parsnips and hazelnut-Parmesan crumble. Vintage ceiling fans add to the wonderful retro vibe. Book ahead.

La Butte aux Piafs   Bistro €

(☎09 83 51 07 50; www.labutteauxpiafs-paris.fr; 31 bd Auge Blanqui, 13e; mains €15-19; ⊙noon-3.30pm & 6pm-midnight Mon-Fri, 6pm-midnight Sat; MPlace d'Italie) A cinematic cluster of cherry-red chairs flags the pavement terrace of this neighbourhood bistro, *the* spot to lap up the quietly fashionable vibe of La Butte aux Cailles. Inside, flip-down cinema seats mix with an eclectic jumble of vintage seating, while menus featuring burgers, meal-sized salads and creative starters come bound in the sleeve of a vinyl single.

Le Beurre Noisette
Bistro €€

(Map p262; ☑01 48 56 82 49; www.restaurant
beurrenoisette.com; 68 rue Vasco de Gama, 15e;
2-/3-course lunch menu €25/34, 3-/5-course
dinner menu €38/46, mains €19; ⊘noon-2pm
& 7-10.30pm Tue-Sat; Ⓜ Lourmel) *Beurre
noisette* (brown butter sauce, named for its
hazelnut colour) features in dishes such as
tender veal loin with homemade fries and
caramelised pork belly tender with braised
red cabbage and apple, at pedigreed chef
Thierry Blanqui's neighbourhood neobistro.
Filled with locals, the chocolate-toned dining room is wonderfully convivial – be sure
to book. Fantastic value.

Le Petit Pan
Modern French €

(Map p262; ☑01 42 50 04 04; www.lepetitpan.
fr; 18 rue Rosenwald, 15e; 2-course lunch menu
€16.50, small plates €2.50-18; ⊘noon-2.30pm
& 7-11.30pm Tue-Sat; Ⓜ Porte de Vanves) Parisians working in the 'hood fill this casual
bistro to bursting at lunchtime thanks to
a fantastic-value lunchtime menu, but it's
after dusk that the gourmet action kicks
in with small plates of tapas *à la française*
designed for sharing: cured ham, duck pâté
with pork trotters or duck hearts fried in
ginger, accompanied by superb wines by
the glass.

Raw Cakes
Vegan €

(Map p262; ☑09 86 12 73 48; 83 rue Daguerre,
14e; pastries & cakes €3-6, mains €10-16, Sun
brunch €25; ⊘10am-8pm Mon, 11am-10pm Tue-
Thu, 10am-4pm Fri, noon-7pm Sun; ⌖; Ⓜ Gaîté)
A pretty lavender-and-fuchsia-pink facade
fronts this much-welcomed cafe and cake
shop where everything is 100% vegan,
gluten-free – and raw. Enticing nut-and-
chickpea burgers, veggie-packed pizzas
and meal-sized salads rub shoulders on
the menu with fresh juices, smoothies and
exquisite uncooked cakes. Sunday brunch
is always a full house.

La Felicità
Italian €

(www.lafelicita.fr; 5 parvis Alan Turing, 13e, off bd
Vincent Auriol; mains €7-18; ⊘12.15-2.30pm Mon
& Tue, 12.15-2.30pm & 6-10.30pm Wed, 12.15-
2.30pm & 6-11pm Thu & Fri, noon-11pm Sat, noon-
10.30pm Sun; 🛜⌖♿; Ⓜ Bibliothèque François
Mitterrand, Chevaleret) At the southern end
of start-up campus Station F (p109),
immense La Felicità (Italian for 'happiness')
sprawls over 4500 sq metres, with 1000
seats, five kitchens and three bars across
a series of spaces including train carriages
that reflect the building's origins as a
railway depot. Styled as a 'food market', it
specialises in pizzas and pastas made from
Italian produce.

L'Assiette
Bistro €€

(Map p262; ☑01 43 22 64 86; www.restaurant-
lassiette.paris; 181 rue du Château, 14e; 2-course
lunch menu €23, mains €25-32; ⊘noon-2.30pm
& 7.30-10.30pm Wed-Fri, 12.30-2.30pm & 7.30-
10.30pm Sat & Sun; Ⓜ Pernety, Gaîté) Consistently hailed as one of Paris' best bistros,
'the Plate' is the culinary powerhouse of
chef David Rathgebe, from Clermont-
Ferrand in the Auvergne. He mixes age-old
traditional French dishes like *cassoulet
maison* (Toulouse sausage and white bean
stew) and *tête de veau* (rolled calf's head)
with the occasional unexpected combo
(sweetbreads with black truffle risotto) to
delicious effect. Reservations essential.

Le Dôme
Brasserie €€€

(Map p262; ☑01 43 35 25 81; www.restaurant-
ledome.com; 108 bd du Montparnasse, 14e; mains
€26-58, seafood platters €85-155; ⊘noon-3pm &
7-11pm; Ⓜ Vavin) A 1930s art deco extrava-
ganza of the formal white-tablecloth and
bow-tied waiter variety, monumental Le
Dôme is one of the swishest places around
for shellfish platters laden with fresh
oysters, king prawns, crab claws and much
more, followed by traditional creamy homemade *millefeuille* for dessert, wheeled in on
a trolley and cut in front of you.

TREASURE HUNT

One of the world's premier
shopping destinations

Treasure Hunt

Paris has it all: broad boulevards lined with international chains, luxury avenues studded with designer fashion houses, famous grands magasins (department stores) and fabulous markets. But the real charm lies in strolling the city's back-streets, where tiny speciality shops and quirky boutiques, selling everything from strawberry-scented wellington boots to heavenly fragranced candles, are wedged between cafes, galleries and churches.

In This Section

Useful Phrases

Look for signs indicating *cabines d'essayage* (fitting rooms).

Most shops offer free (and beautiful) gift wrapping – ask for *un paquet cadeau*.

A *ticket de caisse* (receipt) is essential for returning/exchanging an item (within one month of purchase).

If you're happy browsing, tell sales staff *Je regarde* (I'm just looking).

Montmartre & Northern Paris
Gourmet food shops, art, quintessential souvenirs (p155)

Champs-Élysées & Grands Boulevards
Haute couture houses, famous department stores (p152)

Louvre & Les Halles
Cookware shops, high-street chains, covered arcades (p153)

Le Marais, Ménilmontant & Belleville
Quirky homewares, art galleries, up-and-coming designers (p157)

St-Germain & Les Invalides
Art, antiques and chic designer boutiques (p162)

The Islands
Enchanting gift shops and gourmet boutiques (p161)

Latin Quarter
Late-opening bookshops and music shops (p161)

Bastille & Eastern Paris
Great markets, Viaduc des Arts workshops (p161)

Opening Hours

Generally, shops open 10am to 7pm Monday to Saturday. Smaller shops may shut on Monday and/or close from around noon to 2pm for lunch. Some larger stores hold *nocturnes* (late-night shopping), usually on Thursday, until 8.45pm. Shops in ZTIs (international tourist zones, eg Le Marais) open late and on Sundays.

Sales

Paris' twice-yearly *soldes* (sales) generally last five to six weeks, starting around mid-January and again around mid-June.

The Best...

Experience Paris' best shopping

Fashion

Galeries Lafayette (p152) Magnificent department store with free fashion shows.
Le Bon Marché (p163) Left Bank department store designed by Gustave Eiffel.
Andrea Crews (p158) Bold art and fashion collective.
Pigalle (p156) Leading Parisian menswear brand.

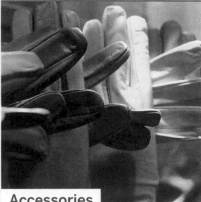

Accessories

JB Guanti (p165) Gorgeous gloves.
Alexandra Sojfer (p165) Handcrafted umbrellas.
Sabbia Rosa (p165) Exquisite lingerie made from French fabrics.
Jamin Puech (p161) One-of-a-kind handbags.

Concept Stores

Merci (p157) Fabulously fashionable and unique: all profits go to a children's charity in Madagascar.
Empreintes (p157) Emporium showcasing some 6000 French artists and designers.
L'Exception (p153) Fashion, homewares, books and more from over 400 French designers.
Hermès (p164; pictured) Housed in an art deco ex-swimming pool.

For Kids

Bonton (p164; pictured) Vintage-inspired fashion, furnishings and knick-knacks for babies, toddlers and children.
Les Petits Bla-Blas (p160) Atelier making children's clothes offering a personalisation service.
Moulin Roty (p158) Flagship store of the beloved French children's brand.

Gourmet Shops

La Grande Épicerie de Paris (p163) Now with a Right Bank outpost, too.

La Manufacture de Chocolat (p161) Alain Ducasse's bean-to-bar chocolate factory.

La Dernière Goutte (p165; pictured) Independent French wines.

Art & Antiques

Marché aux Puces de St-Ouen (p156) One of Europe's largest flea markets, with over 2000 stalls.

Hôtel Drouot (p155) Famous auction house.

Deyrolle (p164; pictured) Historic taxidermist that starred in *Midnight in Paris*.

Vintage & Discount Shops

Frivoli (p153) Brand-name cast-offs by the Canal St-Martin.

Chercheminippes (p163) Several specialist boutiques on one street.

Catherine B (p163) Stocking only Chanel and Hermès vintage pieces.

Lonely Planet's Top Choices

Bouquinistes (p160) Vintage posters and other treasures.

Le Bonbon au Palais (p162) Artisan French sweets.

Shakespeare & Company (p161) A 'wonderland of books'.

🔒 Champs-Élysées & Grands Boulevards

Galeries Lafayette   Department Store

(Map p252; 📞01 42 82 34 56; http://haussmann.
galerieslafayette.com; 40 bd Haussmann, 9e;
⏰9.30am-8.30pm Mon-Sat, 11am-8pm Sun; 📶;
ⓂChaussée d'Antin or RER Auber) Grande-
dame department store Galeries Lafayette
is spread across the main store (its magnificent stained-glass dome is over a century
old), men's store and homewares store
with a gourmet emporium.

Catch modern art in the 1st-floor **gallery**
(📞01 42 82 87 98; www.galeriedesgaleries.com;
⏰11am-7pm Tue-Sun) **FREE**, take in a **fashion
show** (adult/child €12/9; ⏰3pm Fri Mar-Dec by
online reservation), ascend to a free, wind-
swept rooftop panorama or take a break at
one of its many restaurants and cafes.

Guerlain   Perfume

(Map p252; 📞spa 01 45 62 52 57; www.guerlain.
com; 68 av des Champs-Élysées, 8e; ⏰10.30am-
8pm Mon-Sat, noon-8pm Sun; ⓂFranklin D
Roosevelt) Guerlain is Paris' most famous
parfumerie, and its shop (dating from 1912)
is one of the most beautiful in the city. With
its shimmering mirror-and-marble art deco
interior, it's a reminder of the former glory of
the Champs-Élysées. For total indulgence,
make an appointment at its heavenly spa.

Laulhère   Hats

(Map p252; www.laulhere-store.com; 14-16 rue du
Faubourg St-Honoré, 8e; ⏰11am-7pm Mon-Sat;
ⓂMadeleine) Founded in 1840, beret maker
Laulhère still supplies the French army with
the iconic French headwear. Handcrafted
from soft, durable and water-resistant
merino wool, varieties range from plain to
jewel-encrusted versions. The boutique is
hidden within a courtyard.

À la Mère de Famille   Food & Drinks

(Map p254; 📞01 47 70 83 69; www.lamerede
famille.com; 35 rue du Faubourg Montmartre,
9e; ⏰9.30am-8pm Mon-Sat, 10am-7.30pm Sun;
ⓂLe Peletier) Founded in 1761, this is the
original location of Paris' oldest chocolatier. Its beautiful belle époque facade is
as enchanting as the rainbow of sweets,
caramels and chocolates inside.

Guerlain

EGROYS/SHUTTERSTOCK ©

🏛 Louvre & Les Halles

Sézane
Fashion & Accessories

(Map p254; www.sezane.com; 1 rue St-Fiacre, 2e; ⊙11am-8pm Tue-Sat; MGrands Boulevards) 🍃 Affordable French fashion label Sézane, founded by Parisian entrepreneur/designer Morgane Sézalory, has cult status in Paris. Its chic women's tops, trousers, skirts, dresses, knitwear, outerwear, handbags, shoes and homewares such as bed linen, are all sustainably sourced, with many proceeds donated to Demain, its own children's charity (there's also an adjoining charity shop selling seconds and second-hand items).

Didier Ludot
Fashion & Accessories

(Map p254; 🕿01 42 96 06 56; www.didierludot. fr; 24 Galerie de Montpensier, 1er; ⊙10.30am-7pm Mon-Sat; MPalais Royal–Musée du Louvre) In the rag trade since 1975, collector Didier Ludot sells the city's finest couture creations of yesteryear, hosts exhibitions and has published a book portraying the evolution of the little black dress.

L'Exception
Design

(Map p254; 🕿01 40 39 92 34; www.lexception. com; 24 rue Berger, 1er; ⊙10am-8pm Mon-Sat, 11am-7pm Sun; MLes Halles or RER Châtelet–Les Halles) Over 400 different French designers come together under one roof at this light-filled concept store, which showcases rotating collections of men's and women's fashion along with accessories including lingerie and swimwear, shoes, eyewear, gloves, hats, scarves, belts, bags, watches and jewellery. It also sells design books, cosmetics, candles, vases and other gorgeous homewares, and has a small in-house coffee bar.

Legrand Filles & Fils
Food & Drinks

(Map p254; 🕿01 42 60 07 12; www.caves-legrand. com; 1 rue de la Banque, 2e; ⊙11am-7pm Mon, 10am-7.30pm Tue-Sat; MBourse) Tucked inside Galerie Vivienne since 1880, Legrand sells fine wine and all the accoutrements: corkscrews, tasting glasses, decanters etc. It also has a fancy wine bar, *école du vin* (wine

Canal St-Martin

Bordered by shaded towpaths and criss-crossed with iron footbridges, Canal St-Martin wends through the city's northern neighbourhoods. Shopping streets home to offbeat boutiques include rue Beaurepaire: look out for rock 'n' roll fashion at **Liza Korn** (Map p256; www.liza-korn.com; 19 rue Beaurepaire, 10e; ⊙11am-7.30pm Mon-Sat; MRépublique, Jacques Bonsergent) and colour-coded vintage cast-offs at **Frivoli** (www.facebook.com/frivolidepot; 26 rue Beaurepaire, 10e; ⊙1-7pm Mon, 11am-7pm Tue-Fri, 2-7pm Sat & Sun; MRépublique, Jacques Bonsergent). Rue de Marseille is also lined with boutiques such as jewellery studio-showroom **Medecine Douce** (www.bijouxmedecinedouce.com; 10 rue de Marseille, 10e; ⊙11am-7pm Mon-Sat; MJacques Bonsergent). Along the canal itself, check out design bookshop **Artazart** (www.artazart.com; 83 quai de Valmy, 10e; ⊙10.30am-7.30pm Mon-Fri, from 11am Sat, from 1pm Sun; MJacques Bonsergent), and the pastel-shaded **Antoine et Lili** (www.antoineetlili.com; 95 quai de Valmy, 10e; ⊙10.30am-7.30pm Mon-Sat, 11am-7pm Sun; MJacques Bonsergent, Gare de l'Est), stocking clothing for women (pink store) and children (green store), and eclectic homewares (yellow store).

school; courses from €25 for 2½ hours) and *éspace dégustation* with several tastings a month, including ones accompanied by live concerts; check its website for details.

E Dehillerin
Homewares

(Map p254; 🕿01 42 36 53 13; www.edehillerin.fr; 18-20 rue Coquillière, 1er; ⊙9am-12.30pm & 2-6pm Mon, 9am-7pm Tue-Fri, 9am-6pm Sat; MLes Halles) Founded in 1820, this extraordinary two-level store – more like an old-fashioned warehouse than a shiny, chic boutique – carries an incredible selection of professional-quality *matériel de cuisine* (kitchenware).

Top Paris Souvenirs

Art

At major museums, the Boutiques de Musées have painting-and-frame services: browse masterpieces, choose a frame and have replicas mailed to your home.

Perfume

Browse Parisian perfume at new innovators or department stores, or buy a bottle of Champs-Élysées on its namesake street at Guerlain (p152).

Chocolate

Exquisite chocolate boutiques throughout the city include star chef Alain Ducasse's bean-to-bar chocolate factory, La Manufacture de Chocolat (p161).

Candles

Candle-makers from the world's oldest, Cire Trudon (p164), to the scents of Parisian parks and gardens at Kerzon (p157).

Scarves

The ultimate Parisian accessory, whatever the season. Hermès creates timeless designs.

Poultry scissors, turbot poacher, professional copper cookware or an Eiffel Tower–shaped cake tin – it's all here.

La Samaritaine   Department Store

(Map p254; www.lasamaritaine.com; 19 rue de la Monnaie, 1er; [M]Pont Neuf) One of Paris' four big department stores, the 10-storey La Samaritaine is finally emerging from its much contested and drawn-out 14-year over-haul. Pritzker Prize–winning Japanese firm Sanaa has preserved much of the gorgeous art nouveau and art deco exterior, in addition to the glass ceiling topping the central Hall Jourdain.

Hôtel Drouot   Art, Antiques

(Map p254; [J]01 48 00 20 20; www.drouot.com; 7-9 rue Drouot, 9e; ⊙11am-6pm Mon-Wed, Fri & Sat, to 9pm Thu; [M]Richelieu Drouot) Selling everything from antiques and jewellery to rare books and art, Paris' most established auction house has been in business for more than a century. Viewings are from 11am to 6pm the day before and from 11am to noon the morning of the auction. Pick up the cat-alogue *Gazette de l'Hôtel Drouot,* published Fridays, in-house or at newsstands.

⊙ Montmartre & Northern Paris

Fromagerie Alléosse   Cheese

(Map p252; www.fromage-alleosse.com; 13 rue Poncelet, 17e; ⊙9am-1pm & 3.30-7pm Tue-Sat, 9am-1pm Sun; [M]Ternes) On stall-filled foodie street rue Poncelet, heady *fromagerie* Alléosse has its own cheese-ripening *caves* (cellars) spanning 300 sq metres with four separate environments. Its 250-plus cheeses are grouped into five main categories: *fromage de chèvre* (goat's milk), *fromage à pâte persillée* (veined or blue), *fromage à pâte molle* (soft), *fromage à pâte demi-dure* (semihard) and *fromage à pâte dure* (hard).

Belle de Jour   Fashion & Accessories

(Map p250; www.belle-de-jour.fr; 7 rue Tardieu, 18e; ⊙11am-1pm & 2-7pm Tue-Fri, 11am-1pm & 2-6pm Sat; [M]Anvers, Abbesses) Be whisked

---

🛍 Shopping the Triangle d'Or

A stroll around the legendary Triangle d'Or (Golden Triangle; bordered by avs George V, Champs-Élysées and Montaigne, 8e) or on rue du Faubourg St-Honoré constitutes the walk of fame of top French fashion. Rub shoulders with the world's most renowned interna-tional designers at Paris' most influen-tial French fashion houses:

Chanel (Map p252; [J]01 40 70 82 00; www.chanel.com; 42 av Montaigne, 8e; ⊙10am-7pm Mon-Sat, 11am-7pm Sun; [M]George V)

Chloé (Map p252; [J]01 47 23 00 08; www.chloe.com; 50 av Montaigne, 8e; ⊙10.30am-7pm Mon-Sat, 1-7pm Sun; [M]Franklin D Roosevelt)

Dior (Map p252; [J]01 45 63 12 51; www.dior.com; 30 av Montaigne, 8e; ⊙10am-7pm Mon-Sat; [M]George V)

Givenchy (Map p252; [J]01 44 43 99 90; www.givenchy.com; 36 av Montaigne, 8e; ⊙10am-7pm Mon-Sat, 1-7pm Sun; [M]George V)

Hermès (Map p252; [J]01 40 17 46 00; www.hermes.com; 24 rue du Faubourg St-Honoré, 8e; ⊙10.30am-6.30pm Mon-Sat; [M]Concorde)

Lanvin (Map p252; [J]01 44 71 31 73; www.lanvin.com; 22 rue du Faubourg St-Honoré, 8e; ⊙10.30am-7pm Mon-Sat; [M]Concorde)

Louis Vuitton (Map p252; [J]01 53 57 52 00; www.louisvuitton.com; 101 av des Champs-Élysées, 8e; ⊙10am-8pm Mon-Sat, 11am-7pm Sun; [M]George V)

Saint Laurent (Map p252; [J]01 42 65 74 59; www.ysl.com; 38 rue du Faubourg St-Honoré, 8e; ⊙10.30am-7.30pm Mon-Sat; [M]Concorde)

---

back in time to the elegance of belle époque Paris at this Montmartre shop specialising in perfume bottles. Gorgeous 19th-century atomisers, smelling salts and powder boxes in engraved or enamelled Bohemian, Baccarat and Saint-Louis crys-tal share shelf space with more contempo-rary designs. Whether you're after art deco

Flea Markets

Spanning 9 hectares, vast flea market **Marché aux Puces de St-Ouen** (www.marcheauxpuces-saintouen.com; rue des Rosiers, St-Ouen; ⊙Sat-Mon; MPorte de Clignancourt) was founded in 1870 and is said to be Europe's largest. Over 2000 stalls are grouped into 15 *marchés* (markets) selling everything from 17th-century furniture to 21st-century clothing. Each market has different opening hours – check the website for details.

Close by, an abandoned Petite Ceinture train station has been repurposed as eco-hub **La REcyclerie** (www.larecyclerie.com; 83 bd Ornano, 18e; ⊙8am-midnight Mon-Thu, to 2am Fri & Sat, to 10pm Sun early Jan–mid-Dec; MPorte de Clignancourt) ✔ with an urban farm along the old railway line featuring community vegetable and herb gardens and chickens. They provide ingredients for the mostly vegetarian cafe-canteen (tables stretch trackside in summer and the station houses a cavernous dining space). Look out for regular upcycling and repair workshops, flea markets and various other events.

Across town in the city's south, the **Marché aux Puces de la Porte de Vanves** (www.pucesdevanves.fr; av Georges Lafenestre & av Marc Sangnier, 14e; ⊙7am-2pm Sat & Sun; MPorte de Vanves) has over 380 stalls.

Paris' most central flea market is the small Marché aux Puces d'Aligre (p83), adjoining the Marché d'Aligre.

or art nouveau, pink-frosted or painted glass, it's here.

Balades Sonores   Music
(Map p250; ☎01 83 87 94 87; www.baladessonores.com; 1-3 av Trudaine, 9e; ⊙noon-8pm Mon-Sat; MAnvers) One of Paris' best vinyl shops, Balades Sonores sprawls over two adjacent buildings. The ground floor of 1 av Trudaine stocks contemporary pop, rock, metal, garage and French music (all genres). Its basement holds secondhand blues, country, new wave and punk from the '60s to '90s. Next door, No 3 has soul, jazz, funk, hip-hop, electronica and world music.

La Binouze   Drinks
(Map p250; ☎09 53 17 23 18; www.labinouze.fr; 72 rue de Rochechouart, 9e; ⊙noon-10pm Mon-Fri, 11am-11pm Sat, 11am-10pm Sun; MAnvers) Over 600 craft beers from across France and around the world are stocked at this beer emporium. Pick them up to take away or taste them on site, accompanied by tartines (open sandwiches) or cheese and charcuterie sharing boards. Two-hour guided tastings in English or French cost €30.

Pigalle   Fashion & Accessories
(Map p250; www.pigalle-paris.com; 7 rue Henry Monnier, 9e; ⊙noon-8pm Mon-Sat, from 2pm Sun; MSt-Georges) Pick up a hoodie emblazoned with the black-and-white Pigalle logo from this leading Parisian menswear brand, created by designer and basketball player Stéphane Ashpool, who grew up in the 'hood.

O/HP/E   Concept Store
(Map p256; www.facebook.com/ohpeparis10; 27 rue du Château d'Eau, 10e; ⊙2-7pm Tue, 8.30am-7.30pm Wed-Fri, 9.30am-7.30pm Sat, 9.30am-6.30pm Sun; MJacques Bonsergent) White-on-white concept store O/HP/E stocks chic homewares – ceramics, textiles, light fittings, candles and kitchenware (rolling pins, mats, chopping boards, chopsticks et al) – along with cosmetics, stationery and gifts. Also here is an *épicerie* (specialist grocer) with gourmet delicacies (preserves, nougats, sugar-coated olives and chocolates) and a cafe with baked treats such as hazelnut praline tarts.

Spree   Fashion & Accessories
(Map p250; ☎01 42 23 41 40; www.spree.fr; 16 rue de la Vieuville, 18e; ⊙11am-7.30pm Tue-Sat, 3-7pm Sun; MAbbesses) Allow plenty of time to browse this super-stylish boutique-gallery, with a carefully selected collection of designer fashion put together by stylist

Roberta Oprandi and artist Bruni Hadjadj. What makes shopping here fun is that all the furniture – vintage 1950s to 1980s pieces by Eames and other midcentury designers – is also for sale, as is the contemporary artwork on the walls.

🅐 Le Marais, Ménilmontant & Belleville

Merci   Concept Store
(Map p256; 📞01 42 77 00 33; www.merci-merci. com; 111 bd Beaumarchais, 3e; ⊗10am-7.30pm Mon-Sat, noon-7pm Sun; Ⓜ St-Sébastien–Froissart) 🍃 A Fiat Cinquecento marks the entrance to this unique concept store, which donates all its profits to a children's charity in Madagascar. Shop for fashion, accessories, linens, lamps and nifty designs for the home. Complete the experience with a coffee in its hybrid used-bookshop-cafe, a juice at its **Cinéma Café** (Map p256; www.merci-merci.com; 111 bd Beaumarchais, 3e; ⊗11am-7pm Mon-Sat) or lunch in its stylish **La Cantine de Merci** (mains €16-21; ⊗noon-5pm Mon-Fri, to 6pm Sat).

Empreintes   Design
(Map p256; www.empreintes-paris.com; 5 rue de Picardie, 3e; ⊗11am-7pm Mon-Sat; Ⓜ Temple) Covering more than 600 sq metres over four floors, this design emporium has over 1000 items for sale at any one time from more than 6000 emerging and established French artists and designers. Handcrafted jewellery, fashion and art are displayed alongside striking homewares (ceramics, cushions, furniture, lighting and more). Upstairs there's a cafe and a reference library.

Kerzon   Homewares, Cosmetics
(Map p256; www.kerzon.paris; 68 rue de Turenne, 3e; ⊗11.30am-8pm Tue-Sat; Ⓜ St-Sébastien–Froissart) Candles made from natural, biodegradable wax in Parisian scents such as Jardin du Luxembourg (with lilac and honey), Place des Vosges (rose and jasmine) and Parc des Buttes-Chaumont (cedar and sandalwood) make aromatic souvenirs of the city. The pretty white and sage-green boutique also stocks room fragrances, scented laundry liquids, perfumes, soaps, bath oils and other toiletries.

Flea market

Moulin Roty — Toys

(Map p256; www.moulinroty.com; 22 bd des Filles du Calvaire, 11e; ⊙3-7pm Mon, 10am-7pm Tue-Sat; MFilles du Calvaire) Moulin Roty toys are stocked in department stores and boutiques, but this is the company's only premises of its own in Paris. Alongside shelves of soft toys (mice, ducks, cats etc, in beautifully stitched outfits) are animal-adorned backpacks, adorable booties and old-fashioned toys such as rocking horses, tea sets, kaleidoscopes, shadow puppets and cinema projector sets.

Fromagerie Goncourt — Cheese

(Map p256; ✆01 43 57 91 28; www.facebook.com/lafromageriegoncourt; 1 rue Abel Rabaud, 11e; ⊙9am-1pm & 4-8.30pm Tue-Fri, 9am-8pm Sat; MGoncourt) Styled like a boutique, this contemporary *fromagerie* is a must-discover. Clément Brossault ditched a career in banking to become a *fromager* and his cheese selection – 70-plus types – is superb. Cheeses flagged with a bicycle symbol are varieties he discovered in situ during a two-month French cheese tour he embarked on as part of his training.

Paris Rendez-Vous — Gifts & Souvenirs

(Map p254; www.boutique.paris.fr; 29 rue de Rivoli, 4e; ⊙10am-7pm Mon-Sat; MHôtel de Ville) This chic city has its own designer line of souvenirs, sold in its own ubercool concept store inside the Hôtel de Ville (town hall). Shop here for everything from clothing and homewares to Paris-themed books, wooden toy sailing boats and signature Jardin du Luxembourg Fermob chairs. *Quel style!*

Andrea Crews — Fashion & Accessories

(Map p256; www.andreacrews.com; 83 rue de Turenne, 3e; ⊙1-7.30pm Wed-Fri, to 7pm Sat; MSt-Sébastien–Froissart) Using everything from discarded clothing to electrical fittings and household bric-a-brac, this bold art and fashion collective sews, recycles and reinvents to create the most extraordinary pieces. Watch out for 'happenings' in its Marais boutique.

Belleville Brûlerie — Coffee

(Map p256; www.cafesbelleville.com; 10 rue Pradier, 19e; ⊙11am-6.30pm Sat; MPyrénées) With its understated steel-grey facade, this groundbreaking roastery in Belleville

From left: Didier Ludot (p153); Marché aux Puces de la Porte de Vanves (p156); La REcyclerie (p156)

is easy to miss. Don't! Belleville Brûlerie brought good coffee to Paris and its beans go into some of the best espressos in town. Taste the week's selection, compare tasting notes, and buy a bag to take home.

We Are Paris
Concept Store

(Map p256; www.boutiqueweareparis.com; 13 rue Oberkampf, 11e; ☺10am-3pm & 4-8pm Mon-Sat; Ⓜ Filles du Calvaire) ✐ Handcrafted items in this little shop are the work of designers and artisans from Paris and its surrounds. The limited-edition items – from hand-stitched socks to scarves, jewellery, organic cosmetics, candles, ceramics, stationery and delicacies like gourmet popcorn – are made exclusively from chemical-free, eco-friendly French materials.

Candora
Perfume

(Map p256; ☏01 43 48 76 05; www.candora.fr; 1 rue du Pont Louis-Philippe, 4e; ☺2-7pm Tue-Sat; Ⓜ Pont Marie) At this brother-and-sister-run parfumerie near the Seine you can have bespoke scents made up in just 10 minutes. Or learn how to create fragrances yourself during a perfume-making workshop for adults and children. Workshops in English (€79) take place at 2.30pm on Tuesday and Friday, last for 90 minutes and include a 15mL bottle.

Edwart
Chocolate

(Map p256; www.edwart.fr; 17 rue Vielle du Temple, 4e; ☺11am-noon & 1-8pm Mon-Wed, 11am-8pm Thu-Sun; Ⓜ Hôtel de Ville) Wunderkind chocolatiers Edwin Yansané and Arthur Heinze (collectively 'Edwart') take their inspiration from Paris (and – as a global melting pot – by extension, the world). Feisty chocolates using unique ingredients such as Indian curry, Iranian saffron and Japanese whisky are sparingly displayed in their sleek Marais boutique.

Fromagerie Beaufils
Cheese

(Map p256; www.fromagerie-beaufils.com; 118 rue de Belleville, 20e; ☺8.30am-8pm Tue-Sat, to 1pm Sun; Ⓜ Jourdain) The queue outside the door, especially at weekends, says it all. This family-run *fromagerie* and *affineur* (ripener) in Belleville is among the best in Paris, with dozens of lesser-known French and international varieties.

Bouquinistes Along the Seine

With some 3km of forest-green boxes lining the Seine – containing over 300,000 secondhand (and often out-of-print) books, rare magazines, postcards and old advertising posters – Paris' **bouquinistes** (Map p254; quai Voltaire, 7e, to quai de la Tournelle, 5e, & Pont Marie, 4e, to quai du Louvre, 1er; ☺11.30am-dusk), or used-book sellers, are as integral to the cityscape as Notre Dame. Many open only from spring to autumn (and many shut in August), but year-round you'll still find some to browse.

The *bouquinistes* have been in business since the 16th century, when they were itinerant peddlers selling their wares on Parisian bridges; back then their sometimes subversive (eg Protestant) materials could get them into trouble with the authorities. By 1859 the city had finally wised up: official licences were issued, space was rented (10m of railing) and eventually the permanent green boxes were installed.

Today, *bouquinistes* (the official count ranges from 200 to 240) are allowed to have four boxes, only one of which can be used to sell souvenirs. Look hard enough and you just might find some real treasures: old comic books, forgotten first editions, maps, stamps, erotica and prewar newspapers – as in centuries past, it's all there, waiting to be rediscovered.

L'Éclaireur   Fashion & Accessories

(Map p256; ☎01 48 87 10 22; www.leclaireur.com; 40 rue de Sévigné, 3e; ☺11am-7pm Mon-Sat, from 2pm Sun; MSt-Paul) Part art space, part lounge and part deconstructionist fashion statement, this shop is known for having the next big thing first. Two tons of wooden planks, 147 TV screens and walls that move to reveal the men's and women's collection all form part of the stunning interior design by Belgian artist Arne Quinze.

La Cave Le Verre Volé   Wine

(Map p256; www.leverrevole.fr; 38 rue Oberkampf, 11e; ☺4-8.30pm Mon, 10am-1pm & 4-8.30pm Tue-Sat; MOberkampf) One of Paris' largest collections of natural wines is stocked at this wondrous wine shop. Its famous bistro (p128) is located by Canal St-Martin, and its **épicerie** (Map p256; ☎01 48 05 36 55; 54 rue de la Folie Méricourt, 11e; sandwiches €4.90-6.90; ☺11am-2.30pm & 4.30-8pm Mon & Fri, 11am-8pm Tue-Thu & Sat; ☏), where for €7 corkage you can drink bottles purchased here while dining on deli platters and gourmet sandwiches, is just around the corner.

Les Petits Bla-Blas   Children's Clothing

(Atelier Pascaline Delcourt; Map p256; www.atelierpascalinedelcourt.com; 7 rue de Crussol, 11e; ☺11am-7pm Mon-Fri; MFilles du Calvaire) At her 11e atelier, Pascaline Delcourt makes clothing for children (up to six years), bibs, bags and onesies, and also stocks children's jewellery, toys, paper animal lanterns and soft cuddly toys. A personalisation service lets you add a name, date of birth or message to individual items.

Made by Moi   Fashion, Homewares

(Map p256; ☎01 58 30 95 78; www.madebymoi.fr; 86 rue Oberkampf, 11e; ☺4.30-8pm Mon, 10am-8pm Tue-Sat; MParmentier) 'Made by Me', aka handmade, is the driver of this appealing boutique on trendy rue Oberkampf – a perfect address to buy unusual gifts, from women's fashion to homewares such as 'Bobo brunch' scented candles by Bougies La Française and other beautiful objects such as coloured glass carafes, feathered headdresses, funky contact-lens boxes and retro dial telephones.

Jamin Puech Fashion & Accessories
(Map p256; www.jamin-puech.com; 68 rue Vieille du Temple, 4e; ⏰10am-7.30pm Mon-Sat, 1-7pm Sun; MChemin Vert) Established by former theatre and opera costume designers Isabelle Puech and Benoît Jamin, who trained together in Paris, this design house creates beautiful handbags in all manner of bold colours, textures and textiles. For vintage pieces from the 1990s, head to the couple's first boutique at 61 rue d'Hauteville, 10e.

Bring France Home Gifts & Souvenirs
(Map p256; ☎09 81 64 91 09; www.bringfrance home.com; 3 rue de Birague, 4e; ⏰11am-7pm; MBastille) All of the quality items in this terrific little shop are made in France: jewellery, perfume, cards, tea towels, plates, posters, board games, *boules* sets, speciality foodstuffs such as foie gras, tinned sardines, Parisian honey, beer and absinthe kits, and much more.

⊙ Bastille & Eastern Paris

La Manufacture de Chocolat Food
(Map p259; ☎01 48 05 82 86; www.lechocolat-alainducasse.com; 40 rue de la Roquette, 11e; ⏰10.30am-7pm Mon-Sat; MBastille) If you dine at superstar chef Alain Ducasse's restaurants, the chocolate will have been made here at Ducasse's own chocolate factory (the first in Paris to produce 'bean-to-bar' chocolate), which he set up with his former executive pastry chef Nicolas Berger. Deliberate over ganaches, pralines and truffles and no fewer than 44 flavours of chocolate bar.

Fermob Homewares
(Map p259; ☎01 43 07 17 15; www.fermob.com; 81-83 av Ledru-Rollin, 12e; ⏰10am-7pm Mon-Sat; MLedru-Rollin) If you want to create the 'Jardin du Luxembourg look' in your own garden, head for Fermob. It makes French-park-style benches and folding chairs in a range of great colours – from carrot and lemon to fuchsia and aubergine – along

with lovely cushions, rugs, throws, lamps and home accessories. International shipping is available.

⊙ The Islands

Marché aux Fleurs Reine Elizabeth II Market
(Map p254; place Louis Lépin, 4e; ⏰8.30am-7pm Jul-Sep, 9.30am-7pm Oct-Jun; MCité) Blooms have been sold at this flower market since 1808, making it the oldest market of any kind in Paris. On Sunday, there's also a cacophonous bird market, the **Marché aux Oiseaux** (⏰8am-7pm Sun).

38 Saint Louis Food & Drinks
(Map p256; 38 rue St-Louis en l'Île, 4e; ⏰8.30am-10pm Tue-Sat, 9.30am-4pm Sun; MPont Marie) Not only does this contemporary, creamy white-fronted *fromagerie*, run by young, dynamic, food-driven duo Didier Grosjean and Thibault Lhirondelle, have an absolutely superb selection of first-class French cheese; it also offers Saturday wine tastings, artisan fruit juices and prepared dishes to go, such as sheep's-cheese salad with truffle oil, and wooden boxes filled with vacuum-packed cheese to take home.

⊙ Latin Quarter

Shakespeare & Company Books
(Map p260; ☎01 43 25 40 93; www.shakes peareandcompany.com; 37 rue de la Bûcherie, 5e; ⏰10am-10pm; MSt-Michel) Enchanting nooks and crannies overflow with new and secondhand English-language books. The original shop (12 rue l'Odéon, 6e; closed by the Nazis in 1941) was run by Sylvia Beach and became the meeting point for Hemingway's 'Lost Generation'. Readings by emerging and illustrious authors regularly take place and there's a wonderful cafe (p181) next door.

Le Bonbon au Palais Food
(Map p260; ☎01 78 56 15 72; www.lebonbonau palais.com; 19 rue Monge, 5e; ⏰10.30am-7.30pm Tue-Sat; MCardinal Lemoine) Kids and

kids-at-heart will adore this sugar-fuelled *tour de France*. The school-geography-themed boutique stocks rainbows of artisan sweets from around the country. Old-fashioned glass jars brim with treats like *calissons* (diamond-shaped, icing-sugar-topped ground fruit and almonds from Aix-en-Provence), *rigolettes* (fruit-filled pillows from Nantes) and *papalines* (herbal liqueur-filled pink-chocolate balls from Avignon).

Fromagerie Laurent Dubois   Cheese

(Map p260; ☏01 43 54 50 93; www.fromages laurentdubois.fr; 47ter bd St-Germain, 5e; ◷8am-7.45pm Tue-Sat, 8.30am-1pm Sun; Ⓜ Maubert-Mutualité) One of the best *fromageries* in Paris, this cheese-lover's nirvana is filled with to-die-for delicacies, such as St-Félicien with Périgord truffles. Rare, limited-production cheeses include blue Termignon and Tarentaise goat's cheese. All are appropriately cellared in warm, humid or cold environments. Branches include one in the **15e** (Map p262; ☏01 45 78 70 58; 2 rue de Lourmel, 15e; ◷9am-8pm Tue-Sat, 9am-1pm Sun; Ⓜ Dupleix).

Fromagerie Maury   Cheese

(Map p260; ☏09 52 81 84 98; 1 rue des Feuillantines, 5e; ◷2-9pm Tue-Thu, 10.30am-1.30pm & 3-8.30pm Fri & Sat; Ⓜ Censier Daubenton or RER Port Royal) ✐ This wonderful little *fromagerie* feels more like a farm shop you'd find in the countryside than an inner-city Parisian boutique. Organic eggs sit in straw baskets (cartons are available) and owner Christophe Maury insists that you try his amazing range of carefully selected cheeses from small-scale producers in southwestern France, the Jura mountains, Corsica, Italy and Spain before you buy.

ⓐ St-Germain & Les Invalides

La Grande Épicerie de Paris   Food & Drinks

(Map p262; www.lagrandeepicerie.com; 38 rue de Sèvres, 7e; ◷8.30am-9pm Mon-Sat, 10am-8pm Sun; Ⓜ Sèvres-Babylone) The magnificent food hall of Le Bon Marché sells 30,000 rare and/or luxury gourmet products, including 60 different types of bread baked on site

La Grande Épicerie de Paris

HAJAKELY/GETTY IMAGES ©

and delicacies such as caviar ravioli. Its fantastical displays of chocolates, pastries, biscuits, cheeses, and fresh fruit and vegetables are a sight in themselves. Wine tastings regularly take place in the basement.

Le Bon Marché
Department Store

(Map p262; ☎01 44 39 80 00; www.24sevres. com; 24 rue de Sèvres, 7e; ☺10am-8pm Mon-Wed, Fri & Sat, 10am-8.45pm Thu, 11am-7.45pm Sun; MSèvres-Babylone) Built by Gustave Eiffel as Paris' first department store in 1852, this is the epitome of style, with a superb concentration of men's and women's fashions, homewares, stationery, books and toys. Break for a coffee, afternoon tea or a light lunch at the Rose Bakery tearoom on the 2nd floor. The icing on the cake is its glorious food hall.

Magasin Sennelier
Arts & Crafts

(Map p262; ☎01 42 60 72 15; www.magasin sennelier.net; 3 quai Voltaire, 7e; ☺2-6.30pm Mon, 10am-12.45pm & 2-6.30pm Tue-Sat; MSt-Germain des Prés) Cézanne and Picasso were among the artists who helped develop products for this venerable 1887-founded art supplier on the banks of the Seine, and it remains an exceptional place to pick up canvases, brushes, watercolours, oils, pastels, charcoals and more. The shop's forest-green facade with gold lettering, exquisite original timber cabinetry and glass display cases also fuel artistic inspiration.

Cantin
Cheese

(Map p262; ☎01 45 50 43 94; www.cantin. fr; 12 rue du Champs de Mars, 7e; ☺2-7.30pm Mon, 8.30am-7.30pm Tue-Sat, 8.30am-1pm Sun; MÉcole Militaire) ✔ Opened in 1950 and still run by the same family today, this exceptional shop stocks cheeses only made in limited quantities on small rural farms. They're then painstakingly ripened in Cantin's own cellars (from two weeks up to two years) before being displayed for sale. Learn how to concoct the perfect cheeseboard during informative tasting workshops (prices on request).

Vintage Style

Designer and vintage cast-offs at *dépôt-vente* (secondhand) boutiques can yield serious bargains.

Scattered along one street, **Chercheminippes** (Map p262; www. chercheminippes.fr; 102 rue du Cherche Midi, 6e; ☺11am-7pm Mon-Sat; MVaneau) has a string of beautifully presented boutiques selling secondhand pieces by current designers. Each specialises in a different genre (*haute couture*, kids, menswear etc); items are perfectly ordered by size and designer. There are changing rooms.

Fans of Chanel and Hermès should visit **Catherine B** (Map p260; ☎01 43 54 74 18; www.les3marchesdecatherineb.com; 1 rue Guisarde, 6e; ☺noon-6pm Wed-Fri or by appointment; MMabillon), who specialises exclusively in authentic items from these two iconic French fashion houses.

Au Plat d'Étain
Toys

(Map p260; ☎01 43 54 32 06; www.soldats-plomb-au-plat-etain.fr; 16 rue Guisarde, 6e; ☺10.30am-6.30pm Tue-Sat; MMabillon, St-Sulpice) Tiny tin *(étain)* and lead soldiers, snipers, cavaliers, military drummers and musicians (great for chessboard pieces) cram this fascinating boutique. In business since 1775, the shop itself is practically a collectable.

Bonton Surplus
Children's Clothing

(Map p262; ☎01 44 39 09 20; www.bonton.fr; 82 rue de Grenelle, 7e; ☺10am-7pm Mon-Sat; MRue du Bac) What's left of previous seasons' collections from one of Paris' most chic children's fashion shops is sold at reduced prices at this tiny boutique, a riot of colour and fun. The adjoining Bonton Store, also at No 82, stocks the current collection – or head to Bonton's flagship **concept store** (Map p256; 5 bd des Filles du Calvaire, 3e; ☺10am-7pm Mon-Sat; MSt-Sébastien–Froissart) in Le Marais.

🍴 Place de la Madeleine

Ultragourmet food shops garland **place de la Madeleine** (Map p252; place de la Madeleine, 8e; MMadeleine); many have in-house dining options. Notable names include the following.

La Maison de la Truffe (☎01 42 65 53 22; www.maison-de-la-truffe.com; ⊗noon-10.30pm Mon-Sat, closed mid–late Aug) Truffle dealers.

Boutique Maille (www.maille.com; ⊗10am-7pm Mon-Sat) Mustard specialist.

Fauchon (☎01 70 39 38 00; www.fauchon. com; ⊗10am-8.30pm Mon-Sat) Paris' most famous caterer, with mouth-watering delicacies from foie gras to jams, chocolates and pastries.

Patrick Roger (☎09 67 08 24 47; www. patrickroger.com; ⊗10.30am-7.30pm) Extravagant chocolate sculptures.

La Maison du Miel (☎01 47 42 26 70; www.maisondumiel.fr; 24 rue Vignon, 9e; ⊗9.30am-7pm Mon-Sat) Nearby honey specialist.

La Maison de la Truffe
ANNA BRYUKHANOVA/GETTY IMAGES ©

Cire Trudon   Gifts & Souvenirs
(Map p260; ☎01 43 26 46 50; www.trudon.com; 78 rue de Seine, 6e; ⊗11am-7pm Mon, 10am-7pm Tue-Sat; MOdéon) Claude Trudon began selling candles here in 1643, and the company – which officially supplied Versailles and Napoléon with light – is now the world's oldest candle-maker (look for the plaque to the left of the shop's royal-blue awning). A rainbow of candles and candlesticks fill the shelves inside.

Deyrolle   Antiques, Homewares
(Map p262; ☎01 42 22 30 07; www.deyrolle. com; 46 rue du Bac, 7e; ⊗10am-1pm & 2-7pm Mon, 10am-7pm Tue-Sat; MRue du Bac) Overrun with creatures such as lions, tigers, zebras and storks, taxidermist Deyrolle opened in 1831. In addition to stuffed animals (for rent and sale), it stocks minerals, shells, corals and crustaceans, stand-mounted ostrich eggs and pedagogical storyboards. There are also rare and unusual seeds (including many old types of tomato), gardening tools and accessories.

Le Petit Prince   Concept Store
(Map p254; https://le-petit-prince-store-paris. business.site; 8 rue Grégoire Tours, 6e; ⊗11am-7pm Mon-Sat, 1-7pm Sun; MOdéon) Fronted by a midnight-blue facade, this magical boutique is solely devoted to the world of Le Petit Prince (the Little Prince), the golden-haired protagonist from Antoine de Saint-Exupéry's poignant 1943 novella. Its shelves are filled with adorable cuddly toys, figurines, magnets, key rings, T-shirts (for adults and kids), puzzles, crockery, placemats, stationery, posters and various imprints of the classic book.

Hermès   Fashion & Accessories
(Map p262; ☎01 42 22 80 83; www.hermes.com; 17 rue de Sèvres, 6e; ⊗10.30am-7pm Mon-Sat; MSèvres-Babylone) A stunning art deco swimming pool (originally belonging to neighbouring Hôtel Lutetia) now houses luxury label Hermès' inaugural concept store. Retaining its mosaic tiles and iron balustrades, the vast, tiered space showcases new directions in home furnishings, including fabrics and wallpaper, along with classic lines such as its signature scarves. Its cafe, Le Plongeoir (the Diving Board), is equally chic.

JB Guanti   Fashion & Accessories
(Map p262; www.jbguanti.com; 59 rue de Rennes, 6e; ⊗10am-7pm Mon-Sat; MSt-Sulpice) For the ultimate finishing touch, the men's and women's gloves at this boutique, which specialises solely in gloves, are the epitome of both style and comfort, whether unlined,

silk lined, cashmere lined, lambskin lined or trimmed with rabbit fur.

La Dernière Goutte
Wine

(Map p254; ☑01 43 29 11 62; www.facebook.com/dernieregoutteparis; 6 rue du Bourbon le Château, 6e; ◷3-8pm Mon, 10.30am-8pm Tue-Sat, 11am-7pm Sun; Ⓜ Mabillon) 'The Last Drop' is the brainchild of Cuban-American sommelier Juan Sánchez, whose tiny wine shop is packed with exciting, mostly organic French *vins de propriétaires* (estate-bottled wines) made by small independent producers. Wine classes lasting two hours (two white tastings, five red) regularly take place in English (per person €55); it also hosts free tastings with winemakers most Saturdays.

Sabbia Rosa
Fashion & Accessories

(Map p262; ☑01 45 48 88 37; 73 rue des Sts-Pères, 6e; ◷10am-7pm Mon-Sat; Ⓜ St-Germain des Prés) Only French-sourced fabrics (silk from Lyon, lace from Calais) are used by lingerie designer Sabbia Rosa for her ultra-luxe range at this boutique, open since 1976. Every piece is unique; items can be custom-made in 48 hours. The list of clients reads like a who's who: Serge Gainsbourg, Madonna, Naomi Campbell, Claudia Schiffer and George Clooney have all shopped here.

Red Wheelbarrow
Books

(Map p260; ☑01 42 01 81 47; www.theredwheelbarrowbookstore.com; 9 rue de Médicis, 6e; ◷10am-7pm Mon-Wed, 10am-8pm Thu-Sat, 11am-6pm Sun; Ⓜ Odéon, RER Luxembourg) Independent English-language bookshop the Red Wheelbarrow, an institution in Le Marais from 2001 to 2012, delighted its customers when it reopened near the Jardin du Luxembourg in 2018. Its children's section, with French and English titles, remains particularly strong; titles also span contemporary literature, poetry, history and politics. Events and readings take place outside shop hours; check the agenda online.

Alexandra Sojfer
Fashion & Accessories

(Map p262; ☑01 42 22 17 02; www.alexandrasojfer.com; 218 bd St-Germain, 7e; ◷10am-7pm Mon-Sat; Ⓜ Rue du Bac) One-of-a-kind high-fashion *parapluies* (parasols) and *ombrelles* (umbrellas) as well as *cannes* (walking sticks) are handmade by Alexandra Sojfer, who bought this 1834-opened atelier in 2002, and whose family has been in the business for generations. If nothing on display catches your fancy, you can have one custom-made.

⊙ Montparnasse & Southern Paris

Biérocratie
Drinks

(☑01 53 80 16 10; www.bierocratie.com; 32 rue de l'Espérance, 13e; ◷11am-8pm Tue & Thu-Sat, 4-8pm Wed; Ⓜ Corvisart) Craft beers from around the world (such as English Weird Beard, Canadian Dieu du Cieu, Danish Ianø, and Belgian Deus Brut des Flandres) but especially France (including Île-de-France-brewed La Baleine, Distrikt and Parisis) fill this bottle-lined specialist shop. It's run by fun-loving young husband-and-wife team Jaclyn and Pierre. Look out for Friday-evening tastings where you can meet the brewers.

Adam Montparnasse
Arts & Crafts

(Map p262; ☑01 43 20 68 53; 11 bd Edgar Quinet, 14e; ◷9.30am-7pm Mon-Sat; Ⓜ Edgar Quinet) If Paris' art galleries have inspired you, pick up paintbrushes, charcoals, pastels, sketchpads, watercolours, oils, acrylics, canvases and more at this historic shop. Picasso, Brancusi and Giacometti were among Édouard Adam's clients. Another seminal client was Yves Klein, with whom Adam developed the ultramarine 'Klein blue' – the VLB25 'Klein Blue' varnish is sold exclusively here.

BAR OPEN

Coffee roasteries, cocktails, classic cafes
& cutting-edge wine bars

Bar Open

For the French, drinking and eating go together like wine and cheese, and the line between a cafe, salon de thé (tearoom), bistro, brasserie, bar, and even bar à vins (wine bar) is blurred. The line between drinking and clubbing is often nonexistent – a cafe that's quiet midafternoon might have DJ sets in the evening and dancing later on. Many Parisians live in tiny apartments, and cafes and bars have traditionally served as the salon they don't have – a place to meet friends over un verre (glass of wine), read for hours over un café (coffee), debate politics while downing an espresso at a zinc counter, swill cocktails during apéro (aperitif; pre-dinner-drink) time or get the party started aboard a floating club on the Seine.

In This Section

Opening Hours

Many cafes and bars open first thing in the morning, around 7am. Closing time for tends to be 2am, though some have licences until dawn. Club hours vary depending on the venue, day and event.

Previous page: Parisian bar
RAMIRO OLACIREGUI/GETTY IMAGES ©

Montmartre & Northern Paris
Local gems include canal-side cafes (p175)

Champs-Élysées & Grands Boulevards
Swanky hotel bars, glam nightclubs (p172)

Louvre & Les Halles
Eclectic mix of bars and clubs (p173)

Le Marais, Ménilmontant & Belleville
Hip, edgy bars and nightlife venues (p177)

Seine

Eiffel Tower & Western Paris
Classy bars and sunny cafes (p172)

St-Germain & Les Invalides
Historic literary cafes, stylish bars (p183)

Latin Quarter
Spirited student pubs and bars (p181)

Bastille & Eastern Paris
Lively clubs and bars galore (p181)

Montparnasse & Southern Paris
Boulevard-facing brasseries and backstreet cafes (p185)

Costs/Tipping

Costs An espresso/glass of wine/cocktail starts at around €2/3.50/9; a *demi* (half-pint) of beer costs from €3.50. Club admission ranges in price from free to around €20; it's often cheaper before 1am.

Tipping Not necessary at the bar. If drinks are brought to your table, tip as you would in a restaurant.

Useful Phrases

Un café Single shot of espresso.

Un café allongé Espresso with hot water.

Un café au lait Coffee with milk.

Un café crème Espresso with steamed milk.

Un double Double espresso.

Une noisette Espresso with a spot of milk.

The Best...

Experience Paris' finest drinking establishments

Wine Bars

Le Garde Robe (p173) Affordable natural wines and unpretentious vibe.
Le Baron Rouge (p181) Wonderfully convivial barrel-filled wine bar.
Au Sauvignon (p183) Original zinc bar and hand-painted ceiling.

Beer

Paname Brewing Company (p175; pictured) Craft-brewery taproom in a 19th-century waterside granary with a floating pontoon.
Outland (p181) Artisan beer bar serving Outland's own beers.

Cocktails

Experimental Cocktail Club (p173) Speakeasy that spawned an international empire.
Le Syndicat (p175; pictured) Cocktails incorporate rare French spirits.
Tiger (p185) Gin specialist with 130 varieties.
Cod House (p184) Sake-based cocktails pair with gourmet small plates.

Coffee

Beans on Fire (p178) Collaborative roastery and cafe.
La Caféothèque (p179) Coffee house and roastery with an in-house coffee school.
Coutume Café (p183) Artisan roastery with a flagship Left Bank cafe.

Clubs

Le Rex Club (p174; pictured) Renowned house and techno club with a phenomenal sound system.

Concrete (p181) Paris' first club with a 24-hour licence, aboard a barge by Gare de Lyon.

Tearooms

Mariage Frères (p183) Paris' oldest and finest tearoom, founded in 1854.

La Mosquée (p109) Sip sweet mint tea and nibble delicious pastries at Paris' mosque.

Noglu (p185) Cakes, biscuits and savoury treats.

Angelina (p174; pictured) 1903 tearoom now frequented for its decadent hot chocolate.

Pavement Terraces

Chez Prune (p176) The boho cafe that put Canal St-Martin on the map.

Café des Anges (p181) The terrace of this 11e cafe buzzes night and day.

Shakespeare & Company Café (p181; pictured) Live the Parisian Left Bank literary dream.

Lonely Planet's Top Choices

Bar Hemingway (p173) Legendary cocktails inside the Ritz.

Pavillon Puebla (p175) Park-set pavilion.

Le Perchoir (p177) Hip rooftop bar best visited at sunset.

Les Deux Magots (p183) Famous St-Germain literary cafe.

Candelaria (p177) Clandestine cocktail bar.

Eiffel Tower & Western Paris

St James Paris   Bar

(www.saint-james-paris.com; 5 place du Chancelier Adenauer, 16e; ⏰7pm-1am; 🛜; MPorte Dauphine) Hidden behind a stone wall, this historic mansion-turned-hotel opens its bar nightly to nonguests – and the setting redefines extraordinary. Winter drinks are in the wood-panelled library; summer drinks are on the impossibly romantic 300-sq-metre garden terrace with giant balloon-shaped gazebos (the first hot-air balloons took flight here). It has over 70 cocktails and an adjoining Michelin-starred restaurant.

Yoyo   Club

(Map p252; www.yoyo-paris.com; 13 av du Président Wilson, 16e; ⏰hours vary; MIéna) Deep in the basement of the Palais de Tokyo, Yoyo has an edgy, raw-concrete Berlin-style vibe and a capacity of 800. Techno and house dominate, with diversions into hip-hop, electro, funk, disco, R&B and soul. Hours can vary; check the website to see what's happening when.

Bô Zinc Café   Bar

(📞01 42 24 69 05; 59 av Mozart, 16e; ⏰7am-2am; MRanelagh) With its soft sage-green facade and buzzing pavement terrace, Bô Zinc is one of those great hybrid addresses – perfect for hanging with locals over coffee, tea or after-work cocktails. Seating is a mix of wooden bistro chairs and 'flop-in' armchairs, while potted palm trees – inside and out – add a touch of chic. Top-notch nosh too, served until 11pm.

Champs-Élysées & Grands Boulevards

Honor   Coffee

(Map p252; www.honor-cafe.com; 54 rue du Faubourg St-Honoré, 8e; ⏰9am-6pm Mon-Fri, 10am-6pm Sat; MMadeleine) Hidden off ritzy rue du Faubourg St-Honoré in a courtyard adjoining fashion house Comme des Garçons is Paris' 'first and only outdoor independent coffee shop', an

Hôtel Ritz, home to Bar Hemingway

opaque-plastic-sheltered black-and-white timber kiosk brewing coffee from small-scale producers around the globe. It also serves luscious cakes, filled-to-bursting lunchtime sandwiches, quiches and salads (dishes €5 to €10.50), along with fresh juices, wine and beer.

Le PanPan   Bar

(Map p254; ☑01 42 46 36 06; https://lepanpan. business.site; 32 rue Drouot, 9e; ☺10am-3pm & 6pm-midnight Mon-Wed, 10am-3pm & 6pm-2am Thu & Fri, 6pm-2am Sat; ⓂLe Peletier) This unassuming locals' hang-out doesn't even bother with a sign, but it keeps things interesting with activities, like blind taste tests, throughout the week. Happy hour from 6pm to 8pm.

❼ Louvres & Les Halles

Bar Hemingway   Cocktail Bar

(Map p252; www.ritzparis.com; Hôtel Ritz Paris, 15 place Vendôme, 1er; ☺6pm-2am; ☎; ⓂOpéra) Black-and-white photos and memorabilia (hunting trophies, old typewriters and framed handwritten letters by the great writer) fill this snug bar inside the Ritz. Head bartender Colin Peter Field mixes monumental cocktails, including three different Bloody Marys made with juice from freshly squeezed seasonal tomatoes. Legend has it that Hemingway himself, wielding a machine gun, helped liberate the bar during WWII.

Le Garde Robe   Wine Bar

(Map p254; ☑01 49 26 90 60; 41 rue de l'Arbre Sec, 1er; ☺noon-1am Mon-Sat; ⓂLouvre Rivoli) Le Garde Robe is possibly the world's only bar to serve alcohol alongside a detox menu. While you probably shouldn't come here for the full-on cleansing experience, you can definitely expect excellent, afforda-ble *vins naturels* (natural wines) – wines produced from organically grown grapes using few or no pesticides or additives. You can also expect a casual atmosphere and a good selection of food, ranging from cheese and charcuterie plates to

adventurous options (tuna gravlax with black quinoa and guacamole).

Experimental Cocktail Club   Cocktail Bar

(ECC; Map p254; www.experimentalcocktailclub. fr; 37 rue St-Sauveur, 2e; ☺7pm-2am; ⓂRéaumur Sébastopol) With a black curtain facade, this retro-chic speakeasy – with sister bars in London, Ibiza, New York and, *bien sûr,* Paris – is a sophisticated flashback to those *années folles* (crazy years) of Prohibi-tion New York. Cocktails are individual and fabulous, and DJs keep the party going until dawn at weekends. It's not a large space, however, and fills to capacity quickly.

Danico   Cocktail Bar

(Map p254; www.facebook.com/danicoparis; 6 rue Vivienne, 2e; ☺6pm-2am; ⓂBourse) While not exactly a secret, Danico still feels like one – first you'll need to find the hidden, candlelit backroom in **Daroco** (☑01 42 21 93 71; www.daroco.fr; mains €17-47, pizzas €11-17; ☺noon-midnight; ☑) before you get to treat yourself to one of Nico de Soto's extrav-agant cocktails. Chia seeds, kombucha tea, ghost peppers and pomegranate Champagne are some of the more unusual ingredients you'll find on the drink list.

Harry's New York Bar   Cocktail Bar

(Map p252; ☑01 42 61 71 14; www.facebook. com/harrysnewyorkbarparis; 5 rue Daunou, 2e; ☺noon-2am Mon-Sat, 4pm-1am Sun; ⓂOpéra) One of the most popular American-style bars in the prewar years, Harry's once wel-comed writers including F Scott Fitzgerald and Ernest Hemingway, who no doubt sam-pled the bar's unique cocktail and creation: the Bloody Mary. The Cuban mahogany interior dates from the mid-19th century and was brought over from a Manhattan bar in 1911.

Frog & Underground   Pub

(Map p254; www.frogpubs.com; 176 rue Montmar-tre, 2e; ☺8am-1am Mon & Tue, 8am-2am Wed, 8am-3am Thu, 8am-4.30am Fri, 9am-4.30am Sat, 9am-1am Sun; ☎; ⓂGrands Boulevards) FrogPubs has been brewing in Paris since

JANINE EBERLE/LONELY PLANET ©

Paname Brewing Company

1993, and this central rue Montmartre venue is its best yet. Spread over a cavernous ground floor and opening to a terrace, a vaulted cellar with a dance floor and upstairs lounge (spanning 370 sq metres in all), its exciting beers include a wonderfully crisp dry-hopped Hopster pale ale.

Lockwood   Cocktail Bar

(Map p254; ☑01 77 32 97 21; www.lockwood paris.com; 73 rue d'Aboukir, 2e; ◷6pm-2am Mon-Fri, 10am-4pm & 6pm-2am Sat, 10am-4pm Sun; Ⓜ Sentier) Cocktails incorporating premium spirits such as Hendrick's rose- and cucumber-infused gin and Pierre Ferrand curaçao are served in Lockwood's stylish ground-floor lounge and subterranean candle-lit cellar. It's especially buzzing on weekends, when brunch stretches out between 10am and 4pm, with Bloody Marys, coffee brewed with Parisian-roasted Belleville Brûlerie (p158) beans and fare including eggs Benedict and Florentine (dishes €10 to €15).

Le Rex Club   Club

(Map p254; ☑01 42 36 10 96; www.rexclub.com; 5 bd Poissonnière, 2e; ◷11.45pm-7am Wed-Sat; Ⓜ Bonne Nouvelle) Attached to the art deco Grand Rex cinema, this is Paris' premier house and techno venue where some of the world's hottest DJs strut their stuff on a 70-speaker, multidiffusion sound system.

Angelina   Teahouse

(Map p252; ☑01 42 60 82 00; www.angelina-paris.fr; 226 rue de Rivoli, 1er; ◷7.30am-7pm Mon-Fri, 8.30am-7.30pm Sat & Sun; Ⓜ Tuileries) Clink china with lunching ladies, their posturing poodles and half the students from Tokyo University at Angelina, a grande-dame tearoom dating from 1903. Decadent pastries are served here, but it's the super-thick 'African' hot chocolate (€8.20), which comes with a pot of whipped cream and a carafe of water, that prompts the constant queue for a table.

🏛 Montmartre & Northern Paris

Le Syndicat   Cocktail Bar

(Map p254; www.syndicatcocktailclub.com; 51 rue du Faubourg St-Denis, 10e; ⏱6pm-2am Mon-Sat, from 7pm Sun; Ⓜ Château d'Eau) Plastered top to bottom in peeling posters, an otherwise unmarked facade conceals one of Paris' hottest cocktail bars, but it's no fly-by-night. Le Syndicat's subtitle, Organisation de Défense des Spiritueux Français, reflects its impassioned commitment to French spirits. Ingeniously crafted (and named) cocktails include Saix en Provence (Armagnac, chilli syrup, lime and lavender).

Le Très Particulier   Cocktail Bar

(Map p250; ☎01 53 41 81 40; www.hotel-particulier-montmartre.com; Pavillon D, 23 av Junot, 18e; ⏱6pm-2am Tue-Sat; Ⓜ Lamarck–Caulaincourt) The clandestine cocktail bar of boutique Hôtel Particulier Montmartre is an entrancing spot for a summertime alfresco cocktail. Ring the buzzer at the unmarked black gated entrance and make a beeline for the 1871 mansion's flowery walled garden (or, if it's raining, the adjacent conservatory-style interior). DJs spin tunes from 9.30pm Wednesday to Saturday.

Gravity Bar   Cocktail Bar

(Map p256; www.facebook.com/gravitybar; 44 rue des Vinaigriers, 10e; ⏱6pm-2am Tue-Sat; Ⓜ Jacques Bonsergent) Gravity's stunning wavelike interior, crafted from slats of plywood descending to the curved concrete bar, threatens to distract from the business at hand – serious cocktails, such as Back to My Roots (Provence herb-infused vodka, vermouth, raspberry purée and lemon juice), best partaken in the company of excellent and inventive tapas-style small plates such as clam gnocchi.

Pavillon Puebla   Beer Garden

(Map p256; www.leperchoir.tv; Parc des Buttes Chaumont, 39 av Simon Bolivar, 19e; ⏱6pm-2am Wed-Fri, from noon Sat, noon-10pm Sun; 🛜; Ⓜ Buttes Chaumont) Strung with fairy lights, this rustic ivy-draped cottage's two

🍷 French Wine

Wine is easily the most popular beverage in Paris and house wine can cost less than bottled water. Of France's dozens of wine-producing regions, the principal ones are Burgundy, Bordeaux, the Rhône and the Loire valleys, Champagne, Languedoc, Provence and Alsace. Wines are generally named after the location of the vineyard rather than the grape varietal. The best wines are Appellation d'Origine Contrôlée (AOC; currently being relabelled Appellation d'Origine Protégée, AOP), meaning they meet stringent regulations governing where, how and under what conditions they're grown, fermented and bottled.

rambling terraces in the Parc des Buttes Chaumont evoke a *guinguette* (old-fashioned outdoor tavern/dance venue), with a 21st-century vibe provided by its Moroccan decor, contemporary furniture, and DJ beats from Thursdays to Saturdays. Alongside mostly French wines and craft beers, cocktails include its signature Spritz du Pavillon (Aperol, Prosecco and soda).

Paname Brewing Company   Brewery

(www.panamebrewingcompany.com; 41bis quai de la Loire, 19e; ⏱11am-2am; 🛜; Ⓜ Crimée, Laumiere) Spectacularly situated in an industrial 1850s former granary on Bassin de la Villette, Paname's tap room has floor-to-ceiling windows and opens onto a terrace shaded by an ancient cherry tree and a floating table-strewn pontoon. Its five

here on site in the multiethnic La Goutte d'Or neighbourhood adjacent to its cafe. Brews include filter coffee (mug, Aeropress or Chemex) and wacky creations like Bleu d'Auvergne cheese dipped in espresso or tonic water with espresso. Three-hour coffee workshops in French or English (filter techniques, world coffee tours, latte art) start from €72.

Parisian Craft Beer

Beer hasn't traditionally had a high profile in France and mass-produced varieties such as Kronenbourg 1664 (5.5%), brewed in Strasbourg, dominate. Paris' growing *bière artisanale* (craft beer) scene, however, is going from strength to strength, with an increasing number of city breweries, such as **Brasserie BapBap** (Map p256; 01 77 17 52 97; www.bapbap.paris; 79 rue St-Maur, 11e; guided tours €15; ⊙1½hr guided tours 11am Sat, shop 6-8pm Tue-Fri, from 3pm Sat; MRue St-Maur) and **Brasserie la Goutte d'Or** (Map p250; 09 80 64 23 51; www.brasserielagouttedor.com; 28 rue de la Goutte d'Or, 18e; ⊙5-7pm Thu & Fri, from 2pm Sat; MChâteau Rouge, Barbès-Rochechouart) FREE, microbreweries and cafes offering limited-production brews on tap and by the bottle. The city's artisan-beer festival, **Paris Beer Week** (www.laparisbeerweek.com; ⊙early Jun), takes place in brasseries, bars and specialist beer shops, usually in early June. An excellent resource for hopheads is www.hoppyparis.com.

seasonal beers typically include a Pilsner, session, Märzen, Berliner Weisse, pale ale or IPA (look out for them around Paris too).

Café Lomi — Coffee

(09 51 27 46 31; www.lomi.paris; 3ter rue Marcadet, 18e; ⊙8am-6pm Mon-Fri, 10am-7pm Sat & Sun; MMarcadet–Poissonnière) Lomi's internationally sourced beans are roasted

Chez Prune — Bar

(Map p256; 36 rue Beaurepaire, 10e, cnr quai de Valmy; ⊙8am-2am Mon-Sat, 10am-2am Sun; MJacques Bonsergent, République) This boho cafe put Canal St-Martin on the map and its good vibes, original mosaic-tiled interior and rough-around-the-edges look show no sign of disappearing in the near future. Chez Prune remains one of those timeless classic Paris addresses, fabulous for hanging out and people-watching any time of day. Weekend brunch buzzes.

La Fontaine de Belleville — Coffee

(Map p256; www.cafesbelleville.com; 31-33 rue Juliette Dodu, 10e; ⊙8am-10pm; MColonel Fabien) Beans roasted by Belleville Brûlerie are the toast of Paris and the roastery has since opened its own cafe near Canal St-Martin, updating a long-standing local corner spot with gold lettering, woven sky-blue-and-cream bistro chairs and matching tables, and retaining its vintage fittings. Spectacular coffee is complemented by sandwiches, salads and small sharing plates.

CopperBay — Cocktail Bar

(Map p256; www.copperbay.fr; 5 rue Bouchardon, 10e; ⊙6pm-2am Tue-Sat; MStrasbourg–St-Denis) This sleek cocktail bar's floor-to-ceiling windows, polished pale-wood decor and glistening copper fixtures and fittings inject a generous dose of design flair into proceedings. The cocktail menu mixes classics with house specials such as L'Orangeraie (Japanese pepper-infused gin, ginger, lemon juice and orange blossom water) and Le Bouillon (coriander-infused vodka, red lentil purée, verjus, mescal and zaatar syrup).

Hardware Société   Coffee

(Map p250; ☎01 42 51 69 03; 10 rue Lamarck,
18e; ⏱9am-4pm Thu-Mon; ☎; MChâteau Rouge)
With its black-and-white floor, Christian
Lacroix butterflies fluttering across one
wall and perfect love-heart-embossed
cappuccinos, this is a fine spot around
the Sacré-Cœur to linger over superb
barista-crafted coffee (yes, that is a Slayer
espresso machine). It's the Paris outpost
of Melbourne's Hardware Société, with
bountiful breakfasts and brunches served
at marble-topped tables.

Lipstick   Cocktail Bar

(Map p250; www.facebook.com/lipstickbar; 5
rue Frochot, 9e; ⏱6pm-5am Tue-Sat; MPigalle)
If the name isn't a clue, the decor certainly
is: its bordello-like leopard-print lounges,
red velour drapes and a pole in the centre
of the bar reflect its former incarnation as a
brothel in this gentrifying red-light district.
Stupendous cocktails include Queen P
(rose syrup, gin, Aperol, ginger ale and
grapefruit juice).

🍷 Le Marais, Ménilmontant & Belleville

Candelaria   Cocktail Bar

(Map p256; www.quixotic-projects.com; 52 rue
de Saintonge, 3e; ⏱bar 6pm-2am, taqueria noon-
10.30pm Sun-Wed, to 11.30pm Thu-Sat; MFilles
du Calvaire) A lime-green taqueria serving
homemade tacos, quesadillas and tostadas
conceals one of Paris' coolest cocktail bars
through an unmarked internal door. Phenomenal cocktails made from agave spirits,
including mezcal, are inspired by Central
and South America, such as a Guatemalan
El Sombrerón (tequila, vermouth, bitters,
hibiscus syrup, pink-pepper-infused tonic
and lime). Weekend evenings kick off with
DJ sets.

Le Perchoir   Rooftop Bar

(Map p256; ☎01 48 06 18 48; www.leperchoir.tv;
14 rue Crespin du Gast, 11e; ⏱6pm-2am Tue-Sat;
☎; MMénilmontant) Sunset is the best time
to head up to this 7th-floor bar for a drink

Chez Prune

overlooking Paris' rooftops, where DJs spin on Saturday nights. Greenery provides shade in summer; in winter, it's covered by a sail-like canopy and warmed by fires burning in metal drums. It's accessed off an inner courtyard via a lift (or a spiral staircase).

Beans on Fire   Coffee
(Map p256; www.thebeansonfire.com; 7 rue du Général Blaise, 11e; ⊘8.30am-5pm Mon-Fri, 9.30am-6pm Sat & Sun; 🛜; MSt-Ambroise) Outstanding coffee is guaranteed at this innovative space. Not only a welcoming local cafe, it's also a collaborative roastery, where movers and shakers on Paris' reignited coffee scene come to roast their beans (ask about two-hour roasting workshops, available in English, if you're keen to roast your own). Overlooking a park, the terrace is a neighbourhood hotspot on sunny days.

La Commune   Cocktail Bar
(Map p256; www.syndicatcocktailclub.com; 80 bd de Belleville, 20e; ⊘6pm-2am Tue-Sat; 🛜; MCouronnes) An atrium-style covered timber deck strewn with plants and comfy sofas marks the entrance to La Commune. Like its 10e sibling Le Syndicat (p175), cocktails made from French spirits are its raison d'être. Here, the speciality is punch bowls containing five to eight glasses, such as Bisso Na Bissap (Corsican cedar brandy, apricot liqueur, French whisky, bissap juice and fresh citrus).

Le Loir dans La Théière   Cafe
(Map p256; www.leloirdanslatheiere.com; 3 rue des Rosiers, 4e; ⊘9am-7.30pm; 🛜; MSt-Paul) The *Alice in Wonderland*–inspired Dormouse in the Teapot is a wonderful old space filled with retro toys, wooden tables, mismatched chairs and comfy couches. Its dozen different teas, poured in the company of excellent savoury tarts and desserts including its signature lemon meringue pie, ensure a constant queue on the street outside, especially for weekend brunch.

The Hood   Cafe
(Map p256; www.thehoodparis.com; 80 rue Jean-Pierre Timbaud, 11e; ⊘8am-6pm Mon, Wed & Sun, to 10pm Thu-Sat; 🛜; MParmentier) First and foremost this light-filled local hangout is about the coffee (Parisian-roasted Belleville Brûlerie beans are brewed to absolute perfection here), but it takes its music just as seriously with a great vinyl collection, spontaneous jam sessions and acoustic Sunday-afternoon 'folkoff' gigs. Fantastic lunches might include cinnamon-roasted chicken with red cabbage and soba noodles. Ask about English-language coffee-brewing workshops.

Boot Café   Coffee
(Map p256; 19 rue du Pont aux Choux, 3e; ⊘10am-6pm; 🛜; MSt-Sébastien–Froissart) The charm of this three-table cafe is its facade. An old cobbler's shop, its original washed-blue exterior, 'Cordonnerie' lettering and fantastic red-boot sign above are beautifully preserved. The excellent coffee is roasted in Paris, to boot.

Café Charbon   Bar
(Map p256; www.lecafecharbon.fr; 109 rue Oberkampf, 11e; ⊘8am-2am Sun-Wed, to 4am Thu, to 6am Fri & Sat; 🛜; MParmentier) Canopied by a gold-stencilled navy-blue awning, Charbon was the first of the hip bars to catch on in Ménilmontant and it remains one of the best. It's always crowded and worth heading to for the belle époque decor (high ceilings, chandeliers and leather booths) and sociable atmosphere. Happy hour is 5pm to 8pm; DJs and musicians play Friday and Saturday.

La Belle Hortense   Bar
(Map p256; www.cafeine.com/belle-hortense; 31 rue Vieille du Temple, 4e; ⊘5pm-2am; MHôtel de Ville) Behind its charming chambray-blue facade, this creative wine bar named after a Jacques Roubaud novel fuses shelf after shelf of literary novels with an excellent wine list, rare varieties of Armagnac, cognac, Calvados and pastis, and an enriching weekly agenda of book readings, signings and art events.

La Caféothèque — Coffee

(Map p256; ☏ 01 53 01 83 84; www.lacafe
otheque.com; 52 rue de l'Hôtel de Ville, 4e;
⏲ 8.30am-7.30pm Mon-Fri, 8.30am-9.30pm Sat,
10am-7.30pm Sun; 🛜; Ⓜ Pont Marie, St-Paul)
From the industrial grinder to elaborate
tasting notes, this coffee house and roastery is serious. Grab a seat, and pick your
bean, filtration method (Aeropress, V60
filter, piston or drip) and preparation style.
The in-house coffee school has tastings of
different crus and various courses including two-hour Saturday-morning tasting
initiations (five terroirs, five extraction
methods) for €60 (English available).

Le Mary Céleste — Cocktail Bar

(Map p256; www.quixotic-projects.com/venue/
mary-celeste; 1 rue Commines, 3e; ⏲ 6pm-2am,
kitchen 7-11.30pm; Ⓜ Filles du Calvaire) Snag
a stool at the central circular bar at this
uberpopular brick-and-timber-floored
cocktail bar or reserve one of a handful of
tables online. Innovative cocktails such as
Ahha Kapehna (grappa, absinthe, beetroot,
fennel and Champagne) are the perfect
partners to tapas-style 'small plates'
(grilled duck hearts, devilled eggs) to share.

Little Red Door — Cocktail Bar

(Map p256; ☏ 01 42 71 19 32; www.lrdparis.
com; 60 rue Charlot, 3e; ⏲ 6pm-2am Sun-Thu,
to 3am Fri & Sat; Ⓜ Filles du Calvaires) Behind
an inconspicuous timber facade, a tiny
crimson doorway is the illusionary portal
to this low-lit, bare-brick drinking den filled
with flickering candles. Ranked among the
World's 50 Best Bars, it's a must for serious
mixology fans. Its annual collection of 11
cocktails, in themes from 'art' to 'architecture', are intricately crafted from ingredients such as glacier ice and paper syrup.

Ob-La-Di — Coffee

(Map p256; www.facebook.com/obladiparis;
54 rue de Saintonge, 3e; ⏲ 8am-5pm Mon-Fri,
9am-6pm Sat & Sun; Ⓜ Filles du Calvaire) Coffee roasted by Paris' Café Lomi is the big
draw of this pocket-sized coffee shop, clad
with large mirrors, geometric blue-and-
white tiles and glass vases of fresh flowers.

⚲ LGBTI+ Venues

Le Marais, especially the areas around
the intersection of rue Ste-Croix de
la Bretonnerie and rue des Archives,
and eastwards to rue Vieille du Temple,
has long been Paris' main centre of
gay nightlife and is still the epicentre
of LGBTI+ life in Paris. There's also a
handful of bars and clubs within walking
distance of bd de Sébastopol. The lesbian scene is less prominent than its gay
counterpart, and centres on a few cafes
and bars, particularly along rue des
Écouffes. Bars and clubs are generally
all LGBTI-friendly.

These are some of our top choices:

Open Café (Map p256; www.facebook.
com/opencafeparis; 17 rue des Archives,
4e; ⏲ 11am-2am Sun-Thu, to 3am Fri & Sat;
Ⓜ Hôtel de Ville) The wide terrace is prime
for talent-watching.

Gibus Club (Map p256; ☏ 01 77 15 73 09;
www.gibusclub.fr; 18 rue du Faubourg du
Temple, 11e; admission from €13; ⏲ 11pm-
7am Thu-Sat; Ⓜ République) One of Paris'
biggest gay parties.

3w Kafé (Map p256; www.facebook.com/
3wkafe; 8 rue des Écouffes, 4e; ⏲ 7pm-3am
Wed & Sun, to 4am Thu, to 6.30am Fri &
Sat; Ⓜ St-Paul) Flagship lesbian cocktail
bar-pub.

Bar on rue des Archives
EMAD ALJUMAH/GETTY IMAGES ©

It's not designed for hanging out with your
laptop, but the crowd is hip, and the *café*,
cookies, cakes, and dishes like poached
pear, ricotta and honey on toast, superb.

Paris in a Glass

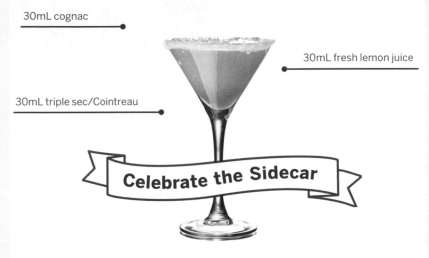

30mL cognac

30mL fresh lemon juice

30mL triple sec/Cointreau

Celebrate the Sidecar

HORTIMAGES/SHUTTERSTOCK ©

The Sidecar

This enduring classic was allegedly invented in 1923 by the Ritz' first head bar tender, Frank Meier, for an American regular who arrived by sidecar. When current head bartender Colin Peter Field updated it in 2001, his 'Ritz Sidecar', using pre-phylloxera cognac, became a Guinness World Record holder for the world's most expensive cocktail (now €1500 at Bar Hemingway).

★ Best Bars for a Sidecar

Bar Hemingway (p173)

Harry's New York Bar (p173)

Le Syndicat (p175)

Harry's New York Bar
TERRY SMITH IMAGES/ALAMY STOCK PHOTO ©

❷ Bastille & Eastern Paris

Concrete   Club
(www.concreteparis.fr; 69 Port de la Rapée, 12e; ⏰from 10pm Thu-Mon; MGare de Lyon) Moored by Gare de Lyon on a barge on the Seine, this wild-child club with two dance floors is famed for introducing an 'after-hours' element to Paris' somewhat staid clubbing scene, with the country's first 24-hour licence. Watch social media for world-class electro DJ appearances and all-weekend events.

Le Baron Rouge   Wine Bar
(Map p259; www.lebaronrouge.net; 1 rue Théophile Roussel, 12e; ⏰5-10pm Mon, 10am-2pm & 5-10pm Tue-Fri, 10am-10pm Sat, 10am-4pm Sun; MLedru-Rollin) Just about the ultimate Parisian wine-bar experience, this wonderfully unpretentious local meeting place, where everyone is welcome, has barrels stacked against the bottle-lined walls and serves cheese, charcuterie and oysters in season. It's especially busy on Sunday after the Marché d'Aligre wraps up. For a small deposit, you can fill up 1L bottles straight from the barrel for less than €5.

Outland   Craft Beer
(Map p259; www.outland-beer.com; 6 rue Émile Lepeu, 11e; ⏰6pm-2am Mon-Sat, to midnight Sun; MCharonne) Of the 12 beers on tap at this artisanal beer bar, eight are Outland's own, brewed just east of central Paris in Fontenay-sous-Bois near the Bois de Vincennes. Among them are a double IPA, a session pale ale, a porter and a fabulously fermented plum göse. Soak them up with tapas like duck liver pâté, organic burrata and stuffed calamari.

Café des Anges   Cafe
(Map p259; ☎01 47 00 00 63; www.cafedes angesparis.com; 66 rue de la Roquette, 11e; ⏰7.30am-2am; 🛜; MBastille) With its pastel-shaded paintwork and locals sipping coffee beneath the terracotta-coloured awning on its busy pavement terrace, Angels Cafe lives up to the 'quintessential Paris cafe' dream. In winter snuggle

beneath a blanket outside, or squeeze through the crowds at the zinc bar to snag a coveted table inside. Happy hour runs from 5pm to 9pm.

Bluebird   Cocktail Bar
(Map p259; 12 rue St-Bernard, 11e; ⏰6pm-2am; MFaidherbe-Chaligny) The ultimate neighbourhood hang-out. Bluebird is styled like a 1950s apartment with retro decor, a giant fish tank along one wall, and a soundtrack of smooth lounge music. Cocktail recipes date from the 1800s and early 1900s and change seasonally, but the menu always features six gin-based creations, six with other spirits, and three low-alcohol wine- and Champagne-based drinks.

Le Pure Café   Cafe
(Map p259; www.lepurecafe.fr; 14 rue Jean Macé, 11e; ⏰7am-2am; MCharonne) A classic Parisian corner cafe, Le Pure is a charming spot to drop into for a morning coffee, aperitif, contemporary bistro meal or Sunday brunch. Its selection of natural and organic wines by the glass is particularly good. Film buffs might recognise its cherry-red facade and vintage-wood and zinc bar from the Richard Linklater film *Before Sunset*.

❷ Latin Quarter

Shakespeare & Company Café   Cafe
(Map p260; www.shakespeareandcompany. com; 2 rue St-Julien le Pauvre, 5e; ⏰9.30am-7pm Mon-Fri, to 8pm Sat & Sun; 🛜; MSt-Michel) ✈ Instant history was made when this literary-inspired cafe opened in 2015 adjacent to magical bookshop Shakespeare & Company (p161), designed from long-lost sketches to fulfil late bookshop founder George Whitman's 1960s dream. Organic chai tea, turbo-power juices and specialist coffee by Parisian roaster Café Lomi (p176) marry with soups, salads, bagels and pastries by **Bob's Juice Bar** (Map p256; ☎09 50 06 36 18; www. bobsjuicebar.com; 15 rue Lucien Sampaix, 10e; dishes €3.50-6, pastries €1.75-3; ⏰8am-3pm Mon-Fri, 9.30am-4.30pm Sat; ☒; MJacques Bonsergent).

L'Académie de la Bière — Pub

(☎01 43 54 66 65; www.academie-biere.
com; 88bis bd de Port Royal, 5e; ⊗10am-2am;
ⓂVavin or RER Port Royal) Serious students
of Belgian beer should head to this 'beer
academy' to try its 12 on tap or choose
from more than 150 bottled varieties,
including Trappist (Monk-made) beers like
prized Westmalle, abbey beers including
Grimbergen and Leffe, fruit beers, and Can-
tillon gueuze (double-fermented Lambic
beer made in Brussels). Happy hour is an
early starter, from 3.30pm to 7.30pm.

Nuage — Cafe

(Map p260; ☎09 82 39 80 69; www.nuagecafe.
fr; 14 rue des Carmes, 5e; per hr/day €5/25;
⊗9am-7pm Mon-Fri, 11am-8pm Sat & Sun;
🛜; ⓂMaubert-Mutualité) One of a crop of
co-working cafes to mushroom in Paris,
Nuage (Cloud) lures a loyal following of
nomadic digital creatives with its cosy,
homelike spaces in an old church (and subsequent school where Cyrano de Bergerac
apparently studied). Payment is by the
hour or day, craft coffee is by Parisian
roaster Coutume and gourmet snacks
stave off hunger pangs.

Le Verre à Pied — Cafe

(Map p260; ☎01 43 31 15 72; www.vie-mouffe
tard.fr; 118bis rue Mouffetard, 5e; ⊗9am-9pm
Tue-Sat, to 3.30pm Sun; ⓂCensier Daubenton)
This café-tabac (cafe plus a tobacconist) is
a pearl of a place where little has changed
since 1870. Its nicotine-hued mirrored wall,
moulded cornices and original bar make
it part of a dying breed, but it epitomises
the charm, glamour and romance of an old
Paris everyone loves, including stallholders
from the rue Mouffetard market who yo-yo
in and out.

Strada Café — Coffee

(Map p260; www.facebook.com/stradacafe94;
24 rue Monge, 5e; ⊗8am-6.30pm Mon-Fri,
10am-6.30pm Sat & Sun; 🛜; ⓂCardinal Lemoine)
Beans from Parisian roastery L'Arbre à Café
and Lyon's Mokxa roastery underpin the
success of this sunlit corner cafe, strewn
with an eclectic mix of armchairs and
wooden-chair seating. Electrical sockets
are plentiful (no laptops at weekends) and

Les Deux Magots

international baristas are passionate about their brews. Breakfast, salad-and-soup lunch (€11.50 to €13.50), weekend brunch (€22) and gluten-free cakes.

St-Germain & Les Invalides

Les Deux Magots   Cafe
(Map p262; ☑01 45 48 55 25; www.lesdeux magots.fr; 6 place St-Germain des Prés, 6e; ⊘7.30am-1am; MSt-Germain des Prés) If ever there was a cafe that summed up St-Germain des Prés' early-20th-century literary scene, it's this former hang-out of anyone who was anyone. You'll spend substantially more here to sip *un café* (€4.80) in a wicker chair on the pavement terrace shaded by dark-green awnings and geraniums spilling from window boxes, but it's an undeniable piece of Parisian history.

Au Sauvignon   Wine Bar
(Map p262; ☑01 45 48 49 02; www.ausauvignon. com; 80 rue des Sts-Pères, 7e; ⊘8am-11pm Mon-Sat, 9am-10pm Sun; MSèvres-Babylone) Grab a table in the evening light at this wonderfully authentic wine bar or head to the quintessential bistro interior, with original zinc bar, tightly packed tables and hand-painted ceiling celebrating French viticultural tradition. A plate of *casse-croûtes au pain Poilâne* (toast with ham, pâté, terrine, smoked salmon and foie gras) is the perfect accompaniment.

Bar Joséphine   Cocktail Bar
(Map p262; www.hotellutetia.com; 45 bd Raspail, 6e; ⊘11am-1am; ☎; MSèvres–Babylone) Named for former regular, entertainer and French Resistance activist Josephine Baker, glamorous Bar Joséphine is within the grand 1910-built Hôtel Lutetia, which reopened in 2018 (the bar's pastel frescoes have been restored). Jazz (live and recorded) is a fitting soundtrack to accompany a signature cocktail such as a Rive Gauche (Guillotine vodka, St-Germain liquor, citrus and celery shrub, and Champagne).

Coffee & Tea

Coffee has always been Parisians' drink of choice to kick-start the day. So it's surprising, particularly given France's fixation on quality, that Parisian coffee long lagged behind world standards, with burnt, poor-quality beans and unrefined preparation methods. However, Paris' coffee revolution has seen local roasteries like Belleville Brûlerie and Coutume priming cafes citywide for outstanding brews made by professional baristas, often using cutting-edge extraction techniques. Caffeine fiends are now spoilt for choice and while there's still plenty of substandard coffee in Paris, you don't have to go far to avoid it.

Surprisingly, too, tea – more strongly associated with France's northwestern neighbours the UK and Ireland – is extremely popular in Paris. Tearooms offer copious varieties; learn about its history at the tea museum within the original Marais branch of **Mariage Frères** (Map p256; www.mariagefreres.com; 30, 32 & 35 rue du Bourg Tibourg, 4e; ⊘noon-7pm; MHôtel de Ville).

Coutume Café   Coffee
(Map p262; ☑01 45 51 50 47; www.coutumecafe. com; 47 rue de Babylone, 7e; ⊘8.30am-5.30pm Mon-Fri, 9am-6pm Sat & Sun; ☎; MSt-François Xavier) ✔ The Parisian coffee revolution is thanks in no small part to Coutume, artisanal roaster of premium beans for scores

⛩ Nightlife in Paris

Paris' residential make-up means nightclubs aren't ubiquitous. Lacking a mainstream scene, clubbing here tends to be underground and extremely mobile. The best DJs and their followings have short stints in a certain venue before moving on, and the scene's hippest *soirées clubbing* (clubbing events) float between venues – including the many dance-driven bars. In 2017 floating club Concrete (p181) became France's first to have a 24-hour licence. Dedicated clubbers may also want to check out the growing suburban scene – much more alternative and spontaneous in nature but also harder to reach.

Wherever you wind up, the beat is strong. Electronic music is of a particularly high quality in Paris' clubs, with some excellent local house and techno. Funk and groove are also popular, and the Latin scene is huge; salsa-dancing and Latino-music nights pack out plenty of clubs. World music also has a following in Paris, where everything – from Algerian raï to Senegalese *mbalax* and West Indian *zouk* – goes at clubs. R&B and hip-hop pickings are decent, if not extensive.

Track tomorrow's hot 'n' happening soirée with these finger-on-the-pulse Parisian-nightlife links.

Paris Bouge (www.parisbouge.com) Comprehensive listings site.

Paris DJs (www.parisdjs.com) Free downloads to get you in the groove.

Sortir à Paris (www.sortiraparis.com) Click on 'Soirées & Bars', then 'Nuits Parisiennes'.

Tribu de Nuit (www.tribudenuit.com) Parties, club events and concerts galore.

of establishments around town. Its flagship cafe – a light-filled, post-industrial space – is ground zero for innovative preparation methods including cold extraction and siphon brews. Couple some of Paris' finest coffee with tasty, seasonal cuisine and the place is always packed out.

Cod House   Cocktail Bar

(Map p260; ☏ 01 42 49 35 59; www.thecodhouse. fr; 1 rue de Condé, 6e; ☺ noon-2.30pm & 6-11pm; Ⓜ Odéon) 'Oh my cod!' screams the turquoise-neon 'tag' on the wall, and indeed, this Japanese-inspired cocktail and tapas bar with eggshell-blue and exposed-stone interior does excite. Sake-based cocktails play around with matcha-infused cachaca, ginger-infused pisco, homemade lemongrass syrup and fresh yuzu. Creative small plates (€5 to €16) might include shrimp tempura, yellowtail carpaccio with fresh chilli, and deep-fried chicken wontons.

Le Bar des Prés   Cocktail Bar

(Map p262; ☏ 01 43 25 87 67; www.lebardespres. com; 25 rue du Dragon, 6e; ☺ noon-2.30pm & 7-11pm; Ⓜ St-Sulpice) Sake-based craft cocktails and tantalising shared plates (€24 to €39) by a Japanese chef create buzz at the chic cocktail-bar arm of Cyril Lignac's foodie empire on rue du Dragon – his glam, 1950s-styled **bistro** (Map p262; ☏ 01 45 48 29 68; www.restaurantauxpres.com; 27 rue du Dragon, 6e; mains €17-39; ☺ noon-2.30pm & 7-11pm Mon-Sat, 11.30am-3pm & 7-11pm Sun; Ⓜ St-Sulpice) is right next door. The scallops with caramelised miso, avocado and fresh coriander are heavenly, as is the yellow tail sashimi, jellied eel and other sushi.

Café de Flore   Cafe

(Map p262; ☏ 01 45 48 55 26; www.cafedeflore. fr; 172 bd St-Germain, 6e; ☺ 7.30am-1.30am; Ⓜ St-Germain des Prés) The red-upholstered benches, mirrors and marble walls at this art deco landmark haven't changed much since the days when Jean-Paul Sartre and Simone de Beauvoir essentially set up office here, writing in its warmth during the Nazi occupation. Watch for monthly English-language *philocafé* (philosophy discussion) sessions.

Castor Club
Cocktail Bar

(Map p260; ☑09 50 64 99 38; 14 rue Hautefeuille, 6e; ⊗7pm-2am Tue & Wed, 7pm-4am Thu-Sat; ⓂOdéon) Discreetly signed, this superb underground cocktail bar has an intimate English gentleman's club–style upstairs bar with vintage wall lamps and slinky red velour stools. But it's downstairs, in the 18th-century stone cellar with hole-in-the-wall booths, that the real cocktail-sipping action happens. Blues tracks add to the already cool vibe.

La Palette
Cafe

(Map p254; www.cafelapaletteparis.com; 43 rue de Seine, 6e; ⊗8am-2am; 🛜; ⓂMabillon) In the heart of gallery-land, this timeless fin de siècle cafe and erstwhile stomping ground of Paul Cézanne and Georges Braque attracts a grown-up set of fashion-industry professionals and local art dealers. Its summer terrace is beautiful.

Noglu
Cafe

(Map p262; ☑01 58 90 18 12; www.noglu.fr; 69 rue de Grenelle, 6e; ⊗8.30am-7pm Mon-Fri, 9am-7pm Sat, 10am-6pm Sun; ⓂRue du Bac) Put the kick back in your shopping stride with a coffee break at Noglu, a pretty-in-pink, mirrored cafe and *salon de thé* (tearoom) with – drumroll – almond, soya or rice milk only and strictly gluten-free cakes, cookies and savoury lunchtime fare. It also serves breakfast (the porridge, scones, croissants and sweet brioches are all gluten-free and organic).

Prescription Cocktail Club
Cocktail Bar

(Map p254; ☑09 50 35 72 87; www.prescription cocktailclub.com; 23 rue Mazarine, 6e; ⊗7pm-2am Mon-Thu, 7pm-4am Fri & Sat, 8pm-2am Sun; ⓂOdéon) With bowler and flat-top hats as lampshades and a 1930s speakeasy New York air to the place, this cocktail club – run by the same mega-successful team as Experimental Cocktail Club (p173) – is very Parisian-cool. Getting past the doorman can be tough, but once in, it's friendliness and old-fashioned cocktails all round.

Tiger
Cocktail Bar

(Map p260; www.tiger-paris.com; 13 rue Princesse, 6e; ⊗6.30pm-2am Mon-Sat; ⓂMabillon) Suspended bare-bulb lights and fretted timber make this split-level space a stylish spot for specialist gins (130 varieties). Signature cocktails include a Breakfast Martini (gin, triple sec, orange marmalade and lemon juice) and Oh My Dog (white-pepper-infused gin, lime juice, raspberry and rose cordial and ginger ale). Dedicated G&T aficionados can work their way through a staggering 1040 combinations.

⊖ Montparnasse & Southern Paris

Bateau El Alamein
Club

(www.bateauelalamein.com; opposite 11 quai François Mauriac, 13e; ⊗5.30pm-2am mid-May–mid-Oct, 8pm-2am mid-Oct–mid-May; ⓂBibliothèque François Mitterrand) Strung with terracotta pots of flowers, this deep-purple boat has a Seine-side terrace to sit amid tulips and enjoy live bands (flyers are stuck on the lamp post at the front). Concerts starting at 9pm (no reservations) span jazz, world and Piaf-style *chansons*. Hours can vary.

Simone La Cave
Wine Bar

(☑01 43 37 82 70; www.simoneparis.com; 48 rue Pascal, 13e; ⊗5pm-midnight Tue-Sat; ⓂLes Gobelins) Tucked away in the 13e, Simone La Cave lures a loyal wine-loving set keen to try its latest, outstanding natural and biodynamic wine selection. *Planches* (platters, €10 to €15) stacked high with cured meats and boutique cheeses, oysters, parsley-marinated anchovies and homemade terrines provide the perfect accompaniment.

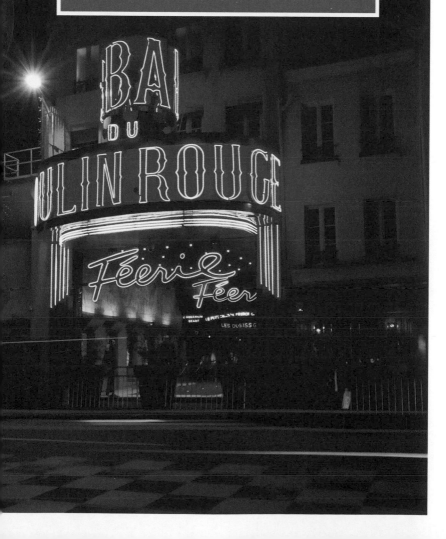

SHOWTIME

Renowned ballet, opera, jazz clubs, street performers & buskers

Showtime

Catching a performance in Paris is a treat. French and international opera, ballet and theatre companies and cabaret dancers take to the stage in fabled venues, and a flurry of young, passionate, highly creative musicians, thespians and artists make the city's fascinating fringe art scene what it is. Paris became Europe's most important jazz centre after WWII and the city has some fantastic jazz clubs, as well as venues for stirring French chansons, dazzling cabarets including the iconic Moulin Rouge, cutting-edge cultural centres, wonderful independent cinemas, and dozens of orchestral, organ and chamber-music concerts each week.

In This Section

Tickets & Booking Websites

The most convenient way to purchase concert, theatre and other cultural and sporting-event tickets is at electronics and entertainment megashop Fnac (www.fnactickets.com), in person at the *billeteries* (ticket offices) or by phone or online. There are branches throughout Paris, including in the Forum des Halles. Tickets generally can't be refunded.

Previous page: Moulin Rouge (p192)

Le Grand Rex (p191)

Jazz Clubs

Café Universel (p195) Intimate club with unpretentious vibe and no cover.

New Morning (p192) Solid and varied line-up of everything from postbop and Latin to reggae.

Le Baiser Salé (p191) Reputable venue that focuses on Caribbean and Latin sounds.

Sunset & Sunside (p191) Blues, fusion and world sounds, as well as straight-up jazz.

Cave du 38 Riv' (p194) Rue de Rivoli jazz club with concerts and jam sessions.

Lonely Planet's Top Choices

Palais Garnier (p190) Paris' premier opera house is an artistic inspiration.

Point Éphémère (p192) Cool cultural centre on the banks of Canal St-Martin.

Moulin Rouge (p192) The cancan creator razzle-dazzles with spectacular sets, costumes and choreography.

La Seine Musicale (p190) State-of-the-art concert venue on a Seine island.

✪ Eiffel Tower & Western Paris

La Seine Musicale   Concert Venue
(📞01 74 34 54 00; www.laseinemusicale.com; Île Seguin, Boulogne-Billancourt; MPont de Sèvres) A landmark addition to Paris' cultural offerings, La Seine Musicale opened on the Seine island of Île Seguin in 2017. Constructed of steel and glass, the egg-shaped auditorium has a capacity of 1150, while the larger, modular concrete hall accommodates 6000. Ballets, musicals and concerts from classical to rock are all staged here, alongside exhibitions.

Outside are amphitheatres, while up above is a panoramic rooftop garden with landscaped lawns. There's an excellent cafe, riverside restaurant and bar on the premises.

It's the first of several arts venues including a contemporary art museum planned as part of the Île Seguin's transformation from a Renault factory to a cultural island.

✪ Champs-Élysées & Grands Boulevards

Palais Garnier   Opera, Ballet
(Map p252; www.operadeparis.fr; place de l'Opéra, 9e; MOpéra) The city's original opera house (p100) is smaller than its Bastille counterpart, but has perfect acoustics. Due to its odd shape, some seats have limited or no visibility – book carefully. Ticket prices and conditions (including last-minute discounts) are available from the **box office** (📞international calls 01 71 25 24 23, within France 08 92 89 90 90; ⊙10am-6.30pm Mon-Sat). Online flash sales are held from noon on Wednesdays.

Théâtre Marigny   Theatre
(Map p252; 📞01 76 49 47 12; www.theatre marigny.fr; av de Marigny, 8e; MChamps-Élysées–Clemenceau) Built in 1883 by Charles Garnier (who designed the Palais Garnier), this 12-sided pavilion-style building reopened in 2018 following five years of renovations. The main theatre, with a

La Seine Musicale , designed by architect Shigeru Ban

capacity of 1023, hosts musicals and opera, while the smaller studio, seating 311 people, presents concerts and plays.

✪ Louvre & Les Halles

Le Baiser Salé   Live Music

(Map p254; ☎01 42 33 37 71; www.lebaisersale. com; 58 rue des Lombards, 1er; MChâtelet) Known for its Afro and Latin jazz, and jazz fusion concerts, the Salty Kiss combines big names and unknown artists. The place has a relaxed vibe, with sets usually starting at 7.30pm or 9.30pm.

La Place   Cultural Centre

(Map p254; ☎01 70 22 45 48; www.laplace.paris; 10 passage de la Canopée, Forum des Halles, 1er; ⊙bar 1-7pm Tue-Sat, concert hours vary; MLes Halles or RER Châtelet–Les Halles) The overhaul of the vast shopping mall Forum des Halles (p77) saw the launch of Paris' inaugural hip-hop cultural centre under its custard-yellow glass canopy, with a 400-capacity concert hall, a 100-capacity broadcast studio, several recording studios and street-art graffiti workrooms, along with a relaxed bar. Some concerts are free, while ticket prices vary for others – check the program online.

Le Grand Rex   Cinema

(Map p254; ☎01 45 08 93 58; www.legrandrex. com; 1 bd Poissonnière, 2e; tours adult/child €11/9, cinema tickets adult/child €11/4.50; ⊙tours 10am-6pm Wed, Sat & Sun, extended hours during school holidays; MBonne Nouvelle) Blockbuster screenings and concerts aside, this 1932 art deco cinematic icon runs 50-minute behind-the-scenes tours (English soundtracks available) during which visitors – tracked by a sensor slung around their neck – are whisked up (via a lift) behind the giant screen, tour a sound-stage and experiment in a recording studio. Whizz-bang special effects along the way will stun adults and kids alike.

Sunset & Sunside   Live Music

(Map p254; ☎01 40 26 46 60; www.sunset-sunside.com; 60 rue des Lombards, 1er; ⊙hours

vary; MChâtelet) There are two venues in one at this well-respected club, which hosts electric jazz, fusion and occasional salsa at Sunset, in the vaulted cellar, and acoustics and concerts on the ground floor at Sunside.

✪ Montmartre & Northern Paris

La Cigale   Live Music

(Map p250; ☎01 49 25 89 99; www.lacigale.fr; 120 bd de Rochechouart, 18e; MPigalle) Now classed as a historical monument, this music hall dates from 1887 but was redec-orated a century later by Philippe Starck. Artists who have performed here include Ryan Adams, Ibrahim Maalouf and the Dandy Warhols.

 Discount Theatre Tickets

Pick up half-price tickets for same-day performances of ballet, opera and music at **Kiosque Théâtre Madeleine** (Map p252; www.kiosqueculture. com; opposite 15 place de la Madeleine, 8e; ⊙12.30-2.30pm & 3-7.30pm Tue-Sat, 12.30-3.45pm Sun Sep-Jun, closed Sun Jul & Aug; MMadeleine), a freestanding kiosk by place de la Madeleine.

Palais Garnier (p190)

JULIE MAYFENG/SHUTTERSTOCK ©

Le Divan du Monde
Live Music

(Map p250; ☑01 40 05 08 10; www.divan dumonde.com; 75 rue des Martyrs, 18e; MPigalle) Take some cinematographic events and *nouvelles chansons françaises* (new French songs). Add in soul/funk fiestas, air-guitar face-offs and rock parties of the Arctic Monkeys/Killers/Libertines persuasion... You may now be getting some idea of the inventive, open-minded approach at this excellent cross-cultural venue in Pigalle.

Le Louxor
Cinema

(Map p250; ☑01 44 63 96 98; www.cinema louxor.fr; 170 bd de Magenta, 10e; tickets adult/child €9.70/5; MBarbès-Rochechouart) Built in neo-Egyptian art deco style in 1921 and saved from demolition by a neighbourhood association seven decades later, this historical monument is a palatial place to catch a new release, classic, piano-accompanied 'ciné-concert', short-film festival, special workshop (such as singalongs) or live-music performance. Don't miss a drink at its bar, which opens onto an elevated terrace overlooking Sacré-Cœur.

Moulin Rouge
Cabaret

(Map p250; ☑01 53 09 82 82; www.moulinrouge. fr; 82 bd de Clichy, 18e; show only from €87, lunch & show from €165, dinner & show from €190; ⊙show only 2.45pm, 9pm & 11pm, lunch & show 1.45pm, dinner & show 7pm; MBlanche) Immortalised in Toulouse-Lautrec's posters and later in Baz Luhrmann's film, Paris' legendary cabaret twinkles beneath a 1925 replica of its original red windmill. Yes, it's packed with bus-tour crowds, but from the opening bars of music to the last high cancan kick, it's a whirl of fantastical costumes, sets, choreography and Champagne. Book in advance and dress smartly (no trainers or sneakers). No entry for children under six.

Philharmonie de Paris
Concert Venue

(☑01 44 84 44 84; www.philharmoniedeparis.fr; 221 av Jean Jaurès, 19e; ⊙box office noon-6pm Tue-Fri, 10am-6pm Sat & Sun, plus concerts; MPorte de Pantin) Major complex the Cité de la Musique – Philharmonie de Paris hosts an eclectic range of concerts, from classical to North African and Japanese, in the Philharmonie building's Grande Salle Pierre Boulez, with an audience capacity of 2400 to 3600. The adjacent Cité de la Musique's Salle des Concerts has a capacity of 900 to 1600.

Point Éphémère
Live Music

(☑01 40 34 02 48; www.pointephemere.org; 200 quai de Valmy, 10e; ⊙noon-2am Mon-Sat, to 11pm Sun; ☎; MJaurès, Louis Blanc) On the banks of Canal St-Martin in a former fire station and later squat, this arts and music venue attracts an underground crowd for concerts, dance nights and art exhibitions. Its rockin' restaurant, **Animal Kitchen**, fuses gourmet cuisine with music from Animal Records (Sunday brunch from 1pm is a highlight).

New Morning
Jazz, Blues

(Map p254; ☑01 45 23 51 41; www.newmorning. com; 7-9 rue des Petites Écuries, 10e; ⊙hours vary; MChâteau d'Eau) This highly regarded auditorium with excellent acoustics hosts big-name jazz concerts as well as a variety of blues, rock, funk, salsa, Afro-Cuban and Brazilian music.

La Scala Paris
Performing Arts

(Map p256; ☎01 40 03 44 30; www.lascala-paris.
com; 13 bd de Strasbourg, 10e; ⓜStrasbourg–
St-Denis) Dance, circus arts, concerts and
multimedia productions all feature at this
550-capacity theatre.

✪ Le Marais,
Ménilmontant & Belleville

La Bellevilloise
Cultural Centre

(☎01 46 36 07 07; www.labellevilloise.com;
19-21 rue Boyer, 20e; ⓒ7pm-1am Wed & Thu,
to 2am Fri, 11am-2am Sat, 11.30am-midnight
Sun; ⓜGambetta) Gigs, concerts, theatrical
performances, exhibitions, readings, dance
classes and workshops: this arts centre is
where it all happens after dark in Ménilmontant. The trendy cafe-restaurant, with
its sunlit tables beneath 100-year-old olive
trees, is packed during Sunday brunch's
two sittings (11.30am or 2pm, adult/child
€29/13), which is accompanied by live jazz.
Advance reservations are recommended.

Le Bataclan
Live Music

(Map p256; ☎01 43 14 00 30; www.bataclan.fr; 50
bd Voltaire, 11e; ⓜOberkampf, Filles du Calvaire)
Built in 1864, intimate concert, theatre and
dance hall Le Bataclan was Maurice Cheva-
lier's debut venue in 1910. The 1497-capacity
venue reopened with a concert by Sting on
12 November 2016, almost a year to the day
following the tragic terrorist attacks that
took place here on 13 November 2015, and
once again hosts French and international
rock and pop legends.

Le Carreau
du Temple
Cultural Centre

(Map p256; ☎01 83 81 93 30; www.carreaudu
temple.eu; 2 rue Perrée, 3e; ⓒbox office
10am-9pm Mon-Fri, to 7pm Sat; ⓜTemple)
The quarter's old covered market with
gorgeous art nouveau ironwork has been
transformed into a striking cultural centre
and entertainment venue. The place where
silks, lace, leather and other materials were
sold in the 19th century is now a vast stage
for exhibitions, concerts, sports classes
and theatre.

Point Éphémère

 Cinema in Paris

The film lover's ultimate city, Paris has some wonderful movie houses to catch new flicks, avant garde cinema and priceless classics.

Foreign films (including English-language films) screened in their original language with French subtitles are labelled 'VO' *(version originale)*. Films labelled 'VF' *(version française)* are dubbed in French.

L'Officiel des Spectacles lists the full crop of Paris' cinematic pickings and screening times; online, check out http://cinema.leparisien.fr.

The city's film archive, the **Forum des Images** (Map p254; ☑01 44 76 63 00; www.forumdesimages.fr; Forum des Halles, 2 rue du Cinéma, Porte St-Eustache, 1er; cinema tickets adult/child €6/4; ☺5-9pm Tue & Thu, 1-9pm Wed, 4-9pm Fri, 10.30am-9pm Sat & Sun; Ⓜ Les Halles or RER Châtelet–Les Halles), screens films set in Paris.

English speakers can catch new-release French films at independent cinemas around Paris through events run by Lost in Frenchlation (www.lost infrenchlation.com/), which include drinks before or after the screening; check the schedule online.

Forum des Halles, by Patrick Perger and Jacques Anziutti
HUANG ZHENG/SHUTTERSTOCK ©

Cave du 38 Riv'   Jazz
(Map p256; ☑01 48 87 56 30; www.38riv.com; 38 rue de Rivoli, 4e; concerts €15-30; ☺concerts from 8.30pm Mon-Sat, from 5pm Sun; Ⓜ Hôtel de Ville) In the heart of Le Marais on busy rue de Rivoli, a tiny street frontage gives way to a fantastically atmospheric vaulted stone cellar with jazz concerts most nights; check the agenda online. Jam sessions with free admission typically take place on Mondays, Thursdays and Fridays.

Le Vieux Belleville   Live Music
(Map p256; ☑01 44 62 92 66; www.le-vieux-belleville.com; 12 rue des Envierges, 20e; ☺concerts 8.30pm-2am Tue, Fri & Sat; Ⓜ Pyrénées) This old-fashioned bistro at the top of Parc de Belleville is an atmospheric venue for performances of *chansons* featuring accordions and an organ grinder three times a week. It's a lively favourite with locals, so booking ahead is advised.

La Java   World Music
(Map p256; ☑01 42 02 20 52; www.la-java.fr; 105 rue du Faubourg du Temple, 11e; concerts free-€10; ☺8pm-dawn Mon-Sat; Ⓜ Goncourt) Built in 1922, this is the dance hall where Édith Piaf got her first break, and it now reverberates to the sound of live salsa, rock and world music. Live concerts usually take place at 8pm or 9pm during the week. Afterwards a festive crowd gets dancing to electro, house, disco and Latino DJs.

✪ Bastille & Eastern Paris

Opéra Bastille   Opera
(Map p259; ☑international calls 01 71 25 24 23, within France 08 92 89 90 90; www.operade paris.fr; 2-6 place de la Bastille, 12e; ☺box office 11.30am-6.30pm Mon-Sat, 1hr prior to performances Sun; Ⓜ Bastille) Paris' premier opera hall, Opéra Bastille's 2745-seat main auditorium also stages ballet and classical concerts. Online tickets go on sale up to three weeks before telephone or box-office sales (from noon on Wednesdays; online flash sales offer significant discounts). Standing-only tickets (*places débouts;* €5) are available 90 minutes before performances. French-language 90-minute **guided tours** (tours adult/child €17/12; ☺Sep–mid-Jul) take you backstage.

Significant discounts are available for those aged under 28 and over 65.

La Cinémathèque
Française   Cinema

(📞01 71 19 33 33; www.cinematheque.fr; 51 rue
de Bercy, 12e; adult/child €7/5.50, museum
€5/2.50; ⊙museum noon-7pm Wed-Mon;
Ⓜ Bercy) This national institution is a temple
to the 'seventh art' and always screens its
foreign offerings in their original versions.
Up to 10 films a day are shown, usually
retrospectives (eg Spielberg, Altman,
Eastwood) mixed in with related but more
obscure films.

✪ Latin Quarter

Café Universel   Jazz, Blues

(Map p260; 📞01 43 25 74 20; www.facebook.
com/cafeuniversel.paris05; 267 rue St-Jacques,
5e; ⊙concerts from 8.30pm Tue-Sat, cafe
8.30am-3pm Mon, 8.30am-1am Tue-Fri,
4.30pm-1am Sat, 1.30pm-1am Sun; 🛜; Ⓜ Censier
Daubenton or RER Port Royal) Café Universel
hosts a brilliant array of live concerts with
everything from bebop and Latin sounds
to vocal jazz sessions. Plenty of freedom is
given to young producers and artists, and
its convivial, relaxed atmosphere attracts
a mix of students and jazz lovers. Concerts
are free, but you should tip the artists when
they pass the hat around.

Le Champo   Cinema

(Map p260; www.cinema-lechampo.com; 51
rue des Écoles, 5e; tickets adult/child €9/4;
Ⓜ Cluny–La Sorbonne) This is one of the
most popular of the many Latin Quarter
cinemas, featuring classics and retrospectives looking at the films of such actors and
directors as Alfred Hitchcock, Jacques Tati,
Alain Resnais, Frank Capra, Tim Burton and
Woody Allen. One of the two *salles* (cinemas) has wheelchair access.

✪ St-Germain
& Les Invalides

Le Lucernaire   Cultural Centre

(Map p262; 📞01 45 44 57 34; www.lucernaire.
fr; 53 rue Notre Dame des Champs, 6e;
⊙bar 9am-9pm Mon, 9am-12.30am Tue-Fri,
10am-12.30am Sat, 11am-9pm Sun; Ⓜ Notre

Dame des Champs) Sunday-evening concerts
are a fixture on the impressive repertoire
of the dynamic Centre National d'Art et
d'Essai (National Arts Centre). Whether it's
classical guitar, Baroque, French *chansons*
or East Asian music, these weekly concerts
starting from 4pm (hours vary) are a real
treat. Art and photography exhibitions, cinema, theatre, lectures, debates and guided
walks round off the packed cultural agenda.

✪ Montparnasse
& Southern Paris

EP7   Arts Centre

(📞01 43 45 68 07; www.ep7.paris; 133 av de
France, 13e; ⊙9.30am-midnight Mon-Thu,
10am-2am Fri & Sat, 10am-midnight Sun; 🛜;
Ⓜ Bibliothèque) The capital's first piece of
'interactive architecture', this cultural cafe
and concert venue was unveiled in 2018.
Contemporary works of pixel art prance
across 12 giant screens covering the
facade, creating a dazzling digital gallery.
Inside the complex, named after the vintage vinyl format 'extended play', you'll find
art exhibitions and happenings, DJ sets, a
bistro and a bar.

Fondation Jérôme
Seydoux-Pathé   Cinema

(📞01 83 79 18 96; www.fondation-jerome
seydoux-pathe.com; 73 av des Gobelins, 13e; cinema & exhibition tickets adult/child €6.50/4.50,
exhibition only €3, guided tour €7/4.50; ⊙1-8pm
Tue, 1-7pm Wed-Fri, 11.30am-7pm Sat; Ⓜ Place
d'Italie) This striking cinema has a small
exhibition devoted to the history of cinema
and screens silent B&W movies accompanied by a live pianist. The Pathé Foundation
is hidden in a former theatre and cinema
dating to 1869, but only the facade –
sculpted by Rodin – remains. The rest of
the building is an unbelievable five-storey
contemporary creation by world-class
architect Renzo Piano.

Guided architecture tours take place
on Saturday at noon. The family-friendly
ciné-concerts (films) at weekends are
particularly enchanting.

ACTIVE
PARIS

Picturesque parks, sporting highlights
and unique local-led tours

Active

As Paris gears up to host the 2024 Summer Olympics and Summer Paralympics, you'll find increasing opportunities to watch spectator sports or take part yourself. To unwind with the Parisians, check out the city's glorious parks and two vast forests, the Bois de Boulogne and Bois de Vincennes, which act as its 'green lungs'. The city also has some stunning swimming pools, both historic and new, and a rapidly expanding network of cycling lanes.

As one of the world's most visited cities, Paris is well set up for visitors with a host of guided tours, from bike, boat, bus, scooter and walking tours (including some wonderful local-led options in off-the-beaten-track areas) to various themed options.

In This Section

What to Watch

From late May to early-June, the French Open hits up at the Stade Roland Garros (p200) in the Bois de Boulogne. The Tour de France races up the Champs-Élysées towards the end of July every year. The main football (soccer) season runs from August through to April.

Fondation Louis Vuitton (p225) in the Bois de Boulogne (p202)

Spectator Sports

Local teams include football's Paris Saint-Germain (www.psg.fr), and rugby's sky-blue-and-white-clad Racing 92 (www.racing92.fr) and pink-clad Stade Français Paris (www.stade.fr). Catch France's national football team, Les Bleus (www.fff.fr), at the Stade de France (p200).

For upcoming events, click on Sports & Games (under the Going Out menu) at https://en.parisinfo. com/what-to-do-in-paris/ sports-and-games-in-paris.

Parks for Activities & Sports

Bois de Boulogne (p202) Sprawling western forest.

Bois de Vincennes (p201) Eastern forest, home to a zoo and the kid-packed Parc Floral.

Jardin du Luxembourg (p68) Paris' most popular park.

Parc des Buttes Chaumont (p201) Hilly haven with t'ai chi vibes.

Swimming Etiquette

If you plan to go swimming at either your hotel or in a public pool, you'll need to don a *bonnet de bain* (bathing cap) – even if you don't have any hair. They are generally sold at most pools. Men are required to wear skin-tight trunks (Speedos); loose-fitting Bermuda shorts are not allowed.

🟢 Spectator Sports

Stade de France   Stadium
(📞01 55 93 00 45; www.stadefrance.com; St-Denis La Plaine; stadium tours adult/child €15/10; M St-Denis-Porte de Paris) This 80,000-seat stadium was built for the 1998 FIFA World Cup, and hosts major sports and music events. Stadium tours lasting 90 minutes take you behind the scenes, providing no event is under way. Tours in English depart from Gate H; confirm times and book tickets in advance online.

Stade Roland Garros   Stadium
(www.rolandgarros.com; 2 av Gordon Bennett, 16e, Bois de Boulogne; M Porte d'Auteuil) The **French Open** (www.rolandgarros.com; ⏰late May-early Jun; M Porte d'Auteuil) is held on clay at the Stade Roland Garros from late May to early-June. Much-needed renovations began in 2016 and will incorporate a new Court No 1 with 15,000 seats and a retractable roof, among other changes. Legal challenges have delayed construction and completion won't be until 2020 at the earliest; the tournament will continue during that time.

🟢 Swimming Pools

Piscine de la Butte aux Cailles   Swimming
(📞01 45 89 60 05; www.paris.fr/equipements/piscine-de-la-butte-aux-cailles-2927; 5 place Paul Verlaine, 13e; adult/child €3.50/2, 10 entrances €28/16; ⏰hours vary; M Place d'Italie) Built in 1924, this art deco swimming complex – a historical monument – takes advantage of the lovely warm artesian well water nearby. It has a spectacular vaulted indoor pool and, since 2017, Paris' only Nordic pool. In the depths of winter Parisians head here to swim 25m laps in a five-lane outdoor pool, heated to a toasty 28°C. Check schedules online.

Piscine Joséphine Baker   Swimming
(📞01 56 61 96 50; www.piscine-baker.fr; quai François Mauriac, 13e; adult/child €6.20/3.10; ⏰7-9am & 10am-11pm Mon-Fri, 10am-8pm Sat & Sun Jun-Sep, shorter hours rest of year; M Quai de la Gare) Floating on the Seine, this striking swimming pool is named after the 1920s American singer. The 25m-by-10m, four-lane pool and large sun deck are especially popular in summer when the roof slides back. Also here is a children's paddling pool. In July and August, plus weekends from late May to September, admission is limited to two hours.

🟢 Parks

Parc de la Villette   Park
(www.lavillette.com; 211 av Jean Jaurès, 19e; ⏰6am-1am; M Porte de la Villette, Porte de Pantin) Spanning 55 hectares, this vast city park is a cultural centre, kids' playground and landscaped urban space at the inter-section of two canals, the Ourcq and the St-Denis. Its futuristic layout includes the colossal mirrorlike sphere of the Géode cinema and the bright-red cubical pavilions known as *folies*. Among its themed gardens are the Jardin du Dragon (Dragon Garden), with a giant dragon's tongue slide for kids, Jardin des Dunes (Dunes Garden) and Jardin des Miroirs (Mirror Garden).

Parc Monceau   Park
(Map p252; www.paris.fr/equipements/parc-monceau-1804; 35 bd de Courcelles, 8e; ⏰7am-10pm May-Aug, to 9pm Sep, to 8pm Oct-Apr; M Monceau) Marked by a neoclassical rotunda at its main bd Courcelles entrance, beautiful Parc Monceau sprawls over 8.2 lush hectares. It was laid out by Louis

Carrogis Carmontelle in 1778–79 in English style with winding paths, ponds and flower beds. An Egyptian-style pyramid is the only original folly remaining today, but other distinctive features include a bridge modelled after Venice's Rialto, a Renaissance arch and a Corinthian colonnade. There are play areas, a carousel and scheduled puppet shows for kids.

Promenade Plantée   Park

(La Coulée Verte René-Dumont; Map p259; cnr rue de Lyon & av Daumesnil, 12e; ⏱8am-9.30pm Mon-Fri, from 9am Sat & Sun Mar-Oct, 8am-5.30pm Mon-Fri, from 9am Sat & Sun Nov-Feb; Ⓜ Bastille, Gare de Lyon, Daumesnil) The disused 19th-century Vincennes railway viaduct was reborn as the world's first elevated park, planted with a fragrant profusion of cherry trees, maples, rose trellises, bamboo corridors and lavender. Three storeys above ground, it provides a unique aerial vantage point on the city. Along the first, northwestern section, above av Daumesnil, art-gallery workshops beneath the arches form the **Viaduc des Arts** (Map p259; www.leviaducdesarts.com; 1-129 av Daumesnil, 12e; ⏱hours vary; Ⓜ Bastille, Gare de Lyon). Staircases provide access (lifts/elevators here invariably don't work).

Parc des Buttes Chaumont   Park

(Map p256; www.paris.fr/equipements/parc-des-buttes-chaumont-1757; rue Manin & rue Botzaris, 19e; ⏱7am-10pm May-Sep, to 8pm Oct-Apr; Ⓜ Buttes Chaumont, Botzaris) One of the city's largest green spaces, Buttes Chaumont's landscaped slopes hide grottoes, waterfalls, a lake and even an island topped with a temple to Sibylle. Once a gypsum quarry and rubbish dump, it was given its present form by Baron Haussmann in time for the opening of the 1867 Exposition Universelle. The tracks of the abandoned 19th-century Petite Ceinture railway line, which once circled Paris, run through the park.

Parc Montsouris   Park

(www.equipement.paris.fr/parc-montsouris-1810; av Reille, 14e; ⏱8am-9.30pm Mon-Fri, 9am-9.30pm Sat & Sun May-Aug, shorter hours rest of

🔭 Scenic Flights

For once-in-a-lifetime views of Paris' rooftops and landmarks, board a helicopter flight with **Helipass** (📞01 40 60 40 00; www.helipass.com; 61 rue Henry Farman, 15e; 90min flight package per 1/2/3/4 people €219/399/597/796; ⏱by reservation; Ⓜ Balard). The 90-minute experience includes 25 minutes of flying time and a short landing near the Château de Versailles before returning to the helipad in the 15e. En route, you'll swoop over the Bois de Boulogne, Longchamp Hippodrome, the Seine, Trocadéro and the Eiffel Tower.

VALERIE LOISELEUX/GETTY IMAGES ©

year; Ⓜ Porte d'Orléans or RER Cité-Universitaire) The name of this sprawling lakeside park – planted with horse-chestnut, yew, cedar, weeping beech and buttonwood trees – derives from *moque souris* (mice mockery) because the area was once overrun with the critters. Today it's a delightful picnic spot and has endearing playground areas, such as a concrete 'road system' where littlies can trundle matchbox cars (BYO cars). On Wednesday, Saturday and Sunday from 3pm to 6pm there are marionette shows and pony rides.

🌳 Forests

Bois de Vincennes   Park

(www.paris.fr/equipements/bois-de-vincennes-6598; bd Poniatowski, 12e; Ⓜ Porte de Charenton, Porte Dorée) In the southeastern

💬 Local Activities

In-Line Skating

Skating, whether on the street or on ice, is a popular activity. Rent a pair of in-line skates at **Nomadeshop** (Map p259; ☑01 44 54 07 44; www.nomadeshop. com; 37 bd Bourdon, 4e; skate rental per day €8; ⊙11am-1.30pm & 2.30-7.30pm Tue-Fri, 10am-7pm Sat, 1-6pm Sun Apr-Oct, closed Sun Nov-Mar; MBastille) and join the Friday-evening skate, **Pari Roller** (Map p262; www.pari-roller.com; place Raoul Dautry, 14e; ⊙9.30pm-midnight Fri; MMontparnasse Bienvenüe) FREE, that zooms through the Paris streets, or join the more laid-back Sunday-afternoon skate, **Rollers & Coquillages** (Map p259; www. rollers-coquillages.org; place de la Bastille; ⊙2.30pm Sun; MBastille).

During the winter holidays several temporary outdoor rinks are installed around Paris. Check www.paris.fr for locations.

Boules

You'll often see groups of earnest Parisians playing boules (France's most popular traditional game, similar to lawn bowls) in the Jardin du Luxembourg and other parks and squares with suitably flat, shady patches of gravel. The **Arènes de Lutèce** (Map p260; 49 rue Monge, 5e; ⊙8am-9.30pm May-Aug, to 8.30pm Apr & Sep, shorter hours rest year; MPlace Monge) FREE boulodrome in a 2nd-century Roman amphitheatre in the Latin Quarter is a fabulous spot to absorb the scene. There are usually places to play at **Paris Plages** (www. parisinfo.com; ⊙mid-Jul–early Sep).

corner of Paris, Bois de Vincennes encompasses some 995 hectares. Originally royal hunting grounds, the woodland was annexed by the army following the Revolution and then donated to the city in 1860 by Napoléon III. A fabulous place to escape the Parisian concrete, Bois de Vincennes also contains a handful of notable sights including a bona fide royal château, **Château de Vincennes** (☑01 48 08 31 20; www.chateau-de-vincennes.fr; 1 av de Paris, Vincennes; adult/child €9/free; ⊙10am-6pm mid-May–mid-Sep, to 5pm mid-Sep–mid-May; MChâteau de Vincennes), with massive fortifications and a moat.

Paris' largest, state-of-the-art zoo, the **Parc Zoologique de Paris** (Zoo de Vincennes; ☑08 11 22 41 22; www.parczoologique deparis.fr; cnr av Daumesnil & rte de Ceinture du Lac Daumesnil, 12e; adult/child €20/15; ⊙9.30am-8.30pm May-Aug, shorter hours Sep-Apr; MPorte Dorée), is also here, as is the magnificent **Parc Floral de Paris** (☑01 49 57 24 84; www.parcfloraldeparisjeux.com; Esplanade du Chateau de Vincennes or rte de la Pyramide; adult/child €2.50/1.50 May-Oct, free Nov-Apr; ⊙9.30am-8pm Apr-Sep, to 6.30pm Oct, to 5pm Nov-Feb, to 6.30pm Mar; MChâteau de Vincennes), a botanical park with exciting playgrounds for older children. The wood also has a lovely lake, with boats to rent and ample green lawns to picnic on.

Bois de Boulogne   Park

(www.paris.fr/equipements/bois-de-boul ogne-2779; bd Maillot, 16e; MPorte Maillot) On the western edge of Paris just beyond the 16e, the 845-hectare Bois de Boulogne owes its informal layout to Baron Haussmann, who was inspired by Hyde Park in London. Be warned that the Bois de Boulogne becomes a distinctly adult playground after dark, especially along the allée de Longchamp, where sex workers cruise for clients.

In the south are two horse-racing tracks, the **Hippodrome de Longchamp** (☑01 44 30 75 00; www.parislongchamp.com; 2 rte des Tribunes, 16e, Bois de Boulogne; MPorte Maillot, Porte d'Auteuil) for flat races and the **Hippodrome d'Auteuil** (☑01 40 71 47 47; www. france-galop.com; Champ de Courses d'Auteuil, 16e, Bois de Boulogne; adult from €5, child free; MPorte d'Auteuil) for steeplechases.

The park is also home to the amusement park **Jardin d'Acclimatation** (☑01

Bois de Vincennes (p201)

40 67 90 85; www.jardindacclimatation.fr; av du Mahatma Gandhi, 16e; admission €5, per attraction €2.90; ⊙11am-6pm Mon, Tue, Thu & Fri, 10am-6pm Wed, Sat, Sun & school holidays; Ⓜ Les Sablons).

❸ Guided Tours

Parisien d'un Jour – Paris Greeters   Walking
(www.greeters.paris; by donation) See Paris through local eyes with these two- to three-hour city tours. Volunteers – mainly knowledgable Parisians passionate about their city – lead groups (maximum six people) to their favourite spots. Minimum two weeks' notice is needed.

Paris Walks   Walking
(☑01 48 09 21 40; www.paris-walks.com; 2hr tours adult/child from €15/10) Long established and well respected, Paris Walks offers two-hour thematic walking tours (art, fashion, chocolate, the French Revolution etc).

Paris à Vélo, C'est Sympa!   Cycling
(Map p256; ☑01 48 87 60 01; www.parisvelo sympa.fr; 22 rue Alphonse Baudin, 11e; 3hr tour adult/child €32/29; Ⓜ Richard Lenoir) Runs three guided bike tours: a Heart of Paris tour, Unusual Paris (taking in artist studios and mansions) and the Contrast tour, combining nature and modern architecture. Tours depart from its bike rental shop (p240).

Localers   Walking
(☑01 83 64 92 01; www.localers.com; tours from €49) Classic walking tours and behind-the-scenes urban discoveries with local Paris experts: *boules*, photo shoots, market tours, cooking classes and more.

REST YOUR HEAD

Top tips for the best accommodation

Rest Your Head

As one of the world's most visited cities, Paris has a wealth of accommodation for all budgets, from a recently reinvigorated hostel scene that now includes purpose-built, state-of-the-art flashpacker pads, to charming old-school hotels, intimate boutique gems, hipster hang-outs, eye-popping designer havens, sleep-drink-dine-dance lifestyle hotels, and deluxe hotels and palaces, some of which rank among the finest in the world. Be sure to reserve as far ahead as possible, especially at busy times including weekends, public and school holidays and the summer months.

Apartment rentals are also very popular in Paris and give you the chance to live like a Parisian, shopping at the local markets and visiting neighbourhood bars. Choosing a central option with good transport links will allow you to maximise your time.

In This Section

Prices/Tipping

A 'budget hotel' in Paris generally costs up to €130 for a double room with en suite bathroom in high season (breakfast not included). For a midrange option, plan on spending €130 to €250. Luxury options cost €250 and higher.

Bellhops usually expect €1 to €2 per bag; it's not necessary to tip the concierge, cleaners or front-desk staff.

VLASTAS/SHUTTERSTOCK ©

Le Grand Hotel

Reservations

Reservations are almost always essential – walk-ins are practically impossible and rack rates are unfavourable relative to online deals (usually best directly via hotels' official websites). Reserve your room as early as possible and make sure you understand the cancellation policy. Check-in is generally in the middle of the afternoon and check-out in the late morning.

Useful Websites

Lonely Planet (www.lonelyplanet.com/france/paris/hotels) Reviews of Lonely Planet's top choices.

Paris Attitude (www.parisattitude.com) Thousands of apartment rentals, professional service, reasonable fees.

Haven In (www.havenin.com) Charming Parisian apartments for rent.

Apartment Rentals

Families – and anyone wanting to self-cater – should consider renting a short-stay apartment. Paris has a number of excellent apartment hotels, including the international chain Citadines (www.citadines.com).

For an even more authentic Parisian experience, home-sharing options are also available, whether a room in someone's apartment or the entire property. Rental agencies (eg Paris Attitude; p207) are among the organisations that list furnished residential apartments for short stays. Apartments often include facilities such as washing machines, and can be good value. The cheapest rates are usually in local neighbourhoods in outer (higher-numbered) *arrondissements*. Many older Parisian buildings don't have lifts/elevators; check the *étage* (floor numb). Parisian apartments are often tiny (in studios, the sofa often doubles as the only bed); confirm the size beforehand. Also establish whether prices include electricity.

Beware of direct-rental scams whereby scammers compile fake apartment advertisements at too-good-to-be-true prices from photos and descriptions on legitimate sites. Book only with reputable companies. Above all, never send money via an untraceable money transfer.

Parisian apartments
WDG PHOTO/SHUTTERSTOCK ©

Accommodation Types

Hotels

Hotels in Paris are inspected by government authorities and classified into six categories, from no stars to five stars. The vast majority are two- and three-star hotels, which are generally well equipped. All hotels must display their rates, including TVA (*taxe sur la valeur ajoutée;* value-added tax), though you'll often get *much* cheaper prices online, especially on the hotels' own websites, which invariably offer the best deals.

Parisian hotel rooms tend to be small by international standards. Families will probably need connecting rooms, but if children are too young to stay in their own room it's possible to make do with triples, quads or suites in some places.

Cheaper hotels may not have lifts/elevators and/or air-conditioning. Virtually all accept credit cards.

Breakfast is rarely included in hotel rates; heading to a cafe often works out to be better value (and more atmospheric).

Hostels

Paris is awash with hostels, and standards are consistently improving. A wave of state-of-the-art hostels includes the design-savvy 950-bed 'megahostel' by leading hostel chain Generator near Canal St-Martin, 10e and, close by, two by the switched-on St Christopher's group.

Some of the more traditional (ie institutional) hostels have daytime lock-outs and curfews; some have a maximum three-night stay. Places that have upper age limits tend not to enforce them except at the busiest of times. Only the official *auberges de jeunesse* (youth hostels) require guests to present Hostelling International (HI) cards or their equivalent.

Not all hostels have self-catering kitchens, but rates generally include a basic breakfast.

Hôtel Off Paris Seine

B&Bs & Homestays

Bed-and-breakfast (B&B) accommodation (*chambres d'hôte* in French) offers an immersive way to experience the city. Paris' tourist office maintains a list of B&Bs; visit https://en.parisinfo.com/where-to-sleep-in-paris.

🖲 Need to Know

Price Ranges

The following price ranges are an indication of accommodation costs in Paris (prices refer to a double room with en suite bathroom in high season, breakfast not included).

Budget Less than €130
Midrange €130–€250
Top End More than €250

Internet Access

Wi-fi (pronounced *wee*-fee in French) is virtually always free of charge at hotels and hostels. You may find that in some hotels, especially older ones, the higher the floor, the less reliable the wi-fi connection.

Smoking

Smoking is officially banned in all Paris hotels.

Taxe de Séjour

The city of Paris levies a *taxe de séjour* (tourist tax) per person per night on all accommodation. The rate depends on the type of accommodation, as outlined below.

Palaces (and similar) €4.40
5 stars €3.30
4 stars €2.53
3 stars €1.65
2 stars €0.99
1 star & B&Bs €0.88
Unrated/unclassified €0.88
3- to 5-star campgrounds €0.66
1- and 2-star campgrounds and marinas €0.22

Neighbourhood	Atmosphere
Eiffel Tower & Western Paris	Close to Paris' iconic sights. Upmarket area with quiet streets. Short on budget and midrange options. Limited nightlife.
Champs-Élysées & Grands Boulevards	Luxury hotels, boutiques and department stores, gastronomic restaurants, great nightlife. Some areas pricey. Can be noisy.
Louvre & Les Halles	Epicentral location, excellent transport links, major museums, shopping galore. Not many bargains. Noise can be an issue.
Montmartre & Northern Paris	Village atmosphere, some parts very touristy. Pigalle's red-light district, though safe, won't appeal to all travellers.
Le Marais, Ménilmontant & Belleville	Buzzing nightlife, hip shopping, fantastic eating options. Lively LGBT+ scene. Very central. Can be noisy.
Bastille & Eastern Paris	Few tourists, allowing you to see the 'real' Paris. Excellent markets, loads of nightlife. Some areas slightly out-of-the-way.
The Islands	As geographically central as it gets. No metro station on the Île St-Louis. Limited self-catering shops, minimal nightlife.
Latin Quarter	Energetic student area, stacks of eating and drinking options, late-opening bookshops.
St-Germain & Les Invalides	Stylish, central location, superb shopping, sophisticated dining, proximity to the Jardin du Luxembourg.
Montparnasse & Southern Paris	Good value, few tourists, excellent links to both major airports. Some areas out of the way and/or not well served by metro.

In Focus

Paris Today   214
Grand-scale plans for the city's infra-structure and green transport initiatives continue apace.

History   216
A saga of battles, bloodshed, grand excesses, revolution, reformation, resistance, renaissance and constant reinvention.

Architecture   221
Paris' cityscape spans Roman baths to medieval wonders, art nouveau splendours and stunning contemporary additions.

Arts   226
The capital's museums and galler-ies – and its streets, parks and metro stations – contain a cache of artistic treasures, while its literary, music and film scenes are flourishing.

Game of *boules* (p202)

ADRIENNE PITTS/LONELY PLANET ©

Paris Today

The City of Light's future is bright: visitor numbers are at a record high, the economy is being revitalised, a raft of infrastructure projects are under way, and the capital is gearing up to host 2023 Rugby World Cup fixtures and the 2024 Summer Olympics and Summer Paralympics. Meanwhile, Paris continues to become greener, with eco-initiatives including more car-free and reduced-traffic areas prioritising pedestrians and cyclists.

Expansive Plans

The gargantuan Grand Paris (Greater Paris) redevelopment project will ultimately connect the outer suburbs beyond the bd Périphérique ring road with the city proper. This is a significant break in the physical and conceptual barrier that the Périphérique has imposed until now, but, due to the steadily growing suburban population (10.5 million, compared to 2.2 million inside the *périphérique*), a real need to redefine Paris, on both an administrative and an infrastructural scale, has arisen.

The crux of Grand Paris is a massive decentralised metro expansion, with four new metro lines, the extension of several existing lines, and a total of 68 new stations, with a target completion date of 2030. The principal goal is to connect the suburbs with one another, instead of relying on a central inner-city hub from which all lines radiate outwards.

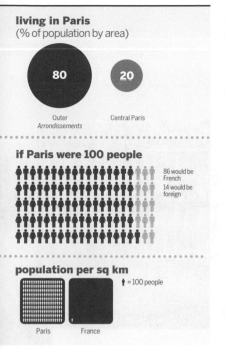

living in Paris
(% of population by area)

80 — Outer Arrondissements

20 — Central Paris

if Paris were 100 people

86 would be French

14 would be foreign

population per sq km

♀ = 100 people

Paris   France

Ultimately, the surrounding suburbs – Vincennes, Neuilly, Issy, St-Denis etc – will lose their autonomy and become part of a much larger Grand Paris governed by the Hôtel de Ville.

Major transport developments also include a high-speed train link between Charles de Gaulle Airport and central Paris by 2024. Orly Airport will be served by metro from 2024 and high-speed train by 2025.

Streamlined Centre

Conversely, inner Paris is shrinking, at least administratively. From 2020, its four central arrondissements, the 1er, 2e, 3e and 4e, will be governed by a single mayor, based at the Mairie du 3e (the 3e's town hall), to better balance services such as childcare based on the number of residents (the 15e has 15 times the population of the 1er arrondissement). The location was voted on by the arrondissements' residents in 2018, who in the same ballot also chose a new name for the district, 'Paris Centre'.

While Paris will only have 17 mayors, the postcodes and addresses of all 20 arrondissements remain the same.

Greener Living

Mayor of Paris Anne Hidalgo is focused on greening the city and minimising car traffic and pollution. Since taking office in 2014, Hidalgo has pedestrianised 3.3km of Right Bank expressway between the Tuileries and Bastille, closed the av des Champs-Élysées on the first Sunday of each month, established an annual car-free day and introduced the Crit'Air Vignette (compulsory anti-pollution sticker) for vehicles registered after 1997 between 8am and 8pm Monday to Friday (older vehicles are banned within the bd Périphérique during these hours).

Ongoing projects include investing €150 million in cycling infrastructure (including an av des Champs-Élysées cycling lane), reducing parking spaces by 55,000 per year, instigating a city-wide maximum speed limit of 30km/h (except along major arteries) by 2020 to minimise noise pollution, and banning diesel cars by 2024 and petrol cars by 2030.

Busy intersections such as place de la Madeleine and Nation have been redesigned to reduce traffic flow. A 'pedestrian peninsula' linking place de la Bastille with the Port de l'Arsenal marina is also scheduled to open in 2020.

Other goals include 100 hectares of green roofs, façades and vertical walls, a third of which will be devoted to urban agriculture.

Hidalgo, who will stand for a second six-year mayoral term in 2020, is also pushing for Paris' four central arrondissements to be pedestrianised.

Château de Versailles (p84)

JIMENA CONTRERAS/500PX ©

History

With its cobbled streets, terraced cafes and iconic landmarks, Paris evokes a sense of timelessness, yet the city has changed and evolved dramatically over the centuries. Paris' history is a saga of battles, bloodshed, grand-scale excesses, revolution, reformation, resistance, renaissance and constant reinvention. This epic is not just consigned to museums and archives: reminders of the capital's and the country's history are evident all over the city.

3rd century BC	**52 BC**	**AD 509**
Celtic Gauls called Parisii arrive in the Paris area and set up wattle-and-daub huts on the Seine.	Roman legions under Titus Labienus crush a Celtic revolt on Mons Lutetius and establish the town of Lutetia.	Clovis I becomes the first king of the Franks and declares Paris the seat of his new kingdom.

Tombeau de Napoléon 1er (p105), Hôtel des Invalides

MANJIK/SHUTTERSTOCK ©

The Beginnings to the Renaissance

Paris was born in the 3rd century BC, when a tribe of Celtic Gauls known as the Parisii settled on what is now the Île de la Cité. Centuries of conflict between the Gauls and Romans ended in 52 BC, when Julius Caesar's legions crushed a Celtic revolt. Christianity was introduced in the 2nd century AD, and Roman rule ended in the 5th century with the arrival of the Germanic Franks. In 508 Frankish king Clovis I united Gaul and made Paris his seat.

France's west coast was beset in the 9th century by Scandinavian Vikings (also known as Norsemen and, later, as Normans). Three centuries later, the Normans started pushing toward Paris, which had risen rapidly in importance: construction had begun on the cathedral of Notre Dame in the 12th century, the Louvre began life as a riverside fortress around 1200, Ste-Chapelle was consecrated in 1248 and the Sorbonne opened in 1253.

The Vikings' incursions heralded the Hundred Years War between Norman England and Paris' Capetian dynasty, bringing French defeat in 1415 and English control of the capital in

1643	**14 July 1789**	**1793**
'Sun King' Louis XIV ascends the throne aged five but only assumes absolute power in 1661.	The French Revolution begins when a mob arms itself with stolen weapons and storms the prison at Bastille.	Louis XVI is tried, convicted and executed; Marie Antoinette's turn comes nine months later.

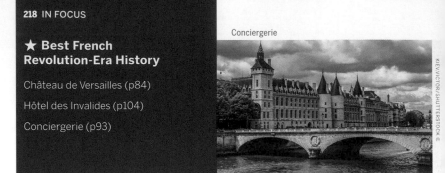

Conciergerie

★ **Best French Revolution-Era History**

Château de Versailles (p84)

Hôtel des Invalides (p104)

Conciergerie (p93)

1420. In 1429 the 17-year-old Jeanne d'Arc (Joan of Arc) rallied the French troops to defeat the English at Orléans. With the exception of Calais, the English were eventually expelled from France in 1453.

The Renaissance helped Paris get back on its feet in the late 15th century. However, turmoil ensued as clashes between Huguenot (Protestant) and Catholic groups culminated in the St Bartholomew's Day massacre in 1572.

The Revolution to a New Republic

A five-year-old Louis XIV (later known as the Sun King) ascended the throne in 1643 and ruled until 1715, virtually emptying the national coffers with his ambitious battling and building, including the construction of his extravagant palace at Versailles. The excesses of this grandiose king and his heirs, including Louis XVI and his Vienna-born queen Marie Antoinette, eventually led to an uprising of Parisians on 14 July 1789, kick-starting the French Revolution. Within four years, the Reign of Terror was in full swing.

The unstable post-revolutionary government was consolidated in 1799 under Napoléon Bonaparte, who declared himself First Consul. In 1804 he had the Pope crown him emperor of the French, and went on to conquer most of Europe before his eventual defeat at Waterloo in present-day Belgium in 1815. He was exiled to St Helena, and died in 1821.

France struggled under a string of mostly inept rulers until a coup d'état in 1851 brought Emperor Napoléon III to power. At his behest, Baron Haussmann razed whole tracts of the city, replacing them with sculptured parks, a hygienic sewer system and – strategically – boulevards too broad for rebels to barricade. Napoléon III embroiled France in a costly war with Prussia in 1870, which ended within months with the French army's defeat and the capture of the emperor, prompting citizens to take to the streets, demanding a republic.

1799

Napoléon Bonaparte overthrows the Directory and seizes control of the government in a coup d'état.

1852–70

During the Second Empire of Napoléon III much of the city is redesigned or rebuilt by Baron Haussmann as the Paris we know today.

1940

Germany launches the battle for France, and the four-year occupation of Paris under direct German rule begins.

Twentieth-Century History

Out of the conflict of WWI, in which 1.3 million French soldiers lost their lives, came increased industrialisation that confirmed Paris' place as a major commercial, artistic and intellectual centre.

This was halted by WWII and the Nazi occupation of 1940. During Paris' occupation, almost half the population evacuated, including General Charles de Gaulle, France's under-secretary of war, who fled to London and set up a government-in-exile. In a radio broadcast he appealed to French patriots to continue resisting, and established the Forces Françaises Libres (Free French Forces) to fight alongside the Allies. Following Paris' liberation, de Gaulle set up a provisional government, but resigned in 1946; he formed his own party and remained in opposition until 1958, when he was returned to power. He was succeeded as president in 1969 by Gaullist leader Georges Pompidou.

After the war, Paris regained its position as a creative nucleus and nurtured a revitalised liberalism that peaked with the student-led uprisings of May 1968 – the Sorbonne was occupied, the Latin Quarter blockaded and a general strike paralysed the country.

Under centre-right President Jacques Chirac's watch, the late 1990s saw Paris seize the international spotlight with the rumour-plagued death of Princess Diana in 1997, and France's first-ever football World Cup victory in July 1998.

The New Millennium

In May 2001 Socialist Bertrand Delanoë was elected mayor, becoming widely popular for making Paris more liveable through improved infrastructure and green spaces.

Chirac's second presidential term, starting in 2002, was marred in 2005 by the fatal electrocutions of two teenagers who were allegedly hiding from police in an electricity substation, which sparked city- then country-wide riots.

Against the backdrop of the global recession, Chirac's successor, Nicolas Sarkozy, struggled to keep the French economy buoyant. His popularity plummeted, paving the way for Socialist Francois Hollande's victory in the 2012 presidential elections. Hollande's own economic policies proved ineffectual, and his popularity likewise plunged. Following the 2014 municipal elections. the election of Socialist Anne Hidalgo, Paris' first female mayor, meant the capital was one of the few cities to remain on the political left.

Turbulent Times

The year 2015 was bookended by tragedy. On 7 January the offices of magazine *Charlie Hebdo* were attacked in response to satirical images it published of the prophet Muhammad. Eleven staff and one police officer were killed and a further 22 people were injured.

25 August 1944
Spearheaded by Free French units, Allied forces liberate Paris and the city escapes destruction.

1968
Paris is rocked by student-led riots; de Gaulle is forced to resign the following year.

2014
Spanish-born Anne Hidalgo becomes the first female mayor of Paris.

★ **Best WWII-Era History**

Hôtel des Invalides (p104)

Bronze plaque, Arc de Triomphe (p42)

Bar Hemingway (p173)

Pont Alexandre III and Hôtel des Invalides

On the night of 13 November 2015 a series of coordinated terrorist attacks occurred in Paris and St-Denis – the deadliest on French soil since WWII. Three explosions shook the Stade de France stadium during a football match. A series of neighbourhood restaurants and their outdoor terraces in the 10e and 11e were attacked by suicide bombers and gunmen. Three gunmen fired into the audience of Le Bataclan, where American band Eagles of Death Metal were performing. Over the course of the evening, 130 people lost their lives (89 in Le Bataclan alone) and 368 were injured, 99 seriously.

Parisians responded by taking to cafe terraces and other public spaces. The hashtag #jesuisenterrasse (I am on the terrace) represented Parisians' refusal to live in fear. The long-planned United Nations Climate Change Conference (COP21) also went ahead shortly afterwards. During the conference leaders from around the world reached an agreement to limit global warming to less than 2°C by the end of the century.

New President, New Directions

France's most recent presidential elections took place in 2017. The traditional parties were eliminated in the first round, with Emmanuel Macron, who launched centrist, pro-EU movement En Marche! (now the party La République en Marche) in 2016, defeating far-right Front National candidate Marine Le Pen 66.1% to 33.9% in the second-round run-off. At age 39, Macron became France's youngest-ever president. La République en Marche went on to field candidates in 2017's legislative elections and secure an absolute majority (308 seats) in the Assemblée Nationale, allowing Macron to forge ahead with economic reforms.

From late 2018, Macron's reforms were tested when *gilets jaunes* ('yellow vests', named for the hi-vis vests French drivers are required to keep in their cars in the event of breakdowns) protested against his government's eco fuel tax, which quickly spread to encompass a broader dissatisfaction felt by citizens affected by high living costs. The government abolished the eco tax, and police resistance helped quell the violence.

Sporting events have been a highlight, with France winning the FIFA football World Cup in 2018. Meanwhile, Paris is preparing to host fixtures for the 2023 Rugby World Cup, and the 2024 Summer Olympics and Summer Paralympics.

2015	**2017**	**2018–19**
Deadly terrorist attacks take place at the offices of *Charlie Hebdo* on 7 January, and in multiple locations on 13 November.	Without the support of an established party, Emmanuel Macron makes history by being elected France's first centrist president.	Protests by *gilets jaunes* ('yellow vests') against economic reforms and inequality take the streets of Paris and France.

Hôtel Drouot (p225)

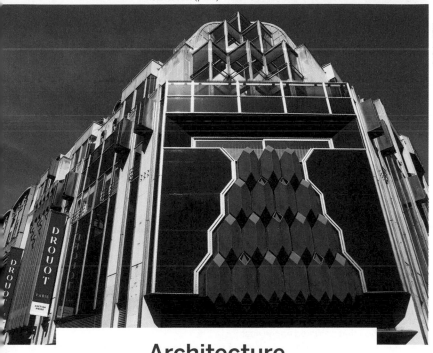

MILAN-POYET ©

Architecture

It took disease, clogged streets and Baron Georges-Eugène Haussmann to drag architectural Paris out of the Middle Ages and into the modern world. Yet ever since Haussmann's radical transformation of the city in the 19th century, Paris has never looked back. Today its skyline shimmers with the whole gamut of architectural styles, from Roman arenas and Gothic cathedrals to post-modernist cubes and futuristic skyscrapers.

Gallo-Roman

Traces of Roman Paris can be seen in the residential foundations in the Crypte Archéologique in front of Notre Dame; in the Arènes de Lutèce; and in the *frigidarium* (cooling room) and other remains of Roman baths dating from around AD 200 at the Musée National du Moyen Âge.

The latter museum also contains the *Pillier des Nautes* (Boatsmen's Pillar), one of the most valuable legacies of the Gallo-Roman period. It is a 2.5m-high monument dedicated to Jupiter and was erected by the boatmen's guild during the reign of Tiberius (AD 14–37) on the Île de la Cité. The boat has become the symbol of Paris, and the city's Latin motto is *'Fluctuat Nec Mergitur'* (Tossed by Waves but Does Not Sink).

Sainte-Chapelle

Merovingian & Carolingian

Although quite a few churches were built in Paris during the Merovingian and Carolingian periods (6th to 10th centuries), very little of them remains.

When the Merovingian ruler Clovis I made Paris his seat in the early 6th century, he established an abbey on the south bank of the Seine. All that remains is the Tour Clovis, a heavily restored Romanesque tower within the grounds of the prestigious Lycée Henri IV just east of the Panthéon.

Romanesque

A religious revival in the 11th century led to the construction of many *roman* (Romanesque) churches, typically with round arches, heavy walls, few (and small) windows and a lack of ornamentation that bordered on the austere.

No remaining building in Paris is entirely Romanesque, but several have important representative elements, including the bell tower of Église St-Germain des Prés.

Gothic

In the 14th century the Rayonnant (Radiant) Gothic style, named after the radiating tracery of the rose windows, developed. Interiors became even lighter thanks to broader windows and more translucent stained glass. One of the most influential Rayonnant buildings was Sainte-Chapelle, which incorporates Paris' finest stained glass. The two transept facades of Cathédrale de Notre Dame de Paris and the vaulted Salle des Gens d'Armes (Cavalrymen's Hall) in the Conciergerie, the largest surviving medieval hall in Europe, are other fine examples of Rayonnant Gothic style.

By the 15th century decorative extravagance led to Flamboyant Gothic, so named because the wavy stone carving made the towers appear to be blazing or flaming *(flamboyant)*. Several *hôtels particuliers* (private mansions) were built in this style, including Hôtel de Cluny, now the Musée National du Moyen Âge.

Renaissance

The Renaissance set out to realise a 'rebirth' of classical Greek and Roman culture and first affected France at the end of the 15th century, when Charles VIII began a series of invasions of Italy, returning with some new ideas.

The Early Renaissance style, in which a variety of classical components and decorative motifs (columns, tunnel vaults, round arches, domes etc) were blended with the rich decoration of Flamboyant Gothic, is best exemplified in Paris by Église St-Eustache on the Right Bank and Église St-Étienne du Mont on the Left Bank.

Mannerism was introduced by Italian architects and artists brought to France around 1530 by François I. In 1546 Pierre Lescot designed the richly decorated southwestern corner of the Cour Carrée at the Musée du Louvre.

The Right Bank district of Le Marais remains the best area for Renaissance reminders in Paris proper, with some fine *hôtels particuliers*, such as Hôtel Carnavalet, housing part of the Musée Carnavalet.

Baron Haussmann

The iconic apartment buildings that line the boulevards of central Paris, with their cream-coloured stone and curvy wrought-iron balconies, are the work of Baron Haussmann (1809–91), prefect of the Seine *département* between 1853 and 1870.

Baroque

During the Baroque period (tail end of the 16th to late 18th century), painting, sculpture and classical architecture were integrated to create structures and interiors of great subtlety, refinement and elegance. With the advent of the Baroque, architecture became more pictorial, with painted church ceilings illustrating the Passion of Christ to the faithful, and palaces invoking the power and order of the state.

Salomon de Brosse, who designed the Palais du Luxembourg in the Jardin du Luxembourg in 1615, set the stage for two of France's most prominent early-Baroque architects: François Mansart, designer of Église Notre Dame du Val-de-Grâce, and his young rival Louis Le Vau, architect of Château de Vaux-le-Vicomte, which served as a model for Louis XIV's palace at Versailles.

Other fine French-Baroque examples include Église St-Louis en l'Île, Chapelle de la Sorbonne, Palais Royal and Hôtel de Sully, with its inner courtyard decorated with allegorical figures.

Neoclassicism

Neoclassical architecture emerged about 1740 and had its roots in the renewed interest in classical forms – a search for order, reason and serenity through the adoption of forms and conventions of Graeco-Roman antiquity: columns, geometric forms and traditional ornamentation.

Among the earliest examples of this style are the Italianate facade of Église St-Sulpice, and the Petit Trianon at Versailles, designed by Jacques-Ange Gabriel for Louis XV in 1761. The domed building in Paris housing the Institut de France is a masterpiece of early French neoclassical architecture, but France's greatest neoclassical architect of the 18th century was Jacques-Germain Soufflot, creator of the Panthéon in the Latin Quarter.

Neoclassicism came into its own under Napoléon, who used it extensively for monumental architecture intended to embody the grandeur of imperial France and its capital: the Arc de Triomphe, the Arc de Triomphe du Carrousel, Église de Ste-Marie Madeleine, the Bourse de Commerce, and the Assemblée Nationale in the Palais Bourbon. The peak of this great 19th-century movement was Palais Garnier, the city's opera house designed by Charles Garnier.

La Seine Musicale (p190) interior

QUENTIN BOULLEGON ©

Art Nouveau

Art nouveau, which emerged in Europe and the USA in the second half of the 19th century under various names (Jugendstil, Sezessionstil, Stile Liberty, Modernisme), caught on quickly in Paris, and its influence lasted until WWI. It was characterised by sinuous curves and flowing, asymmetrical forms reminiscent of creeping vines, water lilies, the patterns on insect wings and the flowering boughs of trees. Influenced by the arrival of exotic objets d'art from Japan, art nouveau's French name came from a Paris gallery that featured works in the 'new art' style.

A lush and photogenic architectural style, art nouveau is expressed to perfection in Paris by Hector Guimard's graceful metro entrances and Le Marais synagogue; the former train station housing the Musée d'Orsay; and department stores including Le Bon Marché, Galeries Lafayette and La Samaritaine.

20th Century

Until 1968, French architects almost exclusively trained at the conformist École de Beaux Arts, reflected in most of the early impersonal and forgettable 'lipstick tubes' and 'upended shoebox' structures erected in the skyscraper district of La Défense and the 210m-tall Tour Montparnasse (1973).

Paris' most notable 20th-century additions were at the behest of the French presidents' *grands projets* ('great works'). Georges Pompidou commissioned the once reviled, now much-loved Centre Pompidou. His successor, Valéry Giscard d'Estaing, was instrumental in transforming the derelict Gare d'Orsay train station into the glorious Musée d'Orsay (1986).

François Mitterrand surpassed all of the postwar presidents with monumental projects. Jean Nouvel's Institut du Monde Arabe (1987), built during this time, mixes modern Arab and Western elements and is arguably one of the city's most beautiful late-20th-century buildings. Mitterrand also oversaw the city's second opera house, tile-clad Opéra Bastille, designed by Carlos Ott in 1989; the monumental Grande Arche de la Défense by Johan-Otto von Sprekelsen (1989); IM Pei's glass-pyramid entrance at the Musée du Louvre (1989); and the four open book-shaped glass towers of the €2 billion Bibliothèque Nationale de France (Dominique Perrault, 1995).

Jacques Chirac orchestrated the magnificent Musée du Quai Branly, a glass, wood and sod structure with a 3-hectare experimental garden, also by Jean Nouvel.

Contemporary

IM Pei's Louvre pyramid paved the way for Mario Bellini and Rudy Ricciotti's magnificent 'flying carpet' roof atop the museum's Cour Visconti in 2012.

Drawing on the city's longstanding tradition of metalwork and glass in its architecture, Canadian architect Frank Gehry used 12 enormous glass 'sails' to design the Fondation Louis Vuitton, which opened in the Bois de Boulogne in late 2014.

Jean Nouvel's Philharmonie de Paris, a state-of-the-art creation with a dazzling metallic facade that took three years to build and that cost €381 million, opened in 2015.

Glass is a big feature of the 1970s-eyesore-turned-contemporary-stunner Forum des Halles shopping centre in the 1er – a curvaceous, curvilinear and glass-topped construction by architects Patrick Berger and Jacques Anziutti, completed in 2016. Another eyesore undergoing renewal is 1970s skyscraper the Tour Montparnasse, due for completion in 2023.

Jean Nouvel is heading the massive Gare d'Austerlitz renovation expected to finish in 2021. One-third of the budget was allocated to repairing the glass roof.

Porte Maillot will be transformed by Mille Arbres (Thousand Trees), a spectacular tree-topped glass structure by Japanese architect Sou Fujimoto and French architect Manal Rachdi. It will provide a pivotal link between central Paris and Grand Paris (Greater Paris) when it opens in 2022.

Hôtel Drouot

A zany structure if ever there was one is auction house **Hôtel Drouot** (www.drouot.com; 9 rue Drouot, 9e). After a late-1970s surrealist facelift by architects Jean-Jacques Fernier and André Biro, the 19th-century Haussmann building was instantly hailed as a modern architectural gem.

Art Deco Renaissance

Recent years have seen a renaissance of some of Paris' loveliest art deco buildings. Neo-Egyptian cinema Le Louxor reopened in 2013. The following year, the luxury McGallery arm of the Accor hotel group opened a five-star hotel and spa in the celebrated Molitor swimming-pool complex in western Paris, where the bikini made its first appearance in the 1930s. In Le Marais, thermal-baths-turned-1980s-nightclub Les Bain Douches, another legendary address, opened as luxury hotel Les Bains after years of being abandoned.

Art deco swimming complexes Piscine de la Butte aux Cailles and Piscine des Amiraux reopened in 2017; the latter was built in 1930 by La Samaritaine architect Henri Sauvage.

Founded in 1870 by Ernest Cognacq and Louise Jaÿ, La Samaritaine's 2019 reopening preserves some 75% of the original art nouveau and art deco exterior.

Vertical Gardens

A signature architectural feature of Paris is the vertical garden, or *mur végétal* (vegetation wall). Seeming to defy gravity, these gardens cover walls in chic boutique interiors, outside museums, within spas and elsewhere. The Seine-facing garden at the Musée du Quai Branly – Jacques Chirac, by Patrick Blanc, is Paris' most famous.

Another standout work of living art by Patrick Blanc is L'Oasis d'Aboukir, on the corner of rue d'Aboukir and rue des Petits-Carreaux, 2e (the northern extension of rue Montorgueil). Installed on a 25m-high blank building facade in 2013, it's subtitled *Hymne à la Biodiversité* (Ode to Biodiversity). The 'living wall' incorporates some 7600 plants from 237 different species. It's since flourished to cover a total surface area of 250 sq metres in greenery.

Daft Punk (p230) in performance

ANDREA RAFFIN/SHUTTERSTOCK ©

Arts

*While art in Paris today means anything and everything –
bold installations in the metro, digital art projections
both inside and outside exhibition spaces, mechanical
sculptures, monumental wall frescoes, tiled Space
Invader tags and other gregarious street art, including in
dedicated street-art museums – the city's rich art heritage
has its roots firmly embedded in the traditional genres of
painting and sculpture.*

Baroque to Neoclassicism

According to philosopher Voltaire, French painting proper began with Baroque painter
Nicolas Poussin (1594–1665), the greatest representative of 17th-century classicism, who
frequently set scenes from ancient Rome, classical mythology and the Bible in ordered
landscapes bathed in golden light.

Jean-Baptiste Chardin (1699–1779) brought the humbler domesticity of the Dutch
masters to French art, while in 1785 neoclassical artist Jacques Louis David (1748–1825)
wooed the public with his vast portraits with clear republican messages. Jean-Auguste-
Dominique Ingres (1780–1867), David's most gifted pupil in Paris, continued the neoclassical tradition.

Romanticism

One of the Louvre's most gripping paintings, *The Raft of the Medusa* by Théodore Géricault (1791–1824), hovers on the threshold of romanticism; his friend Eugène Delacroix (1798–1863), best known for his masterpiece commemorating the July Revolution of 1830, *Liberty Leading the People*, was a leader of the movement.

In sculpture, the work of Paris-born Auguste Rodin (1840–1917) overcame the conflict between neoclassicism and romanticism. One of Rodin's most gifted pupils was his lover Camille Claudel (1864–1943), whose work can be seen with Rodin's in the Musée Rodin.

Realism

The realists were all about social comment. Édouard Manet (1832–83) used realism to depict Parisian middle classes, yet he included in his pictures numerous references to the old masters.

One of the best sculptors of this period was François Rude (1784–1855), creator of the relief on the Arc de Triomphe and several pieces in the Musée d'Orsay. By the mid-19th century, memorial statues in public places had replaced sculpted tombs, making such statues all the rage.

Sculptor Jean-Baptiste Carpeaux (1827–75) began as a romantic, but his work in Paris – such as *The Dance* on the Palais Garnier and his fountain in the Jardin du Luxembourg – recalls the gaiety and flamboyance of the Baroque era.

Impressionism

Paris' Musée d'Orsay is the crown jewel of impressionism. Initially a term of derision, 'impressionism' was taken from the title of an 1874 experimental painting, *Impression: Soleil Levant* (Impression: Sunrise) by Claude Monet (1840–1926). Monet was the leading figure of the school, and a visit to the Musée d'Orsay unveils a host of other members, among them Alfred Sisley (1839–99), Camille Pissarro (1830–1903), Pierre-Auguste Renoir (1841–1919) and Berthe Morisot (1841–95). The impressionists' main aim was to capture the effects of fleeting light, painting almost universally in the open air – and light came to dominate the content of their painting.

Edgar Degas (1834–1917), buried in the Cimetière de Montmartre, was a fellow traveller of the impressionists, but he preferred painting cafe life (*Absinthe*) and in ballet studios (*The Dance Class*) over the great outdoors – several beautiful examples hang in the Musée d'Orsay.

Henri de Toulouse-Lautrec (1864–1901) was a great admirer of Degas but chose subjects one or two notches less salubrious: people in the bistros, brothels and music halls of Montmartre (eg *Au Moulin Rouge*). He is best known for his posters and lithographs, in which the distortion of the figures is both satirical and decorative.

Paul Cézanne (1839–1906) is celebrated for his still lifes and landscapes depicting southern France, though he spent many years in Paris after breaking with the impressionists. The name of Paul Gauguin (1848–1903) immediately conjures up studies of Tahitian and Breton women. Both Cézanne and Gauguin were postimpressionists, a catch-all term for the diverse styles that flowed from impressionism.

Pointillism & Symbolism

Pointillism was a technique developed by Georges Seurat (1859–91), who applied paint in small dots or uniform brush strokes of unmixed colour to produce fine 'mosaics' of warm and cool tones. His tableau *Une Baignade, Asnières* (Bathers at Asnières) is a perfect example.

Metro Art

Art adorns many of the stations of the world-famous Métropolitain. The following is just a sample of the most interesting stations from an artistic perspective.

Abbesses (line 12 metro entrance) The noodlelike pale-green metalwork and glass canopy of the station entrance is one of the finest examples of the work of Hector Guimard (1867–1942), the celebrated French art nouveau architect whose signature style once graced most metro stations.

Bastille (line 5 platform) A 180-sq-metre ceramic fresco features scenes taken from newspaper engravings published during the Revolution, with illustrations of the destruction of the infamous prison.

Chaussée d'Antin-Lafayette (line 7 platform) A large allegorical painting on the vaulted ceiling recalls the Marquis de Lafayette (1757–1834) and his role as general in the American Revolution.

Cluny–La Sorbonne (line 10 platform) A large ceramic mosaic replicates the signatures of Latin Quarter intellectuals, artists and scientists through history, including Molière (1622–73), Rabelais (c 1483–1553) and Robespierre (1758–96).

Concorde (line 12 platform) On the station walls, 45,000 white-and-blue ceramic tiles spell out the text of the *Déclaration des Droits de l'Homme et du Citoyen* (Declaration of the Rights of Man and of the Citizen), setting forth the principles of the French Revolution.

Palais Royal–Musée du Louvre (line 1 metro entrance) The zany entrance on place du Palais by Jean-Michel Othoniel (b 1964) is composed of two crown-shaped cupolas consisting of 800 coloured glass balls.

Henri Rousseau (1844–1910) was a contemporary of the postimpressionists, but his 'naive' art was unaffected by them. His dreamlike pictures of the Paris suburbs and of jungle and desert scenes (eg *The Snake Charmer*) – in the Musée d'Orsay – have influenced art right up to this century. The eerie treatment of mythological subjects by Gustave Moreau (1826–98) can be seen in the artist's studio, now within the Musée Gustave-Moreau in the 9e.

20th-Century Art

Twentieth-century French painting styles included Fauvism, named after the slur of a critic who compared the exhibitors at the 1905 Salon d'Automne (Autumn Salon) in Paris with *fauves* (wild animals) because of their wild brush strokes and radical use of intensely bright colours. Among these 'beastly' painters was Henri Matisse (1869–1954).

Cubism was launched in 1907 with *Les Demoiselles d'Avignon* by Spanish prodigy Pablo Picasso (1881–1973). Cubism, as developed by Picasso, Georges Braque (1882–1963) and Juan Gris (1887–1927), deconstructed the subject into a system of intersecting planes and presented various aspects simultaneously.

Marcel Duchamp (1887–1968) captured the rebellious, iconoclastic spirit of Dadaism – a Swiss-born literary and artistic movement of revolt – in his *Mona Lisa*, complete with moustache and goatee. In 1922 German Dadaist Max Ernst (1891–1976) moved to Paris and worked on surrealism, a Dada offshoot that flourished between the wars. The most influential proponent of this style in Paris was Spanish-born artist Salvador Dalí (1904–89), who arrived in the French capital in 1929 and painted some of his most seminal works while residing here. To see his work, visit the Dalí Espace Montmartre.

Contemporary Art

Street art took off in Paris thanks to Blek le Rat (Xavier Prou; b 1951), whose pioneering stencilled black rats across the city inspired artists such as Banksy, as well as French artist Levalet (Charles Leval; b 1988), who pastes lifelike, site-specific images in Indian ink on craft paper onto walls. Today, street art remains huge; in addition to tiled Space Invader tags and vast murals covering entire high-rise buildings, graffitied streets such Belleville's rue Dénoyez and art-collective canvases including rue Oberkampf's Le MUR, there are now also two street-art museums in the city and companies running dedicated guided tours.

Digital art is also gaining ground: arts centre EP7 screens projections onto its façade, and L'Atelier des Lumières is Paris' first digital-art museum; both opened in 2018.

Literary Arts

Paris has nurtured countless French authors over the centuries who, together with expat writers from Dickens onwards – including the Lost Generation's Hemingway, Fitzgerald and Joyce – have sealed Paris' literary reputation.

Contemporary French writers include Jean Echenoz, Erik Orsenna, Marc Levy, Christine Angot and comedian/dramatist Nelly Alard, whose second novel *Moment d'un couple* (Moment of a Couple), published in 2013, was translated into English as *Couple Mechanics* in 2016.

Delving into the mood and politics of the capital's notable ethnic population is Faïza Guène (b 1985), a French literary sensation who writes in an 'urban slang' style.

Surreal works by ex–French border guard turned author Romain Puértolas (b 1975) include 2015's *La Petite Fille Qui Avait Avalé un Nuage Grand Comme la Tour Eiffel* (The Little Girl Who Swallowed a Cloud as Big as the Eiffel Tower).

Music

Pop

French pop has come a long way since the *yéyé* (imitative rock) days of the 1960s as sung by Johnny Hallyday (1959–2017).

Indie rock band Phoenix, from Versailles, has six hugely successful albums under its belt, including 2017's *Ti Amo*. French psych-punk rock band La Femme's output includes *Mystère* (2016). Nosfell is one of France's most creative and intense musicians, who sings in his own invented language called *'le klokobetz'*.

In 2011 Sylvie Hoarau and Aurélie Saada formed the indie folk duo Brigitte; their 2017 album *Nues* achieved widespread success.

Internationally successful modern pop stars include singer-songwriter Chris (previously Christine and the Queens; aka Héloïse Letissier; b 1988), who released her first album, *Chaleur Humaine,* in 2014 and most recently *Chris* in 2018, and Jain (Jeanne Galice; b 1992), whose debut album, *Zanaka*, was released in 2015, followed by *Souldier* in 2018.

Jazz

Paris was introduced to jazz during WWI, when African-American soldiers from US troops stationed in France came together to play ragtime and jazz in the city's music halls, and really took off during the 1920s, when it attracted US performers such as Josephine Baker who were fleeing segregation. Many returned during the Great Depression, which gave rise to French jazz: Parisian jazz violinist Stéphane Grappelli (1908–97) and Roma guitarist Django Reinhardt (1910–53) jammed together in sessions promoted by the Hot Club of France quintet. Claude Luter and his Dixieland band were hip in the 1950s.

The *chanson française,* a tradition dating from troubadours in the Middle Ages, was eclipsed by the music halls of the early 20th century but was revived in the 1930s by Édith

Cimetière du Père Lachaise

Piaf (1915–63), followed by 'France's Frank Sinatra', Charles Aznavour (1924–2018). In the 1950s Left Bank cabarets nurtured singers like Georges Brassens (1921–81), Jacques Brel (1929–78) and Serge Gainsbourg (1928–91). The genre was revived in the new millennium as *la nouvelle chanson française* by performers like Zaz (Isabelle Geffroy; b 1980), who mixes jazz, soul, acoustic and traditional *chansons*.

Electronica

Paris' electronic dance music is renowned; internationally successful bands such as Daft Punk and Justice head up the scene. David Guetta, Laurent Garnier, Martin Solveig and Bob Sinclar (aka Christophe Le Friant, originally nicknamed 'Chris the French Kiss') are top Parisian electronica producers and DJs who travel the international circuit. Breakbot (Thibaut Berland; b 1981) released his first album in 2012 and gained a rapid following for his remixes. His 2016-released album *Still Waters* includes the track Star Tripper, featured in Disney's *Star Wars*–themed music album *Star Wars Headspace*.

Film

Paris is one of the world's most cinematic cities. The French capital has produced a bevy of blockbuster film-makers and stars and is the filming location of countless box-office hits by both home-grown and foreign directors.

French cinema hasn't looked back since 2012, when *The Artist* (2011), a silent black-and-white romantic comedy set in 1920s Hollywood, became the most awarded film in French cinema history.

One of the most successful French-language films ever is *Intouchables* (Untouchable; 2011). Directed by Parisian Éric Toledano and Olivier Nakache, the comic drama is about a billionaire quadriplegic and his live-in Senegalese carer in Paris. The film scooped Best Foreign Film at both the Golden Globes and the BAFTA Awards in 2013.

France's leading lady is Parisian Marion Cotillard (b 1975), the first French woman since 1959 to win an Oscar, for her role as Édith Piaf in Olivier Dahan's *La Môme* (La Vie en Rose; 2007). The versatile actress went on to play a wide variety of roles including in 2017's *Rock'n Roll*, as the partner of Guillaume Canet (her real-life partner), who plays an actor told by his young co-star that he's no longer 'rock 'n' roll' enough to sell films any more; *Les Fantômes d'Ismaël* (Ismael's Ghosts) as a wife who returns from a 20-year disappearance; and 2018's *Gueule d'Ange* (Angel Face), about a mother who abandons her child.

Film buffs shouldn't miss the Cinémathèque Française, with a film museum and cinema; and the Parisian film archive, Forum des Images.

Entrance to Abbesses metro station (p228)

ARCADY/SHUTTERSTOCK ©

Survival Guide

Directory A–Z

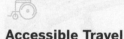

Accessible Travel

o For information about which cultural venues in Paris are accessible to people with disabilities, check Accès Culture (www. accesculture.org).

o Download Lonely Planet's free *Accessible Travel* guide from http://lptravel.to/ accessibletravel.

Discount Cards

Almost all museums and monuments in Paris have discounted tickets *(tarif réduit)* for students and seniors (generally over 60

Book Your Stay Online

For accommodation reviews by Lonely Planet authors, check out http://hotels. lonelyplanet.com/paris. You'll find independent reviews, as well as recommendations on the best places to stay. Best of all, you can book online.

years), provided they have valid ID. Children often get in for free; the cut-off age for 'child' is anywhere between six and 18 years. EU citizens under 26 years get in for free at national monuments and museums.

Paris Museum Pass (www. parismuseumpass.com; two/ four/six days €48/62/74) Gets you into 50-plus venues in and around Paris; a huge advantage is that pass holders usually enter larger sights at a different entrance, meaning you bypass (or substantially reduce) ridiculously long ticket queues.

Paris Passlib' (www.parisinfo. com; two/three/five days €109/129/155) Sold at the **Paris Convention & Visitors Bureau** (Paris Office de Tourisme; ☑01 49 52 42 63; 29 rue de Rivoli, 4e; ⊕9am-7pm May-Oct, 10am-7pm Nov-Apr; ☜; ⓂHôtel de Ville) and on its website, this handy city pass covers unlimited public transport in zones 1 to 3, admission to some 50 museums in the Paris region (aka a Paris Museum Pass), temporary exhibitions at most municipal museums, a one-hour **Bateaux Parisiens** (☑08 25 01 01 01; www.bateauxparisiens.com; Port de la Bourdonnais, 7e; adult/child €15/7; ☜; ⓂBir Hakeim or RER Pont de l'Alma) boat cruise along the Seine, and a one-day hop-on, hop-off open-top bus sightseeing service around central Paris' key sights with **L'Open Tour** (☑01 42 66 56 56; www.paris. opentour.com; 1-day pass adult/ child €34/17, night tour €27/17; ☜). There's an optional €20

supplement for a skip-the-line ticket to levels one and two of the Eiffel Tower.

Electricity

Type E
220V/50Hz

Emergency

Ambulance (SAMU)	☑15
Fire	☑18
Police	☑17
EU-wide emergency	☑112

Health

Hospitals

Paris has some 50 hospitals including the epicentral **Hôpital Hôtel Dieu** (☑01 42 34 82 34; www.aphp.fr; 1 Parvis

Notre Dame – place Jean-Paul-II, 4e; Ⓜ️Cité). It is one of the city's main government-run public hospitals; after 8pm use the emergency entrance at 7 rue de la Cité.

Pharmacies

Pharmacies (chemists) are marked by a large illuminated green cross outside. At least one in each neighbourhood is open for extended hours; see www.parisinfo.com for listings.

Insurance

Comprehensive travel insurance to cover theft, loss and medical problems is highly recommended.

Worldwide travel insurance is available at www.lonelyplanet.com/travel-insurance. You can buy, extend and claim online anytime – even if you're already on the road.

Internet Access

o Wi-fi (pronounced '*wee-fee*' in France) is available in most Paris hotels, usually at no extra cost, and in some museums.

o Many cafes and bars have free wi-fi for customers; you may need to ask for the code.

o Free wi-fi is available in hundreds of public places, including parks, libraries

and municipal buildings; look for a purple 'Zone Wi-Fi' sign. To connect, select the 'PARIS_WI-FI_' network. Sessions are limited to two hours (renewable). For complete details and a map of hot spots, see www.paris.fr/wifi.

o Expect to pay around €1 per hour for access in internet cafes such as **Milk** (www.milklub.com; 31 bd de Sébastopol, 1er; 1hr €1; ⏱️24hr; Ⓜ️Les Halles or RER Châtelet–Les Halles).

o Co-working cafes have sprung up across Paris; you typically pay for a set amount of time, with wi-fi, drinks and snacks included.

Money

o ATMs (*distributeur automatique de billets* in French) are widespread.

o Visa and MasterCard are accepted in most hotels, shops and restaurants; fewer accept American Express. France uses cards with an embedded micro-chip and PIN – few places accept swipe-and-signature. Ask your bank for advice before you leave.

Opening Hours

The following list covers *approximate* standard opening hours. Many businesses

close in August for summer holidays.

Banks 9am to 1pm and 2pm to 5pm Monday to Friday; some open on Saturday morning

Bars & Cafes 7am to 2am

Museums 10am to 6pm; closed Monday or Tuesday

Post Offices 8am to 7pm Monday to Friday, and until noon Saturday

Restaurants noon to 2pm and 7.30pm to 10.30pm

Shops 10am to 7pm Monday to Saturday; they occasionally close in the early afternoon for lunch and sometimes all day Monday. Hours are longer for shops in defined ZTIs (international tourist zones).

Public Holidays

In France a *jour férié* (public holiday) is celebrated strictly on the day on which it falls. Thus if May Day falls on a Saturday or Sunday, no provision is made for an extra day off.

The following holidays are observed in Paris in 2020:

New Year's Day (Jour de l'An) 1 January

Easter Monday (Lundi de Pâques) 13 April

Labour Day (Fête du Travail) 1 May

Victory in Europe Day (Victoire 1945) 8 May

Ascension Thursday (L'Ascension) 21 May (celebrated on the 40th day after Easter)

Practicalities

Smoking Smoking is illegal in indoor public spaces, including restaurants and bars (hence the crowds of smokers in doorways and on pavement terraces outside).

Weights & Measures France uses the metric system.

Whit Monday (Lundi de Pentecôte) 1 June (seventh Monday after Easter)

Bastille Day/National Day (Fête Nationale) 14 July

Assumption Day (L'Assomption) 15 August

All Saints' Day (La Toussaint) 1 November

Armistice Day/Remembrance Day (Le Onze Novembre) 11 November

Christmas (Noël) 25 December

Safe Travel

Overall, Paris is well lit and safe, and random street assaults are rare.

o Stay alert for pickpockets and take precautions: don't carry more cash than you need, and keep credit cards and passports in a concealed pouch.

o Beware of scams such as fake petitions.

o Metro stations best avoided late at night include Châtelet–Les Halles, Château Rouge, Gare du Nord, Strasbourg St-Denis, Réaumur Sébastopol, Stalingrad and Montparnasse

Bienvenüe. Marx Dormoy, Porte de la Chapelle and Marcadet–Poissonniers can be sketchy day and night.

o *Bornes d'alarme* (alarm boxes) are located in the centre of metro/RER platforms and some station corridors.

Telephone

o There are no area codes in France – you always dial the 10-digit number.

o Telephone numbers in Paris always start with 01, unless the number is provided by an internet service provider (ISP), in which case it begins with 09.

o Mobile-phone numbers throughout France commence with either 06 or 07.

o France's country code is 33.

o To call abroad from Paris, dial France's international access code (00), the country code, the area code (drop the initial '0', if there is one) and the local number.

o Note that while numbers beginning with 08 00, 08 04, 08 05 and 08 09 are toll free in France, other numbers beginning with 08 are not.

o Customer-service numbers are generally more expensive than local rates.

o Most four-digit numbers starting with 10, 30 or 31 are free of charge.

o If you can read basic French, directory enquiries are best done via the *Yellow Pages* (www.pagesjaunes.fr; click on *Pages Blanches* for the *White Pages*), which will provide more information, including maps, for free.

o Check with your provider about roaming costs before you leave home, or ensure your phone's unlocked to use a French SIM card (available cheaply in Paris).

Time

o France uses the 24-hour clock in most cases, with the hours usually separated from the minutes by a lower-case 'h'. Thus, 15h30 is 3.30pm, 00h30 is 12.30am and so on.

o France is on Central European Time (like Berlin and Rome), which is one hour ahead of GMT/UTC.

o Daylight-saving time runs from the last Sunday in March, when the clocks move forward one hour, to the last Sunday in October.

Toilets

o Public toilets in Paris are signposted *toilettes* or *WC*. On main roads, *sanisettes* (self-cleaning cylindrical toilets) are open 24 hours and are free of charge. Look for the words *libre* ('available'; green-coloured) or *occupé* ('occupied'; red-coloured).

o Cafe owners do not appreciate your using their facilities if you are not a paying customer (a coffee can be a good investment); however, if you have young children they may make an exception (ask first!). Other good bets are big hotels and major department stores (the latter may incur a charge).

o There are free public toilets in front of Notre Dame cathedral, near the Arc de Triomphe, down the steps at Sacré-Cœur (to the east and west) and at the northwestern entrance to the Jardins des Tuileries.

Tourist Information

Paris' main tourist office, the **Paris Convention & Visitors Bureau** (Paris Office de Tourisme; ☑01 49 52 42 63; www.parisinfo.com; 29 rue de Rivoli, 4e; ◷9am-7pm May-Oct,

10am-7pm Nov-Apr; 🛜; Ⓜ Hôtel de Ville), is at the Hôtel de Ville. It sells tickets for tours and several attractions, plus museum and transport passes.

Visas

There are no entry requirements for nationals of EU countries and a handful of other European countries (including Switzerland). Citizens of Australia, the USA, Canada and New Zealand do not need visas to visit France for up to 90 days.

Everyone else, including citizens of South Africa, needs a Schengen Visa, named after the Schengen Agreement that has abolished passport controls among 26 EU countries and that has also been ratified by the non-EU governments of Iceland, Norway and Switzerland. A visa for any of these countries should be valid throughout the Schengen area, but it pays to double-check with the embassy or consulate of each country you intend to visit. Note that the UK and Ireland are not Schengen countries.

Check www.diplomatie. gouv.fr for the latest visa regulations and the closest French embassy to your current residence.

Transport

Arriving in Paris

Charles de Gaulle Airport
Trains (RER), buses and night buses to the city centre €6 to €18; taxi €50 to €55, 15% higher evenings and Sundays.

Orly Airport Trains (Orlyval then RER), buses and night buses to the city centre €8.70 to €13.25; T7 tram to Villejuif–Louis Aragon then metro to centre (€3.80); taxi €30 to €35, 15% higher evenings and Sundays.

Beauvais Airport Buses (€17) to Porte Maillot then metro (€1.90); taxi during the day/ night around €170/210 (probably more than the cost of your flight!).

Gare du Nord train station
Within central Paris; served by metro (€1.90).

Air

Charles de Gaulle Airport

Most international airlines fly to **Aéroport de Charles de Gaulle** (CDG; ☑01 70 36 39 50; www.parisaeroport.fr), 28km northeast of central Paris. In French the airport is commonly called 'Roissy' after the suburb in which it is located. A high-speed train link between Charles de Gaulle and Gare de l'Est

Climate Change & Travel

Every form of transport that relies on carbon-based fuel generates CO_2, the main cause of human-induced climate change. Modern travel is dependent on aeroplanes, which might use less fuel per kilometre per person than most cars but travel much greater distances. The altitude at which aircraft emit gases (including CO_2) and particles also contributes to their climate change impact. Many websites offer 'carbon calculators' that allow people to estimate the carbon emissions generated by their journey and, for those who wish to do so, to offset the impact of the greenhouse gases emitted with contributions to portfolios of climate-friendly initiatives throughout the world. Lonely Planet offsets the carbon footprint of all staff and author travel.

in central Paris is planned; when complete in 2024, the CDG Express will cut the current 50-minute journey to 20 minutes. Inter-terminal shuttle services are free. A fourth terminal is due to open by 2025.

Bus

There are six main bus lines.

Le Bus Direct line 2 (www. lebusdirect.com; €18, one hour, every 30 minutes from 5.45am to 11pm) Links the airport with the **Eiffel Tower** (16-20 av de Suffren, 15e; MBir-Hakeim or RER Champ de Mars–Tour Eiffel) via the Arc de Triomphe and Trocadéro.

Le Bus Direct line 4 (€18, 50 to 80 minutes, every 30 minutes from 5.45am to 10.45pm from the airport, 5.15am to 9.45pm from Montparnasse) Links the airport with **Gare Montparnasse** (rue du Commandant René Mouchotte, 14e; MMontparnasse Bienvenüe) in southern Paris via **Gare de Lyon** (20bis bd Diderot, 12e;

MGare de Lyon) in eastern Paris (50 minutes).

Noctilien buses 140 and 143 (www.ratp.fr; €8 or four metro tickets) Part of the RATP night service, Noctilien has two hourly or better buses that link CDG with **Gare de l'Est** (rue du 8 Mai 1945, 10e; MGare de l'Est) in northern Paris via nearby **Gare du Nord** (170 rue La Fayette, 10e; MGare du Nord): bus 140 (1am to 4am; from Gare de l'Est 1am to 3.40am) takes 80 minutes, and bus 143 (12.32am to 4.32am; from Gare de l'Est 12.55am to 5.08am) takes 55 minutes.

RATP bus 350 (www.ratp.fr; €6 or three metro tickets, 75 minutes, every 30 minutes from 6.05am to 10.30pm) Links the airport with **Gare de l'Est** (bd de Strasbourg, 10e, Gare de l'Est; MGare de l'Est).

RATP bus 351 (€6 or three metro tickets, 75 minutes, every 30 minutes from 5.30am to 10.30pm) Links the airport with **place de la Nation** (2 av du

Trône, 12e; MNation) in eastern Paris.

Roissybus (€12.50, one hour, from CDG every 15 to 20 minutes from 6am to 12.30am; from Paris every 15 minutes from 5.15am to 12.30am) Links the airport with **Opéra** (11 rue Scribe, 9e; MOpéra).

Taxi

○ A taxi to the city centre takes 40 minutes. Since 2016, fares have been standardised to a flat rate: €50 to the Right Bank and €55 to the Left Bank. The fare increases by 15% between 7pm and 7am and on Sundays.

○ Only take taxis at a clearly marked rank. Never follow anyone who approaches you at the airport and claims to be a driver.

Train

CDG is served by the RER B line (€10.30, child four to nine €7.90, approximately 50 minutes, every 10 to 20 minutes), which connects with central Paris stations including Gare du Nord, Châtelet–Les Halles and St-Michel–Notre Dame. Trains run from 4.50am to 11.50pm (from Gare du Nord 4.53am to 12.15am) every six to 15 minutes.

Orly Airport

Aéroport d'Orly (ORY; ☏01 70 36 39 50; www.parisaeroport.fr) is 19km south of central Paris but, despite being closer than CDG, it is not as frequently used by international airlines, and public-transport options aren't quite as straightforward. That will change by 2024, when metro line 14 will be extended to the airport. A TGV station is due to arrive here in 2025.

Orly's south and west terminals are currently being unified into one large terminal suitable for bigger planes such as A380s.

Bus

Two bus lines serve Orly:

Le Bus Direct line 1 (www. lebusdirect.com; €12, one hour, every 20 minutes from 6.35am to 11.55pm from Orly, 4.40am to 9.40pm from the Arc de Triomphe) Runs to/from the Arc de Triomphe (50 minutes) via **Gare Montparnasse** (rue du Commandant René Mouchotte, 14e; MMontparnasse Bienvenüe) **(30 minutes), La Motte-Picquet** (88 av de Suffren, 15e; MLa Motte-Picquet–Grenelle) and Trocadéro.

Orlybus (€8.70, 30 minutes, every 15 to 20 minutes from 6am to 12.30am from Orly, 5.35am to midnight from Paris) Runs to/from **place Denfert-Rochereau** (3 place Denfert-Rochereau, 14e; MDenfert-Rochereau) in southern Paris.

Taxi

A taxi to the city centre takes roughly 30 minutes. Standardised flat-rate fares since 2016 mean a taxi costs €30 to the Left Bank and €35 to the Right Bank. The fare increases by 15% between 7pm and 7am and on Sunday.

Train

There is currently no direct train to/from Orly; you'll need to change halfway. Note that while it is possible to take a shuttle to the RER C line, this service is quite long and not recommended.

RER B (€13.25, children four to nine €6.60, 35 minutes, every four to 12 minutes) This line connects Orly with the St-Michel–Notre Dame, Châtelet–Les Halles and Gare du Nord stations in the city centre. In order to get from Orly to the RER station (Antony), you must first take the Orlyval automatic train. The service runs from 5.07am to 12.05am. You only need one ticket to take the two trains.

Tram

Tramway T7 (€1.90, 45 minutes, every eight to 15 minutes from 6am to 11.45pm) This tramway links Orly with Villejuif–Louis Aragon metro station in southern Paris; buy tickets from the machine at the tram stop as no tickets are sold on board.

Beauvais Airport

Aéroport de Beauvais (BVA; 08 92 68 20 66; www. aeroportbeauvais.com) is 75km north of Paris and is served by a few low-cost flights. Before you snap up that bargain, though, consider whether the post-arrival journey is worth it.

The Beauvais *navette* (shuttle bus; €17, 1¼ hours) links the airport with **Parking Pershing** (16-24 bd Pershing, 17e; MPorte Maillot) on

central Paris' western edge; services are coordinated with flight times. See the airport website for details and tickets.

Train

Gare du Nord

Gare du Nord (www.gares-sncf.com; rue de Dunkerque, 10e; MGare du Nord) is the terminus for northbound domestic trains as well as several international services.

Located in northern Paris, the London Paris line of the **Eurostar** (www.eurostar. com) runs from St Pancras International to Gare du Nord. Voyages take 2¼ hours.

Thalys (www.thalys. com) trains pull into Paris' Gare du Nord from Brussels, Amsterdam and Cologne.

Other Mainline Train Stations

Paris has five other stations for long-distance trains, each with its own metro station: Gare d'Austerlitz, Gare de l'Est, Gare de Lyon, Gare Montparnasse and Gare St-Lazare; the station used depends on the direction from Paris.

Contact Oui.SNCF (www. oui.sncf) for connections throughout France and continental Europe.

Bus

Eurolines (08 92 89 90 91; www.eurolines.fr; 55 rue St-Jacques, 5e; 10am-1pm & 2-6pm Mon-Fri; MCluny–La Sorbonne) connects all major

European capitals to Paris' international bus terminal, **Gare Routière Internationale de Paris-Galliéni** (28 av du Général de Gaulle, Bagnolet; Ⓜ Galliéni). The terminal is in the eastern suburb of Bagnolet; it's about a 15-minute metro ride to the more central République station.

Major European bus company FlixBus (www.flixbus.com) uses western **Parking Pershing** (16-24 bd Pershing, 17e; Ⓜ Porte Maillot).

Getting Around

Paris' metro and RER trains, trams, buses and night buses are run by RATP (www.ratp.fr), which has an online journey planner. Free transport maps are available at metro ticket windows

and can be downloaded from the website.

Train

Paris' underground network is run by RATP and consists of two separate but linked systems: the metro and the Réseau Express Régional (RER) suburban train line. The metro has 14 numbered lines; the RER has five main lines (but you'll probably only need to use A, B and C). When buying tickets consider how many zones your journey will cover; there are five concentric transport zones rippling out from Paris (zone 5 being the furthest); if you travel from Charles de Gaulle airport to Paris, for instance, you will have to buy a ticket for zones 1 to 5.

For information on the metro, RER and bus systems, visit www.ratp.fr. Metro maps of various sizes

and degrees of detail are available for free at metro ticket windows; several can also be downloaded for free from the RATP website.

Metro

○ Metro lines are identified by both their number (eg *ligne* 1 – line 1) and their colour, listed on official metro signs and maps.

○ Signs in metro and RER stations indicate the way to the correct platform for your line. The *direction* signs on each platform indicate the terminus. On lines that split into several branches (such as lines 7 and 13), the terminus of each train is indicated on the cars and on signs on each platform giving the number of minutes until the next and subsequent train.

○ Signs marked *correspondance* (transfer) show how to reach connecting trains. At stations with many intersecting lines, like Châtelet and Montparnasse Bienvenüe, walking from one platform to the next can take a very long time.

○ Different station exits are indicated by white-on-blue *sortie* (exit) signs. You can get your bearings by checking the *plan du quartier* (neighbourhood maps) posted at exits.

○ Each line has its own schedule, but trains usually start at around 5.30am, with the last train beginning its run between 12.35am and 1.15am (2.15am on Friday and Saturday).

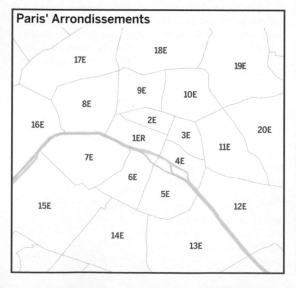

Paris' Arrondissements

17E · 18E · 19E · 9E · 10E · 8E · 16E · 2E · 20E · 1ER · 3E · 11E · 7E · 4E · 6E · 5E · 15E · 12E · 14E · 13E

RER

• The RER is faster than the metro, but the stops are much further apart. Some attractions, particularly those on the Left Bank (eg the Musée d'Orsay, Eiffel Tower and Panthéon), can be reached far more conveniently by the RER than by the metro.

• If you're going out to the suburbs (eg Versailles, Disneyland), ask for help on the platform – finding the right train can be confusing. Also make sure your ticket is for the correct zone.

Tickets & Fares

• The same RATP tickets are valid on the metro, the RER (for travel within the city limits), buses, trams and the Montmartre funicular.

• A ticket – white in colour and called *Le Ticket t+* – costs €1.90 (half price for children aged four to nine years) if bought individually; a *carnet* (book) of 10 costs €14.90 for adults.

• Tickets are sold at all metro stations. Some automated machines take notes and coins, though not all. Ticket windows accept most credit cards; however, machines do not accept credit cards without embedded chips (and even then, not all foreign chip-embedded cards are accepted).

• One ticket lets you travel between any two metro stations (no return journeys)

Tourist Transport Passes

The Mobilis and Paris Visite passes are valid on the metro, the RER, SNCF's suburban lines, buses, night buses, trams and the Montmartre funicular railway. No photo is needed, but write your full name and date of use on the ticket. Passes are sold at larger metro and RER stations, SNCF offices in Paris and the airports. Passes operate by date (rather than 24-hour periods), so activate them early in the day for the best value.

Mobilis Allows unlimited travel for one day and costs €7.50 (for two zones) to €17.80 (five zones). Buy it at any metro, RER or SNCF station in the Paris region. Depending on how many times you plan to hop on/off the metro in a day, a *carnet* (book of 10 tickets) might work out cheaper.

Paris Visite Allows unlimited travel as well as discounted entry to certain museums, and other discounts and bonuses. The 'Paris+Suburbs+Airports' pass includes transport to/from the airports and costs €25.25/38.35/53.75/65.80 for one/two/three/five days. The cheaper 'Paris Centre' pass, valid for zones 1 to 3, costs €12/19.50/26.65/38.35 for one/two/three/five days. Children aged four to 11 years pay half price.

for a period of 1½ hours, no matter how many transfers are required. You can also use it on the RER for travel within zone 1, which encompasses all of central Paris.

• Transfers from the metro to buses or vice versa are not possible.

• Always keep your ticket until you exit from your station; if you are stopped by a ticket inspector, you will have to pay a fine if you don't have a valid ticket.

• Paris is phasing out paper tickets by 2021. The Navigo Easy contactless card (€2) allows infrequent transport users including visitors to prepay for journeys (single or banks of 10) by topping

the card up; there is no expiry date, and cards can be shared between passengers. Frpm October 2019, Navigo Liberté+ will allows passengers to link the card to their bank card, with journey costs automatically deducted.

Bicycle

Vélib'

The **Vélib'** (☏01 76 49 12 34; www.velib-metropole.fr; day/week subscription for up to 5 people €5/15, standard bike hire up to 30/60min free/€1, electric bike €1/2) bike-share scheme changed operators in 2018 and issues with the new system were still ongoing at the time of writing; check the website for the latest information. Ultimately, it will put tens of thousands of bikes (30% of which will be electric) at the disposal of Parisians and visitors at some 1400 stations throughout Paris, accessible around the clock.

○ To get a bike, you first need to purchase a one- or seven-day subscription either at the docking stations or online.

○ The terminals require a credit card with an embedded smart chip (which precludes many North American cards), and, even then, not all foreign chip-embedded cards will work. Alternatively, you can purchase a subscription online before you leave your hotel.

○ After you authorise a deposit (€300) to pay for the bike should it go missing, you'll receive an ID number and PIN code and you're ready to go.

○ Bikes are rented in 30-minute intervals. If you return a bike before a half-hour is up and then take a new one, you will not be charged for a standard bicycle (electric bikes incur charges).

○ Standard bikes are suitable for cyclists aged 14 and over, and are fitted with gears, an antitheft lock with key, reflective strips and front/rear lights. Bring your own helmet (they are not required by law).

○ Electric bikes are also for those aged over 14. They have a top speed of 25km/h and a range of 50km.

Hire

Most bike-hire places will require a deposit. Take ID and bank card/credit card.

Freescoot (📞01 44 07 06 72; www.freescoot.fr; 63 quai de la Tournelle, 5e; 50/125cc scooters per 24hr from €65/75, bicycle/tandem/electric-bike rental per 24hr from €20/40/40; ⏱9am-1pm & 2-7pm Mon-Sat, closed late Jul–mid-Aug & mid-Dec–early Jan; Ⓜ Maubert-Mutualité)

Gepetto et Vélos (📞01 43 54 19 95; www.gepetto-velos.com; 28 rue des Fossées St-Bernard, 5e; bike rental per hr/day/weekend from €4/16/27; ⏱9am-7pm Tue-Sat, 10am-1pm & 2-7pm Sun; Ⓜ Cardinal Lemoine)

Paris à Vélo, C'est Sympa (📞01 48 87 60 01; www.parisvelosympa.fr; 22 rue Alphonse Baudin, 11e; half-day/full day/24hr bike from €12/15/20, electric bike €20/30/40; ⏱9.30am-1pm & 2-6pm Mon-Fri, 9am-7pm Sat & Sun Apr-Oct, shorter hours Nov-Mar; Ⓜ Richard Lenoir)

Boat

Batobus (www.batobus. com; adult/child 1-day pass €17/8, 2-day pass €19/10; ⏱10am-9.30pm late Apr-Aug, shorter hours Sep-late Apr) runs glassed-in trimarans that dock every 20 to 25 minutes at eight small piers along the Seine: Beaugrenelle, Eiffel Tower, Musée d'Orsay, St-Germain des Prés, Notre Dame, Jardin

des Plantes/Cité de la Mode et du Design, Hôtel de Ville, Musée du Louvre and Champs-Élysées.

Buy tickets online, at ferry stops or at tourist offices. Two-day passes must be used on consecutive days. You can also buy a Pass+ that includes **L'Open Tour** (📞01 42 66 56 56; www.paris. opentour.com; 1-day pass adult/child €34/17, night tour €27/17; 📶) buses, to be used on consecutive days. A two-day pass per adult/child costs €47/21; a three day-pass is €51/21.

Bus

Buses can be a scenic way to get around – and there are no stairs to climb, meaning they are more widely accessible – but they're slower and less intuitive to figure out than the metro.

Local Buses

Paris' bus system, operated by the RATP, runs from approximately 5am to 1am Monday to Saturday; services are drastically reduced on Sunday and public holidays. Hours vary substantially depending on the line.

Night Buses

The RATP runs night-bus lines known as Noctilien (www.vianavigo.com); buses depart hourly from 12.30am to 5.30am. The services pass through the main *gares* (train stations) and cross the major axes of the city before leading out to the suburbs. Look for navy-blue N or

Noctilien signs at bus stops. There are two circular lines within Paris (the N01 and N02) that link four mainline train stations – St-Lazare, Gare de l'Est, Gare de Lyon and Gare Montparnasse – as well as popular nightlife areas (Bastille, Champs-Elysées, Pigalle, St-Germain).

Noctilien services are included on your Mobilis or Paris Visite pass for the zones in which you are travelling. Otherwise you pay a certain number of standard €1.90 metro/bus tickets, depending on the length of your journey.

Tickets & Fares

o Normal bus rides embracing one or two bus zones cost one metro ticket; longer rides require two or even three tickets.

o Transfers to other buses – but not the metro – are allowed on the same ticket as long as the change takes place in the 1½ hours between the first and last validation. This does not apply to Noctilien services.

o Whatever kind of single-journey ticket you have, you must validate it in the ticket machine near the driver. If you don't have a ticket, the driver can sell you one for €2 (correct change required).

o If you have a Mobilis or Paris Visite pass, flash it at the driver when you board.

o As with metro tickets, paper tickets will be phased out by 2021, with contact-less cards available from 2019.

Taxi

o The *prise en charge* (flagfall) is €4. Within the city limits, it costs €1.07 per kilometre for travel between 10am and 5pm Monday to Saturday (*Tarif A;* white light on taxi roof and meter).

o At night (5pm to 10am), on Sunday from 7am to midnight and during peak travel times (7am to 10am and 5pm to 7pm Monday to Saturday) in the central 20 *arrondissements*, the rate is €1.29 per kilometre (*Tarif B;* orange light).

o Travel in inner Paris on Sunday night (midnight to 7am Monday) and in the outer suburbs is at *Tarif C,* €1.56 per kilometre (blue light).

o The minimum taxi fare for a short trip is €7.10.

o There are flat-fee fares to/from the major airports (Charles de Gaulle from €50, Orly from €30).

o A fifth passenger incurs a €4 surcharge.

o There's no additional charge for standard-size luggage; larger pieces have a €2 surcharge.

o Flagging down a taxi in Paris can be difficult; it's best to find an official taxi stand.

o To order a taxi, call or reserve online with **Taxis G7** (01 41 27 66 99, 36 07; www.g7.fr) or **Alpha Taxis** (01 45 85 85 85; www.alphataxis.fr).

o An alternative is private driver system Uber taxi (www.uber.com/fr/cities/paris); you order and pay via your phone. However, official taxis continue to protest about the service and there have been instances of Uber drivers and passengers being harassed.

Car & Motorcycle

Driving in Paris is defined by the triple hassle of navigation, heavy traffic and limited parking. Petrol stations are also difficult to locate and access. A car is unnecessary to get around, but if you're heading out of the city on an excursion, then one can certainly be useful. A Crit'Air Vignette (compulsory anti-pollution sticker) is also required in most instances. If you plan on hiring a car, it's best to do so online and in advance.

Language

The sounds used in spoken French can almost all be found in English. There are a couple of exceptions: nasal vowels (represented in our pronunciation guides by 'o' or 'u' followed by an almost inaudible nasal consonant sound 'm', 'n' or 'ng'), the 'funny' u sound ('ew' in our guides) and the deep-in-the-throat r. Bearing these few points in mind and reading our pronunciation guides below as if they were English, you'll be understood just fine. The markers (m) and (f) indicate the forms for male and female speakers respectively.

To enhance your trip with a phrasebook, visit **lonelyplanet.com**. Lonely Planet iPhone phrasebooks are available through the Apple App store.

Basics

Hello.
Bonjour. — bon·zhoor

Goodbye.
Au revoir. — o·rer·vwa

How are you?
Comment allez-vous? — ko·mon ta·lay·voo

I'm fine, thanks.
Bien, merci. — byun mair·see

Please.
S'il vous plaît. — seel voo play

Thank you.
Merci. — mair·see

Excuse me.
Excusez-moi. — ek·skew·zay·mwa

Sorry.
Pardon. — par·don

Yes./No.
Oui./Non. — wee/non

I don't understand.
Je ne comprends pas. — zher ner kom·pron pa

Do you speak English?
Parlez-vous anglais? — par·lay·voo ong·glay

Shopping

I'd like to buy ...
Je voudrais acheter ... — zher voo·dray ash·tay ...

I'm just looking.
Je regarde. — zher rer·gard

How much is it?
C'est combien? — say kom·byun

It's too expensive.
C'est trop cher. — say tro shair

Can you lower the price?
Vous pouvez baisser le prix? — voo poo·vay bay·say ler pree

Eating & Drinking

..., please.
..., s'il vous plaît. — ... seel voo play

   A coffee — *un café* — un ka·fay
   A table for two — *une table pour deux* — ewn ta·bler poor der
   Two beers — *deux bières* — der bee·yair

I'm a vegetarian.
Je suis végétarien/ végétarienne. (m/f) — zher swee vay·zhay·ta·ryun/ vay·zhay·ta·ryen

Cheers!
Santé! — son·tay

That was delicious!
C'était délicieux! — say·tay day·lee·syer

The bill, please.
L'addition, s'il vous plaît. — la·dee·syon seel voo play

Emergencies

Help!
Au secours! — o skoor

Call the police!
Appelez la police! — a·play la po·lees

Call a doctor!
Appelez un médecin! — a·play un mayd·sun

I'm sick.
Je suis malade. — zher swee ma·lad

I'm lost.
Je suis perdu/ perdue. (m/f) — zhe swee pair·dew

Where are the toilets?
Où sont les toilettes? — oo son lay twa·let

Transport & Directions

Where's ...?
Où est ...? — oo ay ...

What's the address?
Quelle est l'adresse? — kel ay la·dres

I want to go to ...
Je voudrais aller à ... — zher voo·dray a·lay a ...

Behind the Scenes

Our Readers

Many thanks to the travellers who used the last edition and wrote to us with helpful hints, useful advice and interesting anecdotes.

Writer Thanks

Catherine Le Nevez

Merci mille fois first and foremost to Julian and to the innumerable Parisians who provided insights, inspiration and great times. Huge thanks too to Dan Fahey, Jennifer Carey and everyone at LP. As ever, a heartfelt *merci encore* to my parents, brother, *belle-sœur, neveu* and *nièce* for sustaining my lifelong love of Paris.

Acknowledgements

Illustrations pp50–51, pp56–57, pp80–81 and pp86–87 by Javier Zarracina and Michael Weldon.

Cover photograph: Palais de Chaillot statue on Trocadéro near the Eiffel Tower, Antonino Bartuccio/4Corners ©

This Book

This book was curated, researched and written by Catherine Le Nevez, with additional research by Christopher Pitts and Nicola Williams. The previous two editions were also curated by Catherine, who researched and wrote the content along with Christopher and Nicola. Damian Harper researched and wrote the Giverny content. This guidebook was produced by the following:

Destination Editors Jennifer Carey, Daniel Fahey

Senior Product Editor Jessica Ryan

Regional Senior Cartographer Mark Griffiths

Product Editors Hannah Cartmel, Shona Gray

Book Designer Lauren Egan

Assisting Editors Janice Bird, Kate Mathews, Louise McGregor, Kirsten Rawlings, Angela Tinson

Assisting Cartographer Alison Lyall

Cover Researcher Brendan Dempsey-Spencer

Thanks to Evan Godt, Victoria Harrison, Liz Heynes, Kate James, Claire Rourke

---

Send Us Your Feedback

We love to hear from travellers – your comments keep us on our toes and help make our books better. Our well-travelled team reads every word on what you loved or loathed about this book. Although we cannot reply individually to postal submissions, we always guarantee that your feedback goes straight to the appropriate authors, in time for the next edition. Each person who sends us information is thanked in the next edition, the most useful submissions are rewarded with a selection of digital PDF chapters.

Visit lonelyplanet.com/contact to submit your updates and suggestions or to ask for help. Our award-winning website also features inspirational travel stories, news and discussions.

Note: We may edit, reproduce and incorporate your comments in Lonely Planet products such as guidebooks, websites and digital products, so let us know if you don't want your comments reproduced or your name acknowledged. For a copy of our privacy policy visit lonelyplanet.com/privacy.

Index

Montmartre

Paris Maps

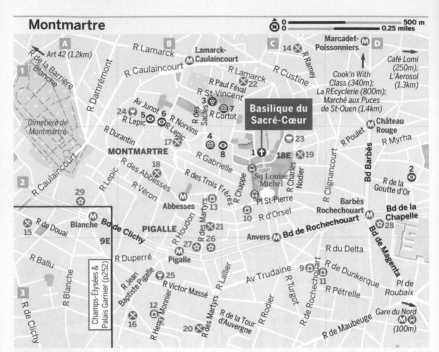

Montmartre

Champs-Élysées & Palais Garnier

Champs-Élysées & Palais Garnier

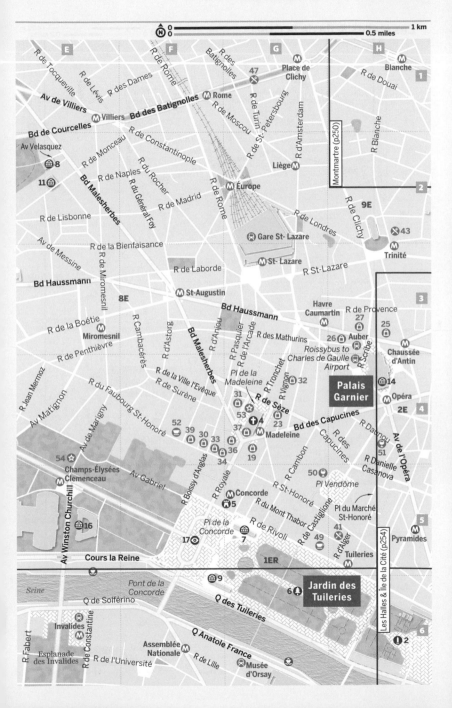

Les Halles & Île de la Cité

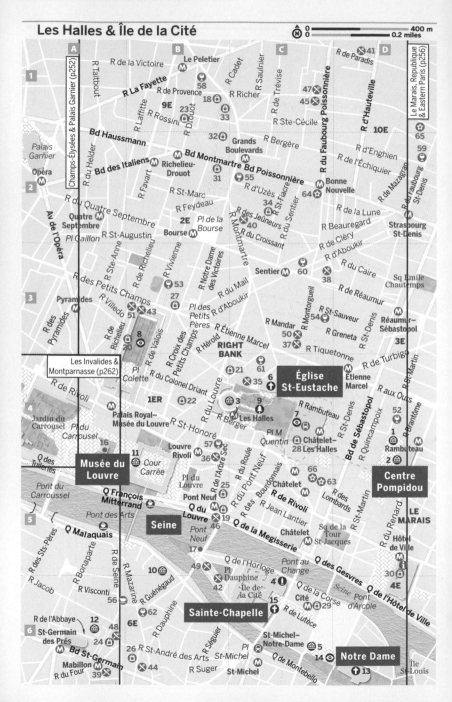

Les Halles & Île de la Cité

Le Marais, Republique & Eastern Paris

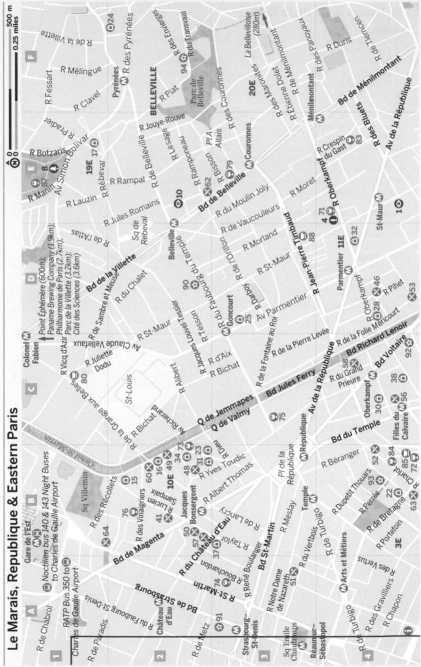

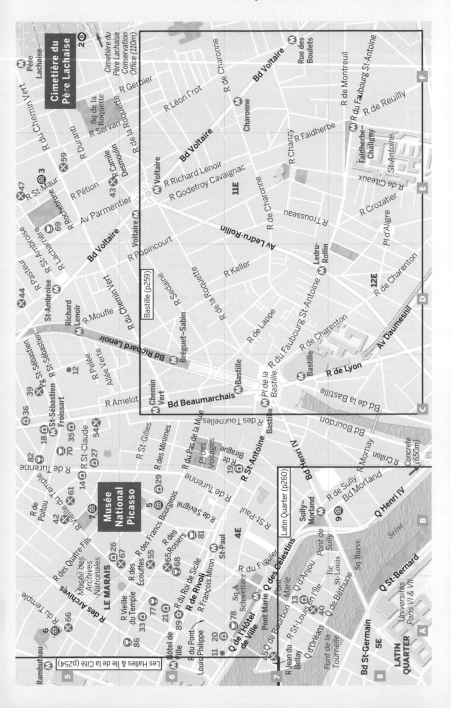

Cimetière du Père Lachaise

Cimetière du Père Lachaise Conservation Office (110m)

Père Lachaise

R du Chemin Vert

R Gerbier

R de Charonne

Bd Voltaire

Rue des Boulets

R de Montreuil

R du Faubourg St-Antoine

R de Reuilly

Sq de la Roquette

R Servan

R Duranti

R de la Roquette

R Léon Frot

Charonne

R Chanzy

R Faidherbe

Faidherbe–Chaligny

St-Antoine

R de Créteaux

R St-Maur

R Rochebrune

R Camille Desmoulin

R Pétion

Av Parmentier

Voltaire

Richard Lenoir

R Godefroy Cavaignac

11E

R de Charonne

R Crozatier

Pl d'Aligre

R Trousseau

12E

R de Charenton

La Folie Regnault

R St-Ambroise

Bd Voltaire

Voltaire

R Poppincourt

Av Ledru-Rollin

Ledru-Rollin

St-Ambroise

Richard Lenoir

R Moufle

R du Chemin Vert

Sédaine

R Keller

R de la Roquette

R de Lappe

R du Faubourg St-Antoine

R de Charenton

Av Daumesnil

St-Sébastien Froissart

Pg St-Sébastien R St-Sébastien

R Pelée

Allée Verte

Bd Richard Lenoir

Bréguet-Sabin

Bastille (p259)

Chemin Vert

R Amelot

Bastille

Pl de la Bastille

R du Faubourg St-Antoine

R de Charenton

Bastille

R de Lyon

Bd Beaumarchais

R des Tournelles

Bastille

Bd Bourdon

Bd de la Bastille

R St-Gilles

R des Minimes

R du Pas de la Mule

Pl des Vosges

R de Birague

R St-Antoine

Bd Henri IV

R Mornay

R Crillon

Concrete (650m)

St-Claude

R du Temple

R de Turenne

R de Poitou

R Vieille du Temple

Musée National Picasso

R de Sévigné

R des Francs Bourgeois

R St-Paul

Latin Quarter (p260)

Sully–Morland

R de Sully

Bd Morland

Q Henri IV

R de Quatre-Fils

Musée des Archives Nationales

R des Écouffes

R des Rosiers

St-Paul

4E

R St-Paul

R du Figuier

Sully

Pont de Sully

Île St-Louis

Sq Barye

Seine

Q St-Bernard

LE MARAIS

R des Archives

R Vieille du Temple

R du Roi de Sicile

R de Rivoli

R François Miron

Sq A Schweitzer

Pont Marie

Marie

Q d'Anjou

Q d'Orléans

Île St-Louis

Q de Béthune

Universités Paris VI & VII

R du Temple

Mairie de l'Hôtel de Ville

R du Pont Louis Philippe

Q de l'Hôtel de Ville

Q de Bourbon

R St-Louis en l'Île

Pont de la Tournelle

Bd St-Germain

5E

LATIN QUARTER

Rambuteau

Les Halles & Île de la Cité (p254)

R Jean du Bellay

Q d'Orléans

Pont de la Tournelle

Le Marais, Republique & Eastern Paris

Bastille

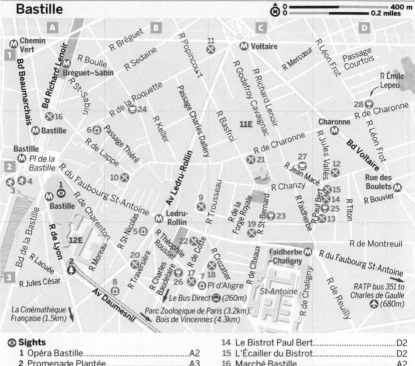

Latin Quarter

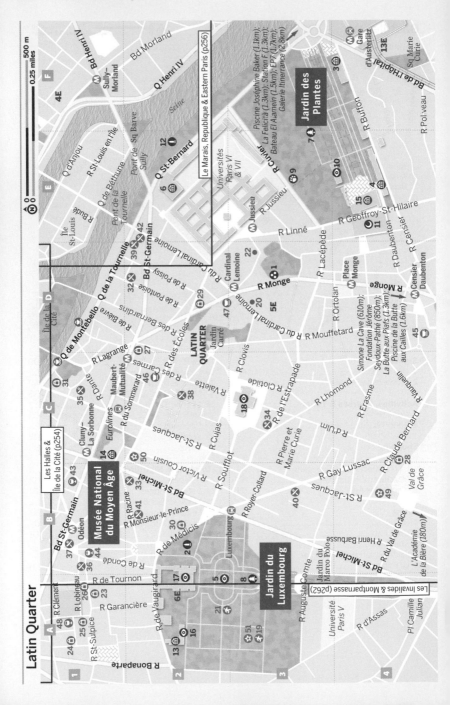

13E

Gare
d'Austerlitz

4E

Le Marais, République & Eastern Paris (p256)

Bd Morland

Bd Henri IV

Q. Henri IV

Sully-
Morland

Seine

Sq St-Bernard

Q. St-Bernard

Pont de Sully

Q de Béthune

R St-Louis en l'Île

Q d'Anjou

Île
St-Louis

Q de la
Tournelle

Pont de la
Tournelle

R Bude

Q de la Tournelle

Bd St-Germain

R du Cardinal Lemoine

Île de la Cité

Q de Montebello

R de Bièvre

R des Bernardins

R de Pontoise

R de Poissy

Piscine Joséphine Baker (1.1km);
La Felicità (1.3km); Station F (1.3km);
Bateau El Aamein (1.5km); EP7 (1.7km);
Galerie Itinérance (2.8km)

**Jardin des
Plantes**

R Cuvier

R Buffon

R Poliveau

Sq Marie
Curie

Bd de l'Hôpital

Universités
Paris VI
& VII

Jussieu

R Jussieu

R Geoffroy-St-Hilaire

R Linné

R Lacépède

R Daubenton

R Censier

R Censier
Daubenton

Cardinal
Lemoine

R Monge

**Place
Monge**

R Ortolan

R Monge

5E

Jardin
Carré

R du Cardinal Lemoine

R Mouffetard

Simone La Cave (610m);
Fondation Jérôme
Seydoux-Pathé (850m);
La Butte aux Piafs (1.3km);
Piscine de la Butte
aux Cailles (1.6km)

**LATIN
QUARTER**

R Lagrange

Maubert-
Mutualité

R des Carmes

R des Écoles

R Clovis

R Clotilde

R de l'Estrapade

R Lhomond

R Erasme

R Vauquelin

R Dante

R du Sommerard

R Valette

R Cujas

R Soufflot

R Clément

R St-Jacques

R Pierre et
Marie Curie

R d'Ulm

Cluny–
La Sorbonne

**Musée National
du Moyen Âge**

Eurolines

R Victor Cousin

Bd St-Michel

R Gay Lussac

R St-Jacques

R Claude Bernard

Val de
Grâce

Les Halles &
Île de la Cité (p254)

Bd St-Germain

Odéon

R Racine

R Monsieur-le-Prince

R Royer-Collard

R Henri Barbusse

R du Val de Grâce

L'Académie
de la Bière (180m)

Luxembourg

R de Médicis

**Jardin du
Luxembourg**

R Auguste Comte

Jardin du
Marco Polo

Université
Paris V

R d'Assas

Pl Camille
Julian

Bd St-Michel

Les Invalides & Montparnasse (p262)

R de Tournon

R de Vaugirard

R de Condé

R Garancière

R St-Sulpice

R Clément

R Lobineau

R Bonaparte

6E

500 m
0.25 miles

Île de la Cité

Latin Quarter

Les Invalides & Montparnasse

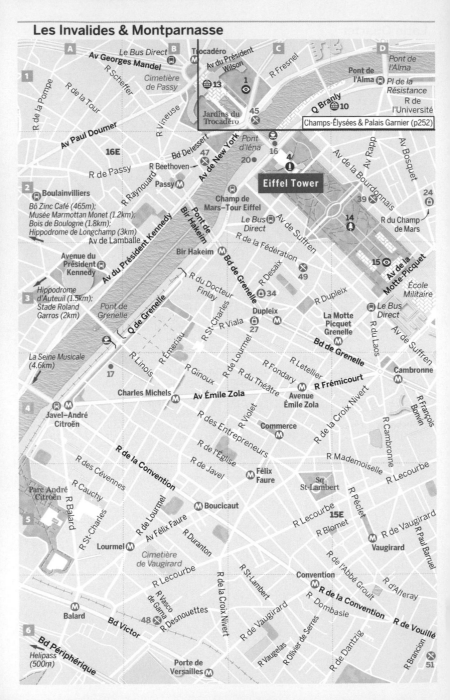

A | B | C | D

1

Av Georges Mandel

Le Bus Direct

Trocadéro

Av du Président Wilson

R Fresnel

Pont de l'Alma

R Scheffer

Cimetière de Passy

13

1

Pont de l'Alma

Pl de la Résistance

R de la Pompe

R de la Tour

Av Paul Doumer

R Vineuse

Jardins du Trocadéro

45

Q Branly

10

R de l'Université

Champs-Élysées & Palais Garnier (p252)

16E

Bd Delessert

47

Pont d'Iéna

16

4

Av Bosquet

R de Passy

R Beethoven

Av de New York

20

Av de la Bourdonnais

Av Rapp

2

Boulainvilliers

R Raynouard

Passy

Eiffel Tower

Bô Zinc Café (465m);
Musée Marmottan Monet (1.2km);
Bois de Boulogne (1.8km);
Hippodrome de Longchamp (3km)

Av de Lamballe

Pont de Bir Hakeim

Champ de Mars-Tour Eiffel

Le Bus Direct

Av de Suffren

39

24

14

R du Champ de Mars

Avenue du Président Kennedy

Bir Hakeim

R de la Fédération

15

Av de la Motte-Picquet

Hippodrome d'Auteuil (1.5km);
Stade Roland Garros (2km)

Av du Président Kennedy

R du Docteur Finlay

Bd de Grenelle

R Desaix

49

34

R Dupleix

École Militaire

Pont de Grenelle

Q de Grenelle

R St-Charles

R Viala

Dupleix

27

La Motte Picquet Grenelle

Le Bus Direct

Av de Suffren

La Seine Musicale (4.6km)

R Émeriau

R Linois

17

R Ginoux

R de Lourmel

R du Théâtre

R Fondary

R Letellier

Bd de Grenelle

R du Laos

Cambronne

Charles Michels

Av Émile Zola

R Violet

Avenue Émile Zola

R Frémicourt

R François Bonvin

4

Javel–André Citroën

R des Entrepreneurs

Commerce

R de la Croix Nivert

R Cambronne

R de l'Église

R de Javel

Félix Faure

Sq St-Lambert

R Mademoiselle

R Lecourbe

Parc André Citroën

R des Cévennes

R Cauchy

R Balard

R St-Charles

R de Lourmel

Av Félix Faure

R Duranton

Boucicaut

R Lecourbe

15E

R Blomet

R Péclet

R de Vaugirard

R Paul Barruel

5

Lourmel

Cimetière de Vaugirard

R Lecourbe

R de la Croix Nivert

R St-Lambert

Convention

R de l'Abbé Groult

R d'Alleray

Vaugirard

R Vasco de Gama

48

R Desnouettes

R de Vaugirard

R de la Convention

R Dombasle

R de Vouillé

Balard

Bd Victor

R de la Croix Nivert

R Vaugelas

R Olivier de Serres

R de Dantzig

R Brancion

6

Bd Périphérique

Helipass (500m)

Porte de Versailles

51

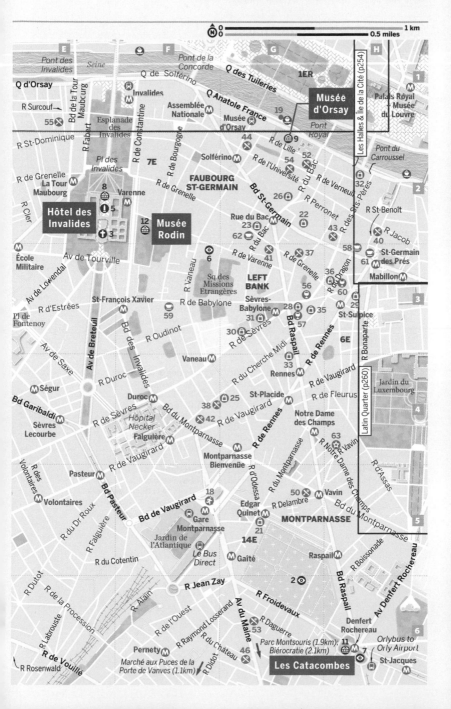

Les Invalides & Montparnasse

Symbols & Map Key

Look for these symbols to quickly identify listings:

- Sights
- Activities
- Courses
- Tours
- Festivals & Events
- Eating
- Drinking
- Entertainment
- Shopping
- Information & Transport

These symbols and abbreviations give vital information for each listing:

- Sustainable or green recommendation
- **FREE** No payment required

- Telephone number
- Opening hours
- Parking
- Nonsmoking
- Air-conditioning
- Internet access
- Wi-fi access
- Swimming pool
- Bus
- Ferry
- Tram
- Train
- English-language menu
- Vegetarian selection
- Family-friendly

Find your best experiences with these Great For... icons.

- Art & Culture
- Beaches
- Budget
- Cafe/Coffee
- Cycling
- Detour
- Drinking
- Entertainment
- Events
- Family Travel
- Food & Drink
- History
- Local Life
- Nature & Wildlife
- Photo Op
- Scenery
- Shopping
- Short Trip
- Sport
- Walking
- Winter Travel

Sights

- Beach
- Bird Sanctuary
- Buddhist
- Castle/Palace
- Christian
- Confucian
- Hindu
- Islamic
- Jain
- Jewish
- Monument
- Museum/Gallery/ Historic Building
- Ruin
- Shinto
- Sikh
- Taoist
- Winery/Vineyard
- Zoo/Wildlife Sanctuary
- Other Sight

Points of Interest

- Bodysurfing
- Camping
- Cafe
- Canoeing/Kayaking
- Course/Tour
- Diving
- Drinking & Nightlife
- Eating
- Entertainment
- Sento Hot Baths/ Onsen
- Shopping
- Skiing
- Sleeping
- Snorkelling
- Surfing
- Swimming/Pool
- Walking
- Windsurfing
- Other Activity

Information

- Bank
- Embassy/Consulate
- Hospital/Medical
- Internet
- Police
- Post Office
- Telephone
- Toilet
- Tourist Information
- Other Information

Geographic

- Beach
- Gate
- Hut/Shelter
- Lighthouse
- Lookout
- Mountain/Volcano
- Oasis
- Park
- Pass
- Picnic Area
- Waterfall

Transport

- Airport
- BART station
- Border crossing
- Boston T station
- Bus
- Cable car/Funicular
- Cycling
- Ferry
- Metro/MRT station
- Monorail
- Parking
- Petrol station
- Subway/S-Bahn/ Skytrain station
- Taxi
- Train station/Railway
- Tram
- Tube Station
- Underground/ U-Bahn station
- Other Transport

Our Story

A beat-up old car, a few dollars in the pocket and a sense of adventure. In 1972 that's all Tony and Maureen Wheeler needed for the trip of a lifetime – across Europe and Asia overland to Australia. It took several months, and at the end – broke but inspired – they sat at their kitchen table writing and stapling together their first travel guide, *Across Asia on the Cheap*. Within a week they'd sold 1500 copies. Lonely Planet was born.

Today, Lonely Planet has offices in Franklin, London, Melbourne, Oakland, Dublin, Beijing and Delhi, with more than 600 staff and writers. We share Tony's belief that 'a great guidebook should do three things: inform, educate and amuse'.

Our Writers

Catherine Le Nevez

Catherine's wanderlust kicked in when she roadtripped across Europe from her Parisian base aged four, and she's been hitting the road at every opportunity since, travelling to around 60 countries and completing her Doctorate of Creative Arts in Writing, Masters in Professional Writing, and postgraduate qualifications in editing and publishing along the way. Over the past dozen-plus years she's written scores of Lonely Planet guides and articles covering Paris, France, Europe and far beyond. Her work has also appeared in numerous online and print publications. Topping Catherine's list of travel tips is to travel without any expectations.

Christopher Pitts

Born in the year of the Tiger, Chris' first expedition in life ended in failure when he tried to dig from Pennsylvania to China at the age of six. Hardened by reality but still infinitely curious about the other side of the world, he went on to study Chinese at university, living for several years in Kunming, Taiwan and Shanghai. A chance encounter led to a Paris relocation, where he lived with his wife and two children for over a decade before the lure of Colorado's sunny skies and outdoor adventure proved too great to resist.

Nicola Williams

Border-hopping is a way of life for British writer, runner, foodie, art aficionado and mum-of-three Nicola Williams. Nicola has authored more than 50 guidebooks on Paris, Provence, Rome, Tuscany, France, Italy and Switzerland for Lonely Planet and covers France as a destination expert for the *Telegraph*. She also writes for the *Independent*, the *Guardian*, lonelyplanet.com, *Lonely Planet Magazine*, *French Magazine*, *Cool Camping France* and others. Catch her on the road on Twitter and Instagram @tripalong.

Contributing Writer

Damian Harper researched and wrote the Giverny content. Damian has been writing for Lonely Planet for over two decades, covering destinations including China, Vietnam, Thailand, Ireland and London.

STAY IN TOUCH LONELYPLANET.COM/CONTACT

AUSTRALIA The Malt Store, Level 3, 551 Swanston St, Carlton, Victoria 3053
☎03 8379 8000,
fax 03 8379 8111

IRELAND Digital Depot, Roe Lane (off Thomas St), Digital Hub, Dublin 8, D08 TCV4, Ireland

USA 124 Linden Street, Oakland, CA 94607
☎510 250 6400,
toll free 800 275 8555,
fax 510 893 8572

UK 240 Blackfriars Road, London SE1 8NW
☎020 3771 5100,
fax 020 3771 5101

twitter.com/
lonelyplanet

facebook.com/
lonelyplanet

instagram.com/
lonelyplanet

youtube.com/
lonelyplanet

lonelyplanet.com/
newsletter